Winning the Trading Game

Founded in 1807, John Wiley & Sons is the oldest independent publishing company in the United States. With offices in North America, Europe, Australia, and Asia, Wiley is globally committed to developing and marketing print and electronic products and services for our customers' professional and personal knowledge and understanding.

The Wiley Trading series features books by traders who have survived the market's ever changing temperament and have prospered—some by reinventing systems, others by getting back to basics. Whether a novice trader, professional or somewhere in-between, these books will provide the advice and strategies needed to prosper today and well into the future.

For a list of available titles, visit our Web site at www.WileyFinance.com.

Winning the Trading Game

Why 95% of Traders Lose and What You Must Do to Win

NOBLE DRAKOLN

WILEY

John Wiley & Sons, Inc.

For general information on our other products and services or for technical support, please contact our Customer Care Department within the United States at (800) 762-2974, outside the United States at (317) 572-3993 or fax (317) 572-4002.

Wiley also publishes its books in a variety of electronic formats. Some content that appears in print may not be available in electronic books. For more information about Wiley products, visit our web site at www.wiley.com.

ISBN-13 978-0-470-16995-7

Printed in the United States of America.

10 9 8 7 6 5 4 3 2 1

This book is dedicated to my sons, Alex and Zachary—thanks for keeping me focused on the future.

Contents

Preface

"Who am I?" This is one of those questions that sits right up there with "Where do we go after we die?" and "What is my true purpose?" While I may not be able to help you with the second two questions, I hope that I can help you answer the first "Who am I?" I believe that I am uniquely qualified because I can honestly say I am you.

My development as a trader didn't come from the ivory towers of Wall Street or the pits of Chicago. I started my journey as a trader in Los Angeles. I left home when I was 17 years old; for all intents and purposes I was homeless, without direction, and in need of some guidance. At the time I was working at a coffeehouse and had the good fortune of meeting someone in the gold business. He sold gold coins and followed the London gold futures contracts. I was intrigued and I pestered him to no end. He eventually brought me on as an assistant, and I was hooked to the markets.

Soon afterward, I bought Ken Roberts's TWMPMM (The World's Most Powerful Money Manual) course and at the age of 19 got my commodities broker license. A year later I purchased Larry Williams's "Batting .800" course. After watching it and reading it, I really felt that there was a rhyme and a reason to the markets. I quickly became a voracious reader of everything I could find on futures and forex trading. I attended seminars on trading and even got involved in buying and selling actual physical commodities with the knowledge I had gained as a broker and through my books. All the while I searched for a "holy grail," a "perfect system," only to realize that if it did exist, it was beyond my reach.

That's when it became more important for me to have a method to approach the markets, as opposed to a one-size-fits-all solution. I came to the simple conclusion that, like it or not, no one person, no matter how much money he has, can control the markets; what he can control is how he interacts with the market. Once I grasped this idea, I took personal responsibility for how I approached the markets. I developed a whole new perspective in what it took for me to be a true speculator and more importantly what I would need to do to transition into a real trader.

For the first time, I looked at the futures and forex markets differently. Over the course of seven years, I broke these markets down to their base components. I wanted to find exactly where I, the trader, fit in. That is when I changed my perspective from fixating on the perfect entry price, the holy grail, to understanding how best to exploit the underlying needs of the various groups of traders involved with the markets. This was no simple task, but once discovered it made me realize that the mistakes I had made in the past occurred solely because I had brought a stock market investor mentality to futures and forex. This was much like bringing a knife to a gun fight.

Over the years I have worked with hundreds of traders. Each one began the same journey I went through. Most likely, you have experienced the same thing. You have read books, listened to audiotapes, and attended webinars, yet still something is missing. I have been where you are, and I hope that this book can help you fill that void. If you take your time, you will find that this book can be the link that will help you bridge the gap between what you have learned in the past and where you need to go in the future.

Now, more than ever, is the time for you to evolve your understanding of futures and forex. Nationwide investors are facing serious problems. Looming ahead of them are dangers that can be avoided simply by increasing their wealth. Traditional investments of stocks and bonds won't cut it though. We only need to look at the dot-com bubble burst—over $7 trillion in Baby Boomer wealth evaporated—to realize that something out of the ordinary needs to be done to get ahead.

Major stock market problems, potential real estate collapse, and the constant uncertainty of the future of Social Security retirement benefits leads to a need to find investments with higher-than-average returns. This is what leads us to futures and forex. While the stock market has floundered for the past 5 years, commodities, such as oil, gold, and many foreign currencies, are all priced at or near 25-year highs.

These opportunities are exciting, but there is a right way and a wrong way to get involved. In these uncertain times, too many investors are looking to futures and forex to help build their wealth without really understanding what they are getting themselves into. Trading in futures and forex is done with little to no planning and a limited understanding of what it really is all about.

This haphazard approach forces all types of investors to make unnecessary costly mistakes in their trading. Industry statistics say that 90% to 95% of traders who speculate in futures and forex lose their entire investment within six months to a year. While there are many factors that can contribute to such a high failure rate, the core mistake that these losing traders make is the belief in the faulty premise that "success" is based solely on "picking" the right direction of the market.

By focusing just on picking the right direction, investors have completely disregarded, whether willfully or through ignorance, all of the necessary elements of true speculation: money management, technical analysis, and risk management. When investors just pick and "play" markets like they pick and play horses at the racetrack, then they are not truly speculating—they are gambling. The reality is that your hard-earned money, even if it is risk capital, is not something to gamble with, but with the right approach it can be the perfect seed capital for speculating.

The purpose of this book is to end the cycle of gambling in futures and forex trading by getting to the heart of speculation. Each investor will learn how to transition from gambling with futures and forex to speculating and then become a full-fledged professional trader on their own terms.

You will learn specific approaches along with practical skills that experienced and professional traders use to get themselves ahead. This book will teach you how to master the three key elements of futures and forex trading: money management strategies, technical analysis strategies, and risk management strategies. You will also be given tools, along with charts and a prescribed three-month trading program, that will make your transition from investor to trader all the smoother.

The book is divided up into three sections. The first section, Part I: More Life at the End of Your Money, puts a magnifying glass to the Social Security system, major market trends, what it takes to be a trader, and the basics of futures and forex trading. In the second section, Part II: Why 95% of Investors Fail at Futures and Forex, we take a critical look at why everyday stock strategies simply don't work. The chapters in this section then delve into how to develop a proper trading plan and give you the necessary tools to find the markets that work for you. You are also introduced to a trader's two worst enemies, fear and greed, what it takes to overcome them, and, more importantly, what to do if you can't.

In the final section, Part III: Seven Lessons for Trading Success, everything is pulled together to center around three key areas: money management, technical analysis, and risk management. This is where the evolution from investor to trader really takes shape. You learn how to manipulate the daisy chain effect of the markets, you are given insight into the hedging aspects of trading, and, finally, you learn how to really customize your trading the way you want to, and not use some cookie cutter approach.

With this organized approach to the futures and forex markets, the goal is to have the gambler's mentality of just "picking" the right trade take a backseat to a set of systems that guide you when you are winning and losing. Once you are equipped with this new skill set, you are able to take control of your futures and forex trading the same way the professionals do.

Keep in mind that learning how to trade successfully is not easy. There will be pitfalls along the way. Each one is meant to challenge you and help you grow as both a person and a trader. Use the book as a guide and a resource to help you navigate those rough waters. I look forward to hearing your experiences, and I wish you the best of success in all of your endeavors. See you on the trading screen.

Acknowledgments

They say that every journey of a thousand miles begins with the first step. This book was not created in a vacuum; there were many people over the last few years who participated by introducing me to someone I didn't know before, by forcing me to develop my ideas for a seminar, or by contributing to helping me stay in a positive state of mind. If I haven't mentioned you by name, I want to extend my sincerest thank you for the part you have played in helping me along the way.

First, I have to thank God for giving me the courage, the perseverance, and the patience to complete this book. In the face of every adversity, my faith gave me strength to not despair and to stay focused on my goal.

To my family and friends: Ma, your constant support and encouragement, along with your spiritual books, kept my days bright. Lori, honey, you are my rock. How you put up with all of my work I will never know. I love you dearly and thanks for all of your support and contributions. Salim and Nick, thanks for the friendly competition and the genuine friendship we have enjoyed throughout the years. Ralph and Joyce Maldonado, thanks for letting me use your kitchen, dining room, living room, patio—you get the point—to write; you have always been gracious hosts. Rick Akasaka, thank you for your talk; I reflect on it from time to time and it gives me the jolt I need to get the job done.

Thanks, John Kinard, for being a loyal business partner and dealing with clients while I was writing the book; your assistance was greatly appreciated. Thanks, Ralph Savrnoch and Axis Trading, for splitting office space with us; the synergy that our firms created gave me the ability to finish the book a lot faster, and for that I am grateful. Professor Milligan, your statistical analysis and ability to comprehend futures in both lay and professional terms made it easier for me to bounce ideas off of—thanks.

I have to give full acknowledgment to Jeff Bezos for creating Amazon.com. The forum he has provided for niche books is amazing—without his business model, I would not have made it this far. I have to give a heartfelt thanks to Gary Kamen, the first futures professional to read my book, like it, and actually support me all the way. Thank you, Ginger

Szala, for trying out a little-known author as an editor for the "Trends in Futures" newsletter. Oliver Velez, thanks for taking my letter seriously and helping me make the video series. Teodor Ancuta, I appreciate your making the first ever translation of my book *Futures for Small Speculators* to Romanian and inviting me out to speak. You opened my eyes to the international need for this information. Thank you, Lothar Albert, for printing my articles in German and introducing my message to an entirely new audience. Thanks, André Malpel, for all of the hospitality you and your family show me every time I come to speak in Paris at your Technical Analysis Expo. Your promptings inspired me to develop my trading explanations further and better.

Thanks to Dr. Alexander Elder, Ken Roberts, Jack Schwager, and Mark Douglas for writing books, giving lectures, and promoting futures. You have all had an influence on how I trade, and more importantly, you have shaped how I wanted to deliver my message.

Kevin Commins, thanks a lot for taking my book proposal seriously. You and Emilie Herman could have looked at it as another futures book, but you didn't. You put up with my tight schedule and late chapters, and still you took the time to understand my message. I appreciate you both for doing that.

Last, but not least, I have to thank Larry Williams. A daisy chain of events occurred that led me to you in Germany almost two years ago. When I mentioned to you in a passing e-mail that I was thinking of writing another book, you went out of your way to get it to your publisher. You didn't have to do that, but you did anyway. I hope I can do the same for someone else in the future.

PART I

More Life at the End of Your Money

One of the marvels of the twenty-first century is the ability of the medical world to prolong human life. It's been said that if we were to apply what we currently know about medicine and human anatomy, the average person could live to be 115 to 120 years old. This is both exciting and scary. While a long life is a good thing, the ability to have a great quality of life is essential. That means you need money—and lots of it.

In a world of uncertainty, investors are finding themselves more likely than ever to find themselves retiring earlier, whether forced or by choice, with the prospect of outliving their money. The traditional investments of stocks and bonds have a difficult time of just beating inflation, much less being capable of producing the necessary double-digit returns in order to make retirement a success.

In the following chapters, you will be exposed to the current pitfalls of following conventional wisdom when it comes to long-term investing. More importantly, you will be exposed to the global investment trends that are evolving right before your eyes. Finally, you will be exposed to how and what it will take from you to use futures and forex to catch these global investment trends and to safeguard your money in the long run.

In the past, being wealthy was believed to be a luxury that only a few could achieve. This is no longer the case. With careful planning and a shift in your thinking, you must do everything in your power to make your money work harder than ever before.

CHAPTER 1

The Need to Build Wealth

I n 2004, President George W. Bush and other political pundits claimed that the Social Security fund was on the verge of collapsing. President Bush and the Republican senators pushed for Social Security reform and privatization. Their rationale was to establish a way for Social Security to give a fair return for future retirees and to make sure that future generations would be able to enjoy the benefits of their Social Security contributions directly.

Whether you agree or disagree with the assessment of Social Security collapse, it is no secret that Social Security benefits have decreased over the years. With the decline in benefits intersecting with longer life spans and the negative savings rate, Americans have few choices to improve their long-term economic prospects. In the end, there are really only two solutions.

The first solution is to save more; the second solution is to make more money. While doing one does not necessarily exclude the other, this book is about making more money. While the future may look bleak, there are ways to boost your 401(k) account and individual retirement account (IRA). There are also ways to take your risk capital and make it work harder than ever. Futures and forex can do that for you.

In this chapter we will take a critical look at increasing life spans, the negative savings rate, and problems with Social Security. We will then see how all of this will have a direct impact on your life. This is not a definitive write-up on these subjects, nor is it meant to give you a purely doom-and-gloom view of the world. My goal is to shed a light on what we face as investors for the long haul.

3

When you make any investment decision you must put it into the context of how it can positively or negatively impact your lifestyle in the long run. While futures and forex investing involves risk, you simply need to look at the alternatives to determine if the risk is worth taking or not. At the end of the day your economic well being is what is important.

RETIRING EARLY

There has always been the fantasy of retiring early. Dreams of leaving the 9-to-5 grind abound. The belief is that the sooner you leave the workforce, the more you can get started on enjoying your real life. The problem with this logic is that although the idea of retiring early is appealing, you still have to generate an income that will match or beat the income you received from working.

Many dreams of retiring early crash against the harsh reality of the economic necessity to support yourself and your family. Dr. Ephrem Cheng did a research report on Boeing Corporation. In his research he discovered an unusual fact: Those who were able to retire early, in their fifties, were likely to live well into their eighties. Those who retired after age 55, and every year thereafter, would lose approximately two years off of their life span, until, eventually, those who retired in their 60s would rarely make it past their 70s.

So the reality for those who retire in their fifties is the fact that they will be facing down at least 30 to 40 years—almost half their lifetime—supporting themselves with whatever nest egg they can muster.

Let's look at a simple example: If you require at least $45,000 a year to live on, with no major medical problems or health care needs, you will need a sizeable savings account to cover you. In order to support yourself over the course of 30 to 40 years, you will need inflation-adjusted return that will allow you $45,000 in payments without having to tap your principal.

The rule of thumb is that you need at least 25 to 30 times that amount in reserves. In this case, you would need a portfolio of $1,125,000 set aside, on the low end. Now, of course, if you have other sources of income, such as pensions or Social Security, then you can reassess the $45,000 figure downward. Unfortunately, many of those programs don't kick in until you have reached a minimum age, typically your early sixties.

Many people get by without having such large portfolios, but when you do that, you are typically tapping into your principal, thereby dwindling the future opportunities of returns.

The Teachers Insurance and Annuity Association–College Retirement Equities Fund (TIAA-CREF) has developed a retirement worksheet in the

"Retirement Countdown" section of their web site. It will give you insight into exactly what it will take for you to retire at various ages.

No matter what you do, you have to acknowledge that while early retirement or retirement in general may seem almost glamorous, longer and longer life spans can make it difficult to live the life you are accustomed to. While our scenario looked at income in the $45,000 range, the demographic of the average futures trader is income near or exceeding $100,000 per year. That would mean you would need a $2 to $3 million dollar portfolio to sustain that level of income.

So let's take a look at how realistically investors are matching their retirement needs with their actual deeds.

NEGATIVE SAVINGS RATE

In 2005, the U.S. Commerce Department's Bureau of Economic Analysis put out a disturbing revelation: Americans had spent more than they earned and effectively had created a "negative savings rate" of 0.5% for the year. The only other time that this had occurred was during the Great Depression.

While people were saving money, they had effectively jeopardized their savings and borrowed money in order to make purchases today. This gradual slide began in 1985, when we were saving 11.1% of our disposable income; today's negative saving rate of 0.5% has effectively created a drop of 11.6% in savings in just 20 years, while at the same time inflation has been moving at approximately 3% per year.

In order to understand exactly how a negative savings rate evolves, we must separate income from wealth. If you have property or assets that appreciate in value, you have one of two choices—hold it or sell it. If you sell it and then spend the proceeds, you have decreased your wealth while not increasing your income.

This is the "wealth effect." As the wealth grows, there is a tendency to spend more money. In the short term the impact may be minimal; over time, however, as we spend our wealth while we decrease our income, we effectively end up cannibalizing the capital we need for retirement.

While the idea of a negative savings rate is not new, there are interesting parallels between now and the Great Depression. The unifying theme to both eras is banking. What partly led to the Great Depression was the liberal lending policies of the banks to fuel the aggressive movements in the stock markets. Investors were often allowed to put up only 10 cents on the dollar, with remaining stock used as collateral for the purchase.

This liberal banking policy, coupled with the antispeculation fever in the stock market that followed soon thereafter, forced the Great Depression onto America's shoulders. Now is not so different.

This time around, instead of the stock market, the banks are being liberal with real estate loans. All types of negative amortization loans, adjustable-rate mortgages (ARMs), and 40- and 50-year mortgages, along with liberal refinance packages, have given investors more and more ways to get equity out of properties, while at the same driving the values up on these same properties.

Banks then, banks now. There was speculation then, and there is speculation now.

By pulling equity of properties (wealth), but not increasing their income at the same time, real estate speculators have collaborated with the banks to effectively pay mortgage notes and diminish their ability for long-term savings in order to pay for their retirement needs.

The only way to resolve the issue of diminishing wealth is for the properties to increase in value. It is unlikely that this will be happening anytime soon. The ability for speculators to sell the properties to eliminate their debt or for the property to increase in value in order for their paper wealth to grow is very difficult in the current environment.

Foreclosures, short sales, and tightening lending practices imply that the negative savings rate will increase, not diminish, in the years to come. The consensus is that the only way this problem can be stymied effectively is the transfer of wealth, inheritance, to the Baby Boomers from their parents.

The question you have to ask yourself is: "Do I wait around for someone to die before I shore up my savings, or do I figure out a way to increase my income and my disposable income and simply save more?"

SOCIAL SECURITY

We talked earlier about retiring early. The earlier you retire, the longer you are likely to live. While you need a significant amount of reserves in order to cover your annual expenses, Social Security can be a big help. Depending on your age, you can collect partial or full benefits.

For rough numbers, if you made $45,000 per year, you could expect Social Security benefits in the neighborhood of $15,000 per year. The problem with these benefits is that you wouldn't be able to collect them until you were 62 and you would still need a way to come up with $30,000 in annual income from your personal savings. That is just the tip of the iceberg of the problems with Social Security, though.

In 2004, President Bush enlightened us all to a potential collapse in the Social Security system. Looming on the horizon is the fact that 78 million Baby Boomers will be retiring. In a country of only 302 million people, that is a significant number of retirees. Couple that with the fact that currently there are 3.1 workers to support 1 retired worker, but as time progresses there will be only 2 workers to support 1 retired worker.

Federal Reserve Chairman Ben Bernanke said to Congress, "Unless Social Security and Medicare are revamped, the massive burden from retiring Baby Boomers will place major strains on the nation's budget and the economy."

To put all of this in context, we have to look at what Social Security is and what it isn't. It was established in 1935 by President Franklin D. Roosevelt. It was designed as social insurance that was funded by payroll taxes. This payment went to a "trust fund," which would then redistribute benefits to the retired.

One of the key flaws of the system is the idea of calling it a "trust fund." In truth there is no actual capital in an account to make payments to beneficiaries. The program is a "pay as you go" program. So while we may have contributed to the program for years, our contributions are not set aside for us but actually paid out to current retirees.

The hope is that in the future there will be enough workers to contribute to the program, so that then retirees still will be able to draw benefits. Currently, $500 billion in benefits are paid out to 47.5 million people. Couple the fact that there will be a potential doubling in the number of beneficiaries, which would double the payments, with the fact that the "money" collected to shore up Social Security has been invested in special "nonmarketable U.S. government bonds," and there is a sincere fear that there simply will not be enough money to continue retirement benefits as they currently exist.

Insolvency projections for Social Security range from 2018 to 30 or 40 years from now. Regardless of the "when," the reality is that it will be more and more difficult to fulfill the promises of Social Security. The last time there was a potential crisis in Social Security of this magnitude, back in the 1980s, several reforms were implemented. Taxes were increased, the benefit age was raised, and Social Security benefits, up to 50%, became taxable.

These are some of the same solutions being promoted in today's environment. To understand the magnitude of the problem, currently 7% of the total U.S. economy is allocated to Social Security. In 2030, that number will increase to almost 13%, and by 2050, over 15% of the entire U.S. economy will be allocated to Social Security.

If the U.S. government were running a surplus, this drastic percentage growth would not be so alarming. The problem is that the government is running a budget deficit to the tune of $319 billion dollars a year. With no end in sight to the war on terrorism, this deficit figure does not look like it will be ending anytime soon.

The solutions to "fix" the Social Security system are not that appealing. If taxes are increased, we would effectively see an increase in taxes from 18% of the U.S. budget to 24%, driving us closer and closer to being a purely socialist state.

Privatization of Social Security is also touted as a potential fix to the problem. While plausible, it has little to no bearing on fixing the "pay as you go" system that has been in effect for over 50 years. In fact, it will exacerbate and speed up the need to use the U.S. Treasury bonds to pay current Social Security recipients, with the eventual need to find a way for the United States to honor those bonds.

Those who do have the new private Social Security system will then be responsible for their own investing decisions, even though many of them are currently having difficulties managing their current 401(k)s and IRAs.

Another potential possibility is to increase the age for Social Security distribution to 70, bumping it up from the current 67. While this, on the surface, will delay Social Security payments, it simply means that those who wanted to retire at the traditional age of 65 will be forced to work another five years, which means their private savings will have to sustain them even longer.

Any increase in the normal retirement age will also mean there will be an increase in the age to receive limited benefits as well. If you are forced to retire earlier, you simply have to tough it out and fend for yourself.

None of the proposed solutions to shore up Social Security benefits represents a positive impact or solution for those currently receiving benefits or those Baby Boomers who will be receiving distributions in the future.

CONCLUSION

While none of these things by itself is a problem, it is the combination of a potential Social Security collapse, the changing idea of what retirement may mean, and the negative savings rate that makes it clear that traditional forms of investment, stocks and bonds, need to be supplemented with an alternative that can power boost your overall returns.

Futures and forex investing has the potential to do that for you. With the commensurate potential of boosted returns, you also have to realize that there is increased risk. When it comes to futures, you have the ability to lose what you put in and more, if you are not careful. When it comes to spot forex investing, you are trading on a 24-hour cycle. The speed and discipline you need in order to be successful at spot forex can take some time getting used to, before you ever are able to turn a profit.

When you look at the potential future of your long-term investment goals, the question you have to ask yourself is: "Is the risk worth taking?" Only you know the quality of life and lifestyle to which you have grown accustomed. Only you know what you expect from your investments. Only you know what standard of living you expect as you grow older. Whatever you do, take control of your fate and don't be a victim of the financial whims of others.

CHAPTER 2

Money-Making Megatrends

I n the last chapter we discussed some of the factors that impact retirement. We also looked at the overall difficulty that investors face in seeing their portfolios grow to a level that can sustain their future lifestyle.

While traditional investments such as stocks and bonds are constantly touted as the panacea for everyday problems, the reality is that there are activities occurring worldwide that have the ability to power boost your investment returns.

In much the same way that stocks move in a cyclical fashion, so do futures. The difference between the ups and the downs of stocks and futures hinge on two different ideas, though. Stocks move based on speculation and anticipation of a company's success or lack thereof. Futures and currencies move on the needs of the economic engines of entire countries. It is the difference between micro and macro economics.

Once you understand the encompassing nature of futures and currencies, you begin to pay careful attention to the interrelationship of various economic influences and the economies they affect. You also develop a confidence in the numerous futures and forex opportunities ahead of you.

Jim Rogers, author of the book *Hot Commodities* has stated on numerous occasions that we are in a 25-year bull market for commodities. This may or may not be true, but it is undeniable that the world's prosperity hinges on raw materials, credit liquidity, and currency weakness and strength. All three of these things have lined up in just the right way to create opportunities that didn't exist just a few years ago.

In this chapter we will take a look at industrialization, emerging markets, and alternative fuels. Each one of these topics plagues the front page of the newspaper in one form or another. By putting a spotlight on them, you will begin to see not only the robustness of the opportunities ahead of you, but the relevance. It is difficult to change gears from something as familiar as stocks and bonds. The only way to successfully do it is by showing how common and ubiquitous the world of forex and futures is. Once that is done, we will delve deeper into the "what" and how of futures and forex investing.

INDUSTRIALIZATION

The Industrial Revolution is broken up into two phases. The first typically deals with the industrialization of Britain in the eighteenth century. Three key areas—textiles, steam power, and iron founding—were developed into full-fledged businesses that were dependent on machinery more than people. These developments moved in lock step with the development of the Royal Exchange in Manchester, England. The Royal Exchange was developed as a place for merchants and tradesmen to meet and develop forward contracts, the precursor to today's futures contract.

The second industrialization wave occurred in the nineteenth century, largely impacted by the development of the rail system in the United States and the growth of steel and petroleum. These developments, along with the introduction of electricity, led to the development of the Chicago Board of Trade in 1848.

In both instances, the proliferation of eighteenth- and nineteenth-century technology revolutionized the world and spurred the nascent growth of globalization, all of which had a direct impact on the development of commodity trading and the introduction of two different types of traders: hedgers, who owned or were about to purchase the goods, and speculators.

Fast forward to the twentieth and twenty-first centuries, and the silicon age has done to the world what electricity and steam engines did in the preceding centuries. In 1971, Intel introduced the first computer chip. These micro processors are in everything, from cell phones and cars to coffee makers and toys. This has led to a third industrial/technological revolution in countries that may have missed out on the first and second revolutions but are rapidly gaining ground on the developed first-world countries they hope to emulate.

The five emerging markets that get all of the media attention are China, India, Brazil, Russia, and Mexico. In the past 10 years, each of these countries has seen a huge impact in their imports/exports, development of a middle class, and the overall growth of their economies. This growth does not come without growing pains, though. Their growth has directly impacted supply and demand of key resources in agriculture, energy, and raw production materials.

EMERGING MARKETS

China, India, Brazil, Mexico, Indonesia, Pakistan, and Turkey represent the future of import, export, and currency trends. How they interact with raw material, global resources, and international credit represents the opportunities that individual investors have. By keeping our eyes on their activity, we gain a better understanding of what to trade and, more importantly, why we should trade it.

China

The 1970s were a turning point for China's National Party. In December 1978, the National Party Congress's 11th Central Committee made a conscious decision to modernize their economic growth after Japan, the Republic of Korea, Singapore, Taiwan, and Hong Kong. Their citizens suffered from food shortages and rationed clothing. There was a belief that communism did not have to be abandoned in order to develop a way to participate in the market economy of the world.

Nine short years later, the plan worked; by 1987, there was an increased food supply and various consumer goods that simply didn't exist before. The direct results of these changes have also led to China's becoming the fourth largest economy in the world. In 2006, its economic output was US$2.68 trillion. The poverty rate in China dropped from a high of 53% in 1981 to 8% by 2001.

If China stays on track with its growth, it is predicted to overtake the United States as the world's largest economy by 2040. But this growth comes with a price: There are increased gaps between the rich and poor; there has been a large displacement of citizens in order to develop land and because of pollution; and 7 of the top 10 most polluted cities are in China.

There have also been various economic hiccups for China along the way. With pork being a main dietary staple, the recent run-up in corn prices, because of ethanol speculation, made livestock feed more expensive. This forced the Chinese government to develop subsidies to continuously supply pork to their citizens. Couple that small price fluctuation in corn with the fact that 20% of China's energy needs are supplied by foreigners, and it is easy to see the price sensitivity of China's entire economic program. If they have to subsidize every time there is a shortage of goods or commodities that their citizens rely on, it can be disastrous for the cash reserves they have on hand.

Add to the mix that China finally eased the artificial peg of the Chinese yuan from the U.S. dollar in 2005, and you have the potential for inflation to creep into the economy. Even though the Chinese government has been careful to allow no more than a 0.05% fluctuation in the yuan's value daily against the dollar, in the past two years it has already gained 8% against the U.S. dollar. With Wal-Mart, a U.S.-based company, as their seventh largest trading partner, any weakening of the dollar has a significant impact on their profits.

Opportunities in currency, agriculture, and energy abound in China. It's their dependence on the global economy that has put them both center stage and at odds with their traditions. Walking the fine line will be imperative if China hopes to maintain its identity while at the same time not be left at the whims of the international community.

India

In the past 16 years we have seen India go from limited activity on the world stage to becoming one of the top economic powerhouses. In 1991, they had foreign exchange reserves totaling US$5.8 billion. By June 2007, their foreign reserves had risen to US$208 billion. This rapid growth has led India to become the twelfth largest economy in the world.

In spite of this rapid growth, India still faces some key social problems. India has the highest rate of malnutrition among children under the age of three. This is greater than any other country in the world. Couple that with the fact that 25% of the population lives on less than 40 cents per day, and you have a recipe for disaster.

A secondary problem is that in order to fuel their growth, they import crude oil, fertilizers, and various chemicals. Each of these is price sensitive and can significantly add to the bottom line of their exported products. This can have a negative impact on their export growth.

With problems of poverty, lack of food, and a potential for a global shortage in oil, it is natural to look at India and see a country divided. Even though it has been touted as the largest democracy in the world, there are key flaws that could jeopardize the democracy if the people do not feel there is a fair distribution of the wealth that has been created during this economic boom period.

Brazil

Brazil dominates Latin America. They have the most developed agricultural, mining, and manufacturing sectors. When it comes to economic growth, it is considered on par with both India and China. They are the world's ninth largest economy, and growing. They are also pioneers in alternative fuels and are one of the key exporters of ethanol.

Brazil's unique energy program is a direct result of the oil crisis of 1973. In order to diminish their reliance on oil imports, they developed sugar cane into an ethanol fuel. This ethanol introduction directly reduced the number of cars running on gasoline by 10 million. This is a significant achievement, since Brazil is the 10th largest energy consumer in the world.

In spite of Brazil's progressive energy policy, there has been little to no improvement in Brazil's social problems. Poverty, violence, debts, poor wages, and crime are rampant. Almost 19% of the population lives below the poverty line. Slums abound and the uneven distribution of wealth is clearly seen throughout the country.

This is a country that, while promising, has many social problems that have the potential to throw their entire economic growth into a downward spiral.

Russia

With the collapse of the Soviet Union 16 years ago, Russia has made leaps and bounds in developing a market economy. For the past eight years, the Russian economy has grown at 6.7% annually. They are running a federal budget surplus of 9% of gross domestic product (GDP), and the increase in oil prices has created a windfall of revenues.

In eight short years, 1999 to 2007, Russia's foreign reserves went from $12 billion to $420.2 billion dollars. This growth puts Russia as the ninth largest country in the world. The double-edged sword is that this growth that has been primarily fueled by oil is very precarious.

Although Russia has the largest known natural gas reserves, the second largest coal reserves, and the eighth largest oil reserves in the world, the push to alternative fuels may make the long-term prospect of growth in these areas suspect. This also leaves the Russian ruble to excessive exposure to an energy-based economy in a world that is experiencing energy price fatigue.

Mexico

Mexico has a very strong economy and is recognized as the world's 12th largest economy based on GDP. While Mexico has strong international trade relations, 90% of its exports go to the United States and Canada. This heavy dependence on the United States has had adverse effects on Mexico's economy over the years. The economic downturn in the United States during the dot-com bubble burst cut Mexico's growth almost in half.

In spite of the outward positive appearances, there are key underlying problems in economic disparity. While there has been a consistent decrease in poverty and a growing middle class has evolved, the numbers just don't add up. The top 20% of earners make 55% of all of the money in Mexico. That leaves 80% of the people trying to cut up a wage pie of just 45%. Add to this the large dependence of the Mexican economy on money being sent from workers in the United States—US$20 billon a year—and you see a nation that is hyperdependent on U.S. politics and economic well-being.

All the while there are immigration and border issues with the United States. Human resources have left the country to the tune of 1% of the Mexican population, and no new solutions have been introduced to stem the flow. While on the surface poverty appears to have diminished, everyday life is simply difficult for Mexican citizens. There has become a divide in the economic development of the north versus the south of Mexico, with health issues and extreme poverty running rampant in the south.

Other Emerging-Market Countries

On April 19, 2007, the Grant Thornton International Business Report (IBR) identified Indonesia, Pakistan, and Turkey as the next emerging markets to watch.

Indonesia and Pakistan have been identified as having good-size populations capable of providing the necessary labor that could potentially rival both India and China when it comes to manufacturing.

If they decide to chase the paths of other emerging markets, like China and India, it quickly becomes apparent that inexpensive alternative fuels and energy sources must be discovered in order to sustain the growth of these countries while at the same time preserving the environment.

RESOURCES UNDER FIRE

In 2006, British Defense Secretary John Reid stated with the utmost confidence that dwindling natural resources will lead to the likely outcome of violent conflict over agricultural lands, clean water, and energy.

His feelings were backed up a few years earlier by a report designed for the U.S. Department of Defense. This report intimated that global climate changes have the ability to produce cataclysmic environmental events that could trigger battles over energy, food, and water.

Whatever your feelings on global warming and climate, there is no question that many of the resources that we have taken for granted—oil being one of them—are simply not as cheap as they used to be. The rise in the price of oil, along with many everyday food items such as corn, as well as the huge fluctuations in the price of copper, have had a tremendous impact in our day-to-day lives.

Let's take a look at three common commodities and look at the factors that influence them. We will also look at the charts of their price movement. Finally, we will look at the change of the overall commodity index.

Food

In 2005, an article in *The Guardian* said, "One in six countries is facing food shortage." While we all know that newspapers use sensationalism to sell papers, the facts presented were not encouraging. Thirty-four countries and up to 30 million people are currently experiencing droughts and food shortages.

Countries throughout Africa (e.g., Ethiopia, Zimbabwe, Sudan), as well as countries in Central America and Southeast Asia, have been affected, with many experiencing their worst harvests in more than 10 years. Other countries such as Peru and Ecuador, according to the United Nations, are being monitored for early signs of potential famine.

Without question, the situation is difficult in these developing countries, but even first-world countries such as Spain and Portugal have been affected. In 2005, only half of their crop could be harvested, and they had to apply for European Union food assistance.

No one is immune to the changes in climate that have affected crop yields and arable lands. Without some drastic measures taken, the need for countries to produce food for export becomes increasingly significant. This necessity to use agricultural lands for foodstuffs runs headlong into the quest to use agricultural lands to produce food for fuel. We see this problem particularly with corn.

Corn is seen as a potential raw material in the production of ethanol. If farmers see that there is a built-in premium in growing corn as opposed to other grains, such as wheat or soybeans, they will switch to corn. This produces a fight for a limited product with the simultaneous diminishment/elimination of substitute goods, thereby driving prices up on corn, wheat, and soybeans at the same time as one in six countries faces famine.

Water

In 2003, *USA TODAY* proclaimed, "More than half of humanity will be living with water shortages, depleted fisheries, and polluted coastlines within 50 years because of a worldwide water crisis."

This was an excerpt from the United Nations Environment Programme official report on water and the management of worldwide water supplies.

The report cited data from NASA and the World Health Organization, along with several other agencies. By current estimates, 4 billion people will be affected by severe water shortages by 2050.

The future shortages will only compound present-day problems, where over 40% of humanity lacks adequate sanitation facilities and over half of all coastal regions have been overdeveloped and polluted. All of these problems are exacerbated by third-world countries' poor water supply and irrigation practices.

The World Bank reports that 80 countries now have water shortages that threaten health and economies. According to their estimates, the demand for water is doubling every 21 years. Corporations such as Coca-Cola bottling outfits in India, have faced firsthand how the limited water resources they use to run their operations come face to face with local populations' need to simply survive.

It is expected that water will have to be commoditized just like other resources. The water from free-flowing streams and accessible underground water supplies will have to be packaged, branded, and monetized in order to quench the thirst and feed the hunger of 7 billion people.

Energy

In 2003, I released a simple article on the Internet entitled, "Oil Could Reach as High as $4.37/Gallon." I got hate mail sent to me. In April 2007, Shell gas station in San Francisco was offering premium gasoline at $4.29 and Regular gas was at $4.09. I was 8 cents shy of calling the upper limits of pump gas prices.

It was presumed that we would never have as high gas prices as Europe and that I must be quoting potential oil prices in the United Kingdom or Europe. As we have seen, that has not been the case. The fear that the world is rapidly approaching near the end of its supplies in light sweet crude oil has made the commodity become more pressured than ever, almost to the point of hoarding.

In 2004, the world supply of oil was 83 million barrels a day. This has been the fastest rate of increase in oil supplies in history. Unfortunately, the looming worry that this is the peak of oil production has made countries around the world skittish.

This has led the OPEC (Organization of Petroleum Exporting Countries) nations to have a heavy hand in making sure oil prices sustain high levels. Traditionally, the OPEC nations have traded in U.S. dollars when they sold oil. With the growth of the euro and the expansion of the European Union, OPEC's faith in the U.S. dollar's value rebounding significantly has been diminished. In the end, OPEC feels justified in their position to maintain high oil prices.

OIL COULD REACH AS HIGH AS $4.37/GALLON

Over 30 years ago, October 17, 1973, the Organization of Petroleum Exporting Countries (OPEC) shut the valve on oil to the United States.

The price of a gallon of gasoline went up by 400 percent. United States citizens were forced, by law, to conserve energy. What triggered that event? The Arab-Israeli war.

It's starting all over again. President Bush is frustrated at our inability to bring Iraq to stability even though we have placed 250,000 troops in the area.

On the other hand, our Arab allies are frustrated that Bush is uninterested in completely resolving the Israeli-Palestinian conflict and the failing occupation of Iraq.

In their minds, the United States' war against Iraq and Israel's war against Palestine are linked, and they are beginning to come to the same conclusions that Saudi Arabia's King Faisal came to in 1973.

With just the hint of war, we have already seen the price of gas go up 69 percent and the price of a barrel of oil reach $40. When that first shot was fired, a barrel of oil soared in price. Now that we cannot stabilize the region, as one shoe leads, the other follows.

The Arabs will finally protest against the mismanagement of Iraq and the failing resolution of the Israeli-Palestinian conflict, not with picket signs, but with an oil embargo. Oil can easily reach $50–60 per barrel.

Gas at the pump could be as high as $3–4/gallon. Only savvy investors will know what to do. In fact, United Parcel Service, along with other major corporations, has already purchased gasoline future contracts to protect themselves.

Written by Noble DraKoln, 2004, http://www.internetworldstats.com/articles/art022.htm.

Ethanol—The Gasoline Alternative

In 1956, geophysicist Marion Hubbert made a simple postulation that oil production would follow a bell curve. In the beginning, when the oil reserves were discovered, the production would be great; soon afterward, it would "peak" and fall into a rapid exponential decline. This is known as "peak theory."

While originally scoffed at, Dr. Hubbert made a simple prediction that came true. Based on his calculations, oil discovery and full exploitation would take 35 years, and in the United States the "peak" period would occur anywhere from 1965 to 1970. Thus far, he was accurate; the oil production peak occurred in the United States in 1970. He further posited that 50 years after his publication there would be a world peak.

Mr. Hubbert's theory and subsequent play-out of his theory in real numbers has led the world to look for viable alternatives to the potential decline and eventual disappearance of oil as a primary fuel. One of the key front runners is ethanol.

Ethanol is not particularly special. It has been made in multiple ways, either through fermentation or through petrochemical reactions. As the price of oil has increased, more traditional forms of ethanol production have been explored along with multiple resources.

In the United States, corn has been explored as an ethanol resource. In Brazil, where sugar cane is prevalent, sugar cane is used in the production in ethanol. Many European countries, along with Japan, are looking to their excess wine supply (grapes) and sake (rice wine) to produce ethanol.

The level of desperation to find an alternative has clouded some commercial judgment in deciding that ethanol is the way to go. A clear example of the cart getting ahead of the horse is the level of product needed in order to produce ethanol. In the United States, since corn is the primary crop to produce ethanol, the input/output ratio is skewed. It takes 35 liters of corn (1 bushel) to produce 10 liters of ethanol. Over two-thirds of the corn is effectively wasted as ancillary by-products, none of which is fuel.

To reduce this disparity, scientists are attempting to use less essential foodstuffs, such as corn and sugar, and develop ways to break down their by-products (husk and fibers) into a more efficient form of ethanol, along with fast-growing weeds such as switchgrass.

In 2006, 69% of the world's ethanol supply came from the United States and Brazil. They have the ability to produce 5.1 billion gallons of ethanol per year, with an expected rollout of another 3.8 billion gallons by 2009.

Of course, ethanol production is not without its detractors. The key problems cited are crop yield, efficiency, and using agricultural land for fuel. Regardless of these potential problems, the world has embraced the idea of ethanol as an alternative fuel source, which alone spells opportunity.

FUTURES, FOREX, OR STOCKS?

There are many emerging-market funds and hot stocks associated with the countries and resources discussed in this chapter. The average investor would scour through hundreds, if not thousands, of different stocks and mutual funds domestically and abroad to find just the right opportunity.

As long as the management is competent, and hopefully not corrupt, and they have the right combination of marketing and competitive advantage over the next corporation, you might just have a chance at exploiting different current-event opportunities like these and many others.

However, you can go straight to the source. If you want to trade ethanol, there are ethanol futures—no need for a corporate middleman. If you want to invest in the growing European economy, buy the spot or futures euro currency with ease. If you think there will be a shortage of soybeans worldwide, sell soybean futures.

The simplest and best way to take advantage of today's news is in the futures and forex markets. As you read this book, you will learn the why, the how, and the "what to do" that will give you the confidence to take control of your investments.

CHAPTER 3

What Type of Investor Are You?

While the futures and forex markets are considered "alternative investments," much of the activity that you will be doing with them is "trading." Let's define the differences between investing and trading.

Investing is defined as "the act of committing money or capital to an endeavor (a business, project, real estate, etc.) with the expectation of obtaining an additional income or profit."

Trading is defined as "to engage in buying and selling for profit."

These two activities, investing and trading, have the same end goal of profits, but they approach it from two different directions. When you invest, you are committing to the stock or bond that you are purchasing. This is important to be clear on. The buy-and-hold philosophy of stocks and bonds reconfirms that commitment.

When you are "investing" in futures and forex, you are actually "trading." You are not taking delivery on the tangible goods; 99% of the time, you are simply buying and selling the futures and forex contracts at the first sign of profit or based on your predetermined profit goals.

This fluidity in not becoming committed to an investment but being willing to buy and sell to either make a profit or diminish loss is imperative for your success. The commitment is to profitability, not being right about which direction the market is going. This is a defining factor in how well you adapt to the trading approach presented throughout this book.

This is the underlying strength that it will take for you to transition from being a Type A investor, who is looking to get rich quick without understanding the underlying building blocks of futures and forex trading, and a Type B investor, who embraces the building blocks and adapts them to his own risk/reward profile and ultimate profit goals.

YALE STUDY

Now that we have separated investing and trading, let's look at what some of the great minds of our times think about futures investing. On June 14, 2004, the Yale International Center for Finance put out a white paper entitled "The Facts and Fantasies about Commodity Futures." Gary Gorton of the University of Pennsylvania and K. Geert Rowenhorst of the Yale School of Management came to several insightful conclusions. Of the various questions they attempted to answer, these three questions give us the most insight into the appropriateness of this investment class:

1. What are the returns to investing in commodity futures, and how do these returns compare to investing in stocks and bonds?
2. Are commodity futures riskier than stocks?
3. Can commodity futures provide diversification to other asset classes?

In determining their answers to these questions, they took data from the Commodity Research Bureau (CRB) and created an equally weighted index that extended from 1959 to 2004. They removed various commodity contracts that had come and gone over the years.

Second, they concentrated on only one commodity from one exchange, even if that market was traded in multiple exchanges. Volume and liquidity became their determining factor.

Finally, they focused all of their efforts on the front month or contract with the nearest expiration, disregarding other months that the various commodities were traded on.

What Are the Returns to Investing in Commodity Futures, and How Do These Returns Compare to Investing in Stocks and Bonds?

In their research, Gorton and Rowenhorst discovered that over the past 43 years, commodity futures were comparable to the S&P 500, while at the same time they outperformed corporate bonds. There was an average return of 11.02% for both the S&P 500 and the commodity futures. When calculated based on standard deviation, the S&P 500 returns are slightly higher at 14.9% than commodity futures that returned 12.12%.

Are Commodity Futures Riskier Than Stocks?

During two different time periods, the 1970s and the 1990s, commodity futures outperformed the S&P 500. This is significant because the volatility of the equally weighted commodity futures return is slightly below the volatility of the S&P 500.

So while the average returns of the S&P 500 and the commodity futures index may be on par, the underlying difference in volatility makes stocks slightly more risky.

Can Commodity Futures Provide Diversification to Other Asset Classes?

In determining the correlation of commodity futures returns with stocks and bonds, the authors chose to look at three different time intervals. They evaluated the returns quarterly, annually, and over the course of a five-year interval. They discovered that commodity futures are negatively correlated to the S&P 500 and long-term bonds. As time goes on, the negative correlation increases. Inversely, commodity futures returns are positively correlated with inflation.

They coupled this data with the months that the equity markets had their worst performance and then calculated the relationship between commodity futures and equities for two time frames: 1% and 5%. During 5% of the worst-performance months, stocks fell an average of 9.18%, while commodities returned 1.43%. During 1% of the worst-performance months, stocks fell an average of 13.87%, while commodities returned an average of 2.32%.

Pros and Cons

The information Gorton and Rowenhorst accumulated doesn't stop there. The authors then looked at commodity futures in relation to companies that trade in commodities and attempted to determine which market is the better performer.

By publishing this study, Gorton and Rowenhorst made commodities an accessible asset class based on the numbers. They have dispelled many assumptions and myths and, at the same time, have raised the esteem of the commodity futures market to a level of prominence that goes beyond anecdotal and subjective experiences.

By dissecting commodity futures in this way, we can look to the numbers and develop concrete strategies that can properly incorporate commodity futures into a bond and stock portfolio while managing inflationary pressures with an eye toward optimizing returns and minimizing risk.

The key problem with their report is that they take a fictionalized commodity index. They equally weigh each commodity, and then they ignore the various commodity back months to concentrate on the front months only. While this may work for a white paper, what is available to the average investor is completely different.

The data that they use comes from the CRB, which has two of its own indices. The second index that they developed was created solely to take into account the increased volatility of the energy sector of the past several years.

Other commodity indices such as the Goldman Sachs Commodity Index and the Dow Jones Commodity Index are even more heavily weighted in oil, often having a one-for-one correlation in its movement. It is also important to keep in mind that the private sector will constantly move and shift the weight of its index to match the investment environment at the time. So an index's remaining static over the course of 50 years is unlikely and will include commodity markets that may be eliminated over time.

Even with these flaws, the authors of this white paper have given a kinder face to commodity futures that can allow for a pure stock and bond investor to find a sense of comfort that he may not be able to get anywhere else.

TYPES OF INVESTORS

When a pure stock and bond investor picks up a book like this, he knows that he wants something different, but he can't quite put his finger on it.

He may have missed out on the run-up in gold from $300 to $700, or he may have missed out on the euro's explosion from 88 cents to $1.30, or he may have missed out on the run-up of the oil market from $12 per barrel to $70 per barrel. At each turn, he saw what was happening but really didn't have a clue on how he could participate.

I call this type of investor Type A. There are five different types of Type A investor; the Hare, the Turtle, the Ostrich, the Peacock, and the Mouse. Each of these Type A investors has varying degrees of experience in the market and various motivations, but, unfortunately, they end up with the same result when it comes to futures and forex investing—failure.

Type A Investor

The Type A investor has a balanced portfolio around stocks and bonds. For the most part the diversification plan that he has revolves around the various types of mutual funds and a mix of zero-coupon bonds and corporate bonds. He feels confident that this is the way to go, but he can't wrap his mind around how others are capable of making double-digit returns in their accounts.

As we discussed earlier, the problem with this conservative approach is the fact that many investors will outlive their money. In the past, it was to be expected that the income mix of pensions, Social Security, and a small amount of investments would be enough to support you in your retirement.

Unfortunately, the lack of pensions and the dismal prospects of Social Security mean that your retirement investments have to work three times as hard. When you become too conservative, you actually do yourself a disservice, particularly when you are attempting to live off of your investments.

With current inflation running at 3% per year, it is no secret that after 10 years your money will buy one third less than it buys today. The inflation rate between January 1997 and January 2007 was 27.23%; during that same time frame, the "compound annual rate of growth" for the S&P 500 was 6.64%.

That means almost one half of your gains were being eroded by inflation, and we haven't even begun to account for taxes.

During that same 10-year period, the United States Treasury bond yielded 5.92%, and the United States Treasury bill yielded 4.15%.

It is easy to see that the Type A investor who focuses solely on a stock and bond mix will be sorely disappointed in his long-term returns when he takes into account inflation, taxes, and the need to maintain his standard of living.

So when the average Type A investor begins to look at futures and forex investing, he realizes three things:

1. He has only a limited amount of capital to do anything.

2. He has only a finite amount of time to learn something new or to devote to a new endeavor.

3. There are too many overwhelming commodity and currency opportunities to pick the right one for him.

These three problems combine to give the Type A investor the necessary excuses not to do anything or, even worse, to blame someone else when things go wrong for him in futures and forex investing.

This is unfortunate because while the Type A investor is holding on to his classical investments, Wall Street is constantly developing and creating new financial instruments to figure out more sophisticated ways to transfer wealth from the average investors to their bottom-line profit projections.

Different Type A Investors   Over the years I have met so many different types of Type A investors that I wanted to point out their motivations
and personality traits, as well as the key attitudes that hold them back from
transitioning into a Type B investor.

The Hare

Just like the fable of the hare and the tortoise, this investor-turned-trader
is fixated on the end result, with little regard to anything else. With little
preparation or forethought, the first bit of news that supports his ideas has
him in the market.

He is counting his profits before he makes them and is more concerned
with hype than substance. He likes to be involved with the excitement and
somehow feel like he is in the know with little effort.

The failure of this Type A investor is that there is overreliance on
newsletters, TV programs, or insiders. Little research is done, so all of the
credit is taken for success, but everyone else is to blame for failure, including the market.

The Hares rarely stick around in the futures and forex markets for long.
They have no long-term diversification plan and are typically doomed to
repeat their mistake of jumping into the market based on hype over and
over again if they aren't careful.

The Turtle

This Type A investor has been involved with stocks and bonds all his life.
He knows what he knows and isn't open-minded to anyone telling him how
to invest. He typically takes a while to come to a trading decision in the
futures and forex market, and when he does he is determined to apply his
exact same stock and bond strategies.

For the most part, he is fixated on not taking anyone's advice but his
own on how to trade the markets and has a lot of myopia on what futures
and forex investing is really all about. There is a tendency to a long-term
bias and holding on to losers in this Type A investor.

The Turtle will grind his account down to zero because he could not
adapt to the new environment and will then blame futures and forex as
being impossible to understand. He will always know that there is more
money to be made in adding futures and forex to his portfolio, but he will
assume that since he can't figure it out, no one can.

The Ostrich

This Type A investor is someone who is very traditional in his approach.
He has a balanced mix of stocks and bonds and is getting average returns,
all the while suffering through major market ups and downs.

He has most likely tried out futures and forex in the past, but didn't really understand how to incorporate it into his overall diversification plan. So he may have lost money and been afraid ever since.

This is the most difficult type of Type A investor. The Ostrich simply doesn't trust himself or his own judgment when it comes to trading futures and forex. He would rather bury his head in the sand instead of looking for a different way or approach to trading these markets.

The Peacock

This Type A investor has to be right. He sells himself on the whys and wherefores of the market. Peacocks are very intelligent and very well versed in their areas of expertise, so their typical assumption is that their day-to-day talents can automatically translate into the futures and forex arena.

They are constantly looking for the holy grail and will have opinions about the market direction regardless of what is occurring on the screen. The weakness of the Peacock is that no one can tell him anything. His focus on what he believes should be occurring is so overwhelming that what is happening and his end result of making a profit are overshadowed.

This Type A trader will have the hardest time in understanding that you don't have to be right about the markets direction in order to profit from it.

The Mouse

This Type A investor simply wants to get his toe wet. Regardless of his overall investment portfolio, he will put in the least amount of capital he can get away with. While he thinks he's being prudent, he is actually doing himself a disservice.

There are two reasons why new businesses fail: undercapitalization or overcapitalization. The Mouse is perpetually undercapitalized. By putting in the least amount possible, the Mouse is pigeonholed into markets in which he is most likely not interested. He is also stuck with limited risk management opportunities and is constantly at the mercy of market hiccups.

Of the five types, the Mouse would probably be better off not trading at all. His typical experience will be negative, either constantly being stopped out or blowing out his account, and he will have a difficult time gaining enough confidence in futures and forex trading to be able to put in a reasonable amount of capital to increase his chances of success.

Breaking the Type A Investor Cycle   It is imperative that all of the Type A investors begin to modify and change their approach to their overall portfolio. This takes a paradigm shift in the way they approach the futures and forex markets altogether. This takes a commitment from Type A investors to seriously want to incorporate futures and forex investing as a permanent part of their diversification goals.

Let's look at what I call the Type B investor to see how it's done.

Type B Investor

The Type B investor is not too much different from the Type A investor. He believes in stocks and bonds, and, more importantly, he is aware of the same difficulties in approaching futures and forex investing:

1. He has only a limited amount of capital to do anything.
2. He has only a finite amount of time to learn something new or to devote to a new endeavor.
3. But instead of being "overwhelmed" when it comes to commodity and currency investing, he sees "unlimited" opportunity.

When you look at the various commodity indices, you see that there has been tremendous growth potential. Barclay Trading Group tracks various indices around the world. In their top 50 listed indices there are seven different commodity indices. On the extreme end of the indices, second from the top, Rogers International Commodity Index had a compounded annual return of 19.99%, for a total return 264%, from August 1998 to June 2007.

The worst-performing commodities index is the CRB Total Return Index. From August 1998 to June 2007 it had a compounded annual return of 5.16%, for a total of 56.60% during that time frame.

If you take a look at the euro, you see it move from a low of $0.8228 in 2000, just a year from its inception, to a high of $1.3833 in July of 2007. This 53-cent increase represents a 64% increase in just seven years.

These are tremendous moves. Not all of them can be captured in the stock or bond market. By opening his mind to true diversification, by adding commodities and currencies to his portfolio, the Type B investor is able to bolster his overall returns and beat inflation.

The problem is that the Type A person gets involved with futures and forex on a lark or a hot tip expecting quick results and, more times than not, becomes disappointed or disenfranchised with the results.

How Do You Become a Type B investor?   Going from your typical Type A investor to a Type B investor requires two things. First, you must be aware that the investments that you are currently in are unable to sustain your long-term goals. Second, you have to know yourself. Like any investment, futures and forex investing can be approached in a myriad of different ways.

The first issue we have tackled in depth—retirement problems and the global changes going on around the world. So we'll tackle the second issue head on. It's difficult for many investors to take an active role in their investments. The fact that you have picked up this book puts you ahead of 90% of the investors out there.

Now you have to take it one step further and truly understand what type of investor you are versus what type of investor you want to be. By getting involved in futures and forex, you are making a conscious decision to take an active role in your investment portfolio.

This can be a difficult endeavor if you are the type of investor who simply doesn't have or want to devote the time to monitor your investments. To keep the potential opportunities from overwhelming you, you must put in the time to learn about these investments.

Even if you want a pure buy-and-hold strategy and relinquish control to a futures or forex money manager, you must be able to understand the whys and hows of what they are doing.

If you want to be actively involved in picking and choosing your futures and forex investments, you must have a clear and logical reason for doing what you do.

There is so much hype involved with alternative investing that it becomes easy to overlook the hard work it takes. That is the key difference between being a Type B investor and a Type A investor.

Type B investors realize that anything worth having takes hard work, and they make a commitment to trading futures and forex for the long haul. They refuse to let one bad investment make or break them. They also realize that in order to succeed in futures and forex investing, they have to change their mind-set from being a strict buy-and-hold investor to becoming a speculator willing to trade in and out of their investment when necessary.

Transitioning to a Type B Trader   It is not an impossible task to go from being a Type A investor to a Type B trader. This book is designed to do just that. The goal is to teach you how to develop a proper trading plan and how to use proper money management and risk management techniques. More importantly, it will show you how to use technical analysis to identify trends, countertrends, and entry/exit techniques.

By combining all of these different aspects of trading, you become a complete trader, a holistic trader, who is not overly strong in one area but capable of operating effectively on multiple levels to achieve the type of control in your trading that can lead to success.

FATAL MARKET CONDITIONS

When it comes to trading, who you are and how you interact with the market is tantamount to your success. If you approach the market as one of the Type A investors, you will constantly find yourself discouraged by the enormity of the markets, rarely having time to review your motivations and actions. As you gain control and become more of a Type B investor, you will find the market more malleable to your will.

One of the questions I hear most often is: "If I become a Type B investor, will I no longer exhibit my Type A traits?"

There is no easy answer. Who we are as people rarely ever changes; only in the face of extreme adversity are we able to see if there has been a change. The long way to adversity is for you to trade and be put to the "mettle." A shorter way is to ask yourself hypothetical questions about your potential reactions in various situations.

The following paragraphs include three of the most aggressive moves in history: gold and silver cornering, near collapse of Long-Term Capital Management, and the currency crisis dubbed the Asian Flu. By role-playing what your attitudes and reactions would have been during these particular events, you begin to shape your thinking and eventually your trading.

These are just a handful of events that have shaped our world. You can look to George Soros's breaking the Bank of England or to the oil embargo of the early 1980s, and further, to put yourself through the paces and see how you would have reacted.

Gold and Silver Cornering

After the United States went off the gold standard, a gold auction was held in August 1979. The face of the U.S. dollar had changed. At the same time, gold was in demand more than ever. The auction was a raging success and garnered more attention than expected.

In order to curb this enthusiasm, the commodity exchanges raised minimum margin requirements. This is a common tactic to reduce speculation and to price the smaller participants out of the market. This was a successful move on the Chicago Board of Trade's (CBOT's) part because it forced smaller speculators to sell their holdings and take their profits.

There was an unexpected side effect, though: Large foreign speculators moved in and began buying up contracts at the newly adjusted margin levels. The CBOT was shocked and took even more restrictive measures. They began to limit the number of contracts that could be bought.

Then the 1980 Olympics were boycotted by Russia. The CBOT took the political instability as an opportunity to allow only the closing of long positions. This basically put artificial downward pressure on the gold and silver markets, creating a rapid deflation in price, thereby ruining many physical gold investors and futures speculators.

At the time, silver had reached a high of $68 per ounce and Gold had broken through the $800-per-ounce barrier.

The common feeling is that the Hunt brothers attempted to corner the gold and silver markets and thus caused the collapse. The CBOT was also complicit in helping them reach their untimely demise, and, in fact, they could be painted as the victims of the CBOT's radical change in policies. Nevertheless, because of the Hunt brothers' total financial commitment to the gold and silver markets and the amount of money they had borrowed to pyramid their positions, they were on the verge of collapsing the United States banking system. Out of necessity and economic stability, the Federal Reserve bailed out the Hunt brothers and the banks to the tune of a $1.1 billion loan.

Ask yourself these questions about this market:

- What would a Type A investor do when entering this market?
- How would a Type A investor exit this market?
- What would catch the Type A investor's attention to participate in this market?
- What would a Type B investor do differently?
- When would a Type B investor enter/exit this kind of market?

It's okay if you can't answer these questions right now. Go through the book, sign up for the free trading software, and back-test these markets and learn how you could react and what you would do in order to not get caught on the wrong side of any of these freight trains.

Interest Rate Backfire

Long-Term Capital Management (LTCM) was a hedge fund founded with Nobel Prize winners Myron Scholes and Robert Merton on the board. LTCM had developed a trading style that utilized arbitrage. They focused their efforts on trading U.S., Japanese, and European sovereign bonds. The arbitrage focused on a simple concept: over time, the value of long-dated bonds issued a short time apart would tend to become identical because the bonds that were trading at a premium would decrease in value and the bonds trading at a discount would increase in value. The profits between the two were practically guaranteed. This risk-free profit would become more and more apparent every time a new bond was issued.

Since the profit opportunity was "very" thin, LTCM needed more leverage than most companies in order to make the program worthwhile for their investors. In 1998, the firm started out with equity of US$4.72 billion. They used that equity to borrow over US$124.5 billion and leveraged assets of around \$129 billion. They then used these positions to convince banks to give them off-balance-sheet derivative positions amounting to US\$1.25 trillion.

Initially, this heavily leveraged strategy produced returns in the double digits. These "risk-free" profits stopped in August 1998, when Russia defaulted on their sovereign debt. Investors lost faith in Japanese and European bonds. U.S. Treasury bonds became the bonds of the hour. The expected bond narrowing not only stopped, but quickly began to diverge. LTCM lost US\$1.85 billion in capital.

Because LTCM had daisy-chained so much leverage, if they failed, the effect would not only be a loss of capital, but a banking crisis to the tune of at least US\$1.25 trillion.

To save the global economy, the Federal Reserve Bank of New York, without putting up any taxpayer money, organized a bank-led bailout of US\$3.625 billion. By the end of the fiasco, the total losses were found to be US\$4.6 billion.

Ask yourself these questions about this market:

- What would a Type B investor do when discovering a "risk-free" opportunity?
- How would a Type B investor react to the "risk-free" investment that no longer worked?
- Would a Type B investor hold on in this market until oblivion?
- What would be the money management tools of a Type B investor?
- When would a Type B investor put on a risk management strategy?

In the news and in the media, investors are constantly being bombarded by "surefire" opportunities and "risk-free" opportunities. Even the best minds on the planet can confuse what the market "should be" doing with "what the market is doing."

The moral of the story is that you shouldn't be married to a position. While we all would like to believe it couldn't happen to us, the reality is that traders give back profits and then lose part of their principal frequently. This is what separates the professionals from the novices, most of the time. They are typically not afraid to cut their losses short or to turn a trade into a breakeven before it turns negative on them.

Asian Flu

In late 1996, Asian countries were being noted globally for their unprecedented economic growth. Technology and manufacturing were large contributors to the newfound financial strength in Indonesia, Malaysia, Thailand, and Singapore.

Export/import partners of these countries wondered how long their growth could be sustained. The main business attraction that had encouraged business in those countries in the first place, undervalued currencies, had gotten significantly stronger.

In early 1997, Soros's groups began heavily shorting Thailand's currency, the baht, and Malaysia's currency, the ringgit, using the same highly leveraged tactics that had been used five years earlier against the British pound.

In July 1997, in order to stimulate their weakening economy, Thai officials devalued the baht. This action set off a wave of devaluations throughout Asia, most notably Malaysia.

Prime Minister Mahathir Mohammad of Malaysia declared to the world his disdain for George Soros and his currency-crippling investment strategies.

Ask yourself these questions about this market:

- Who would a Type B investor pay attention to, the concerned exporters and importers or the news?
- How would a Type B investor prepare for an unconfirmed potential currency collapse?
- What tools would a Type B investor use to discern this market's mood?
- What would be the first warning signs for a Type B investor?
- When would a Type B investor set up risk management parameters to protect himself from loss?

WHERE YOU FIT IN

What is futures and forex investing?

The answer is both simple and complex. Once you get past the definitions, it quickly becomes apparent that futures and forex investing is a culture in and of itself. There is a need to abandon your preconceived notions while at the same time fortifying your mind-set when it comes to your approach and goals.

You will have to take a serious look at your stock market experiences and do your best to disregard your conventional wisdom for a whole set of new rules of engagement.

Futures and forex investing is not easy, but it is simple. You must take a methodical step-by-step approach and have set rules of engagement. Once you do that, you will begin to unlock the true potential of this alternative investment for your overall investment portfolio.

PART II

Why 95% of Investors Fail at Futures and Forex

W hat does it take to be successful in life? Do we emulate the worst people, or do we emulate the best? When it comes to trading futures and forex, it seems easy to emulate the worst. Those who have heard about futures and forex trading usually hear it from family members or acquaintances who failed at it. While it is good to keep an open mind, the negativity of the unsuccessful can weigh heavily for those starting out or for those who have experience but still lack a grasp of the basics of how the futures and forex markets work.

There are a myriad of reasons why 95% of traders fail, ranging from undercapitalization or overcapitalization to not being familiar with the vocabulary, bringing old stock ideas into trading decisions, and misunderstanding gambling and speculation. The following chapters will shed light on why 95% of investors fail in their transition to trading futures and forex and more importantly how you can become one of the 5% that can take control of their futures and forex trading, leading them to success.

Becoming one of the elite 5% is easier said than done. That is why you must learn to separate your individual trading experience from your overall trading goals. You will sometimes find yourself losing right along with the other 95% of traders. You won't be able to make heads or tails of the market. What will make the difference is not the loss but how you have prepared for the loss and how you react.

CHAPTER 4

The World of Futures and Forex

W hile today's futures and forex markets are the hottest news items, with the weak dollar, increasing oil prices, and gold making headlines every other day, it has not always been this way. Each of these markets was born out of the necessity of their times.

Forward contracts, the precursor to the futures markets, can be dated as far back as Phoenician times. In sixteenth-century Japan, we see a fully operational rice futures exchange that was functional and had a tremendous impact on the local economy. The countries that adopted forward contracts and later futures contracts, all had one thing in common: strong commodity economies that were impacted by time in some form or fashion.

The same occurred in the forex market. While foreign currency trading is a relatively new phenomenon, approximately 30 years in the making, it also came of age out of the need to accurately reflect the value of various burgeoning economies around the world.

So when the world was smaller, particularly after the end of World War II, import and export numbers were negligible, and thus free-floating currencies were not as important. The moment that the world began to catch up with the United States in manufacturing and exporting goods, so did the need to accurately use currencies to reflect the strength or weakness of a country and then measure their goods and services accordingly.

Two markets, one fuel, growth.

In this chapter we will lay down a brief foundation of how futures and forex trading works. We will also look at the interrelationship among the spot, futures, and option markets in order to round out your understanding of how these markets behave.

By the end of this chapter, your working vocabulary, along with your understanding of the players in these markets, will have a tremendous impact on how you perceive your role as a trader.

FUTURES AND OPTIONS

Ring. Ring.

Ring.

Jim: Hello?

Bob: Hi Jim, this is Bob. Bob down here at the Soybean Ponderosa.

Jim: Oh, Bob! Good to hear from you. What can I do for you today?

Bob: Well, Jim, I am about to put my soybeans in the ground this week, and I wanted to know how many bushels you might want. And what kind of price you could give me for them.

Jim: Bob, I would love to give you what I paid for them last year, but that's not going to work. They say this will be the best crop yet.

Bob: Jim, don't worry about it. I use farm marketing. If you and I can lock in a price today, I'll use the futures to catch any move upward in price.

Jim: That's good, Bob. Let's talk numbers, then. . . .

Futures predate stocks by several thousand years. One of the earliest recognized futures transactions was the Chinese rice futures of 6,000 years ago.

In the seventeenth century, Japan instituted the first organized rice futures exchange. Japanese merchants would store rice in warehouses for future use. Warehouse holders would in turn sell receipts against the stored rice.

Gradually, these "rice tickets" became accepted as general currency, and rules were developed to standardize their exchange. The agricultural problem that existed 6,000 years ago in China—maintaining a year-round supply of a seasonal product—reared its ugly head in the United States' Midwest of the 1800s.

Today's commodity exchanges resemble the rice futures exchange of Japan the most. They have adopted complete standardization for each commodity as well as delivery locations.

While today's commodity contracts come in various amounts, move on differing price scales, and are delivered in various months, they each contain all of these three elements on their ticker symbol: contract name, month of delivery, year, and price. They are all also self-consistent when it comes to their standardization.

Hedgers and Speculators

With globalization there is a challenge of meeting a constant demand for goods and products as well as properly moving supplies around so nothing goes to waste. This demand-and-supply battle affects all types of products or events. From livestock, manufacturing processes, currency, weather, as well as all products that are of a cyclical nature.

The solution to this problem has lead to the development and maturation of futures trading. In the 1840s, we saw the Midwest become the hub for railroads and telegraph lines. We saw the invention of many agricultural tools that increased overall production levels. All of these events combined to make an efficient agricultural acquisition and distribution system.

While futures contracts were already trading in Liverpool, England; Chicago sat in the middle of all of the United States' activity at the time and thus became the hub of futures trading.

In 1848, a central location was developed in Chicago for farmers and dealers to meet and purchase "spot" grains. The farmers would get cash for immediate delivery of the grains. While this was an effective way to get rid of current supplies, the system was flawed in two ways. Farmers had no standard quantities or quality of product. Not having set standards made many farmers have a difficult time in getting the best prices for their goods.

Farmers (sellers) and dealers (buyers) would also make deals for "future" purchases. They would do this to lock in favorable prices ahead of time. This was a big departure from the practice of cash and carry and required a great deal of trust between the two parties. Since delivery and payments could be months in the "future."

For example, a farmer and a dealer would agree on a price for delivery of 1,000 bushels of corn at the end of May. This was acceptable to the farmer (seller) because he knew how much he would be paid for his corn in advance. He could budget for seeds, hired help, planting equipment, and any other necessary expenses a head of time, and then calculate his profit margins accordingly. The dealer (buyer) enjoyed this scenario because he knew his raw material costs in advance and could calculate his necessary resell mark up accordingly. Each side would put up a small amount of money as a good faith deposit to guarantee the agreement. These two groups, farmers and dealers, became known as "hedgers."

By creating these "future" or "forward" contracts the farmer and dealer had essentially created a credit opportunity for each other. Instead of a cash and carry situation fraught with uncertainty, their agreement with each other had essentially made their activity into a business, which could show potential cash flow and could project earnings.

These contracts became well received by the banks and allowed both parties to be eligible for loans and lines of credit. These contracts became so well respected, that both dealers and farmers were able to sell their contracts to third parties. These third parties were often other dealers and farmers willing to deliver or accept delivery on the contracts. Some dealers and farmers would also buy and sell these additional contracts to make sure that they had gotten the best possible price on their original contracts.

Then there were third parties that also purchased and sold contracts solely to capitalize on weather or market conditions that affected the price of the grains. These parties became known as "speculators." They never intended to make or take delivery of the actual grains, nor were they farmers or dealers. They wanted to simply buy high, sell low or sell high, buy low. Sound familiar?

Thus evolved the commodity exchanges and the two party system of trading, the "hedgers," the ones in the know, and the "speculators," the ones that think they are in the know.

The spot market never went away; it was complimented by the futures market, and later the option market. Creating three different ways for farmers and dealers to buy and sell their products.

Over the past 150 years, futures trading has grown from grains to gold, cattle to coffee, and much more. Indices such as the Dow Jones, S&P 500, and Nasdaq 100 are all accessible as futures contracts. Even blue-chip stocks, such as GE, AT&T, and Ford, have a futures component.

Futures Exchanges

The organization of futures exchanges standardized the freely traded forward contracts. They set the quality, quantity, and delivery points of every contract. This made it easier for the hedgers to determine the value of their products and agreements.

Over the past 100 years, U.S. futures exchanges have merged and morphed. While there are regional futures exchanges and specialty futures exchanges, there are three dominant players in the United States.

The Chicago Board of Trade (CBOT) was established in 1848. It is one the world's oldest derivatives exchange. Forty-seven futures and options products trade on the CBOT. In 2001, trading volume exceeded 260 million contracts.

At the outset, the CBOT focused solely on agricultural futures; wheat, corn and oats dominated the landscape. Almost 130 years after the CBOT was formed, the lineup of products was finally expanded. Legislation allowed the CBOT to offer futures on financial instruments for the first time. Futures on U.S. Treasury bonds became the pioneering financial instrument. Today, U.S. Treasury bonds are one of the most actively traded futures around the world.

In 1982, options on futures contracts were finally allowed. Overnight, this changed the way futures were traded.

The CBOT stays on the cutting edge of the industry. It has introduced futures and futures options on the Dow Jones Industrial Average, and upgraded and added an electronic trading system to its infrastructure. This was a huge feat since trading had been done primarily with open outcry, where live traders buy and sell in the pits, for 150 years.

Chicago Mercantile Exchange The Chicago Mercantile Exchange (CME) began in 1898 as the Chicago Butter and Egg Board. Like the CBOT, it offered only agricultural products. The CME finally ventured from basic agricultural products with the introduction of frozen pork belly futures in 1961. This was the first futures contract based on frozen meat. Continuing its pioneering efforts, the CME introduced live cattle futures in 1964. This was the first time futures were offered on a nonstorable commodity.

The CME launched currency futures in 1972; they were the world's first financial futures contracts. Prior to this, the CME traded only commodities such as corn, wheat, and pork bellies. This new development was in direct response to the breakdown of the Bretton Woods Agreement.

On May 16, 1972, seven forex currency futures contracts were listed. The contracts dealt in British pounds, Canadian dollars, German deutsche marks, French francs, Japanese yen, Mexican pesos, and Swiss francs.

The CME has an electronic trading platform that offers trading 24 hours a day, 5 days a week.

In April 2001, the CME expanded forex market coverage by offering electronic access to its full range of currency contracts virtually 24 hours a day via the Globex electronic trading platform. This electronic trading access occurs side by side with floor trading in CME's currency pits during floor trading hours.

In March 2003, the total notional value of forex trading at CME was US$347.5 billion. Currency futures are derivatives on the interbank cash and forward exchange rates.

In 2002, the CME became the first U.S. financial exchange to become publicly traded.

In 2007, the CME and the CBOT merged to form the largest derivatives exchange in the United States.

New York Board of Trade The New York Board of Trade (NYBOT) didn't exist until 1998. It was born through the merger of the Coffee, Sugar, & Cocoa Exchange, Inc. and the New York Cotton Exchange.

The New York Cotton Exchange was founded in 1870 and the Coffee Sugar & Cocoa Exchange, Inc. was founded in 1882. These two pioneered sugar options, frozen concentrated orange juice, and the New York Stock Exchange Composite Index, as well as the Commodity Research Bureau Futures Price Index.

The NYBOT has opened the first full-time electronic market for U.S Treasury and agency futures. The NYBOT is a not-for-profit membership organization. It was established as the parent company for the two merged exchanges and their subsidiaries and divisions.

New York Mercantile Exchange   The New York Mercantile Exchange (NYMEX) began as the Butter and Cheese Exchange of New York. It was founded in 1872 by dairy merchants who wanted to bring order and standardization to their industry. By 1882, the product line had expanded and the group changed its name to the New York Mercantile Exchange.

Today, the NYMEX no longer deals with agricultural products. In 1978, the introduction of heating oil futures set the stage for NYMEX's dominance in the energy sector. It is also dominant in metal futures.

The exchange has two divisions, the NYMEX Division and the COMEX (commodity exchange) Division. The first focuses on energy, platinum, and palladium futures and options. The second handles gold, silver, copper, and aluminum.

What Markets Are Traded?

Futures contracts in the United States and in various other countries fall into six broad categories: agricultural, metallurgical, interest-bearing assets, indices, foreign currency, and security futures.

FOREIGN EXCHANGE (FOREX)

Foreign Exchange n. Abbr. *Forex or FX*
   Transaction of international monetary business, as between governments or businesses of different countries.
   Negotiable bills drawn in one country to be paid in another country.
                    The American Heritage Dictionary of the English Language,
                         4th edition (2000, Houghton Mifflin Company)

The forex market is a relatively new phenomenon. While we can trace futures and stock trading back over 100 years, forex trading history began just 30 years ago. What makes this market tremendously interesting is that it went from nothing to being the largest volume–traded industry in the world, with over US$1.5 trillion traded daily.

While the majority of forex traders know only about the spot forex side, forex began in the futures market. It has a robust spot, futures, and options trading environment. Each market interacts with each other and there are few, if any, real boundaries that affect how they react to the same supply and demand numbers.

What makes it unique is that the spot market for forex allows "speculators" to get involved with little to no investment. This is a function of the over-the-counter market, which has changed the rules of what is required of investors and the proliferation of high speed internet connections that allow anyone to bring currency dealers right into their homes. How did this happen? Was it by design? Or was it by accident?

What Is the Spot Market?

Forex trading falls into three arenas: spot, futures, and options. The majority of new forex traders learn only about spot forex trading. While the spot market has some advantages, don't ignore the futures and options forex markets.

This schism between spot, futures, and option forex developed early on. Banks developed control of the spot forex market in what is known as the over-the-counter (OTC) market. They initially offered spot forex services as a way to provide added value services to their large multinational clients. In the beginning these spot transactions were considered essential for multinational corporations to operate quickly.

The banks also considered OTC forex to be a risk-free way of generating profits. Banks consider the spread between currency bids and asks as free money. Banks have always fought to make sure that foreign currency exchange was seen as an express power of banking, with no need for additional regulatory oversight. With such an aggressive stance by the banks, the OTC market's explosive growth was inevitable.

While much of foreign exchange trading could have been conducted on the regulated exchanges, the banks didn't support it and created their own instruments as substitutes. OTC forex has expanded from its early roots as a spot transaction market for just multinational corporations to include retail investors. Over US$1.5 trillion is traded daily. The majority of this growth has been fueled by independent dealers, which now out number banks in offering OTC currencies.

The spot market operates 24 hours a day, 6 days a week, in 3 different time zones: London, Tokyo, and the United States.

Importers and Exporters

There are three distinct time frames that set up the stage for today's style of currency trading. The first time frame is the precurrency era of the 1950s.

The second time frame is the worldwide volatile political atmosphere of the 1970s. The third time frame is what has occurred in this free market economy since its liberation 30 years ago. In each time frame there have been three catalysts—war, gold, and foreign banks—which have played a significant role in propelling currency development.

In the 1970s, war, U.S. gold reserves, and foreign bank activity played a significant role in the currency market we have today. Each problem began to directly feed off of the other.

The Vietnam War had drained our gold reserves heavily. By 1970, Fort Knox only had US$12 billion.

At the same time, we saw the growth of the oil business along with increased foreign trade. This combined activity caused a boom in the demand for U.S. dollars in foreign banks. During the 1970s, over US$47 billion was sitting in overseas banks.

It was clear to anyone that, at least on paper, our gold reserves were overleveraged by almost 4 to 1. Plus, there was no end in sight and no way to reverse the momentum that had already begun. As a nation, we did not know how to react against such an overbearing demand for our currency.

Our problems were then compounded by the invention of the financial instrument called the "Eurodollar."

At the time, and until this day, foreign banks with U.S. dollars would make low-interest loans in U.S. dollars to importers and exporters. Although the dollars were never intended to be repatriated, the United States in the 1970s was still on the hook to exchange these "credit"-created dollars for the gold we were keeping on reserve at Fort Knox.

Then a miracle in disguise happened. The Bretton Woods Agreement collapsed. The Bretton Woods Agreement had kept an artificial peg to the U.S. dollar all around the globe. Some pegs were strong, some pegs were weak, but at the end of the day they never moved more than 1% in any direction. Like today's problem with the Chinese yuan, the forced peg against the dollar kept a constant controlled flow of U.S. dollars out of the country.

At the same time, gold had a fixed peg to the U.S. dollar as well—one ounce equaled $35.

In the overleveraged gold-dollar environment, many countries began to feel frustrated with the artificial peg. Germany was the first to break away from the artificial peg. Three months later, the dollar went off of the gold standard and other countries quickly eliminated the peg.

With the end of the gold standard, the United States was no longer required to give gold to anyone holding U.S. dollars when they asked for it. Thus began the world of "fiat" money, and a whole set of different problems arose.

In the 30 years since the collapse of the last gentlemanly agreement on currency rates, a few momentous occasions have occurred. The Japanese yen gained prominence because of Japan's heavy export relationship with the United States. The Gulf War occurred, along with the collapse of the overheated Asian economy; the euro was created; and the dot-com bubble affected the global economy.

Each time, currencies have come away with a newfound respect, as well as an element of surprise that keeps you guessing what's next.

Now a new stage has been set. The United States' perpetual war on "terror," the permanent introduction and dominance of the euro currency, as well as the steady Organization of Petroleum Exporting Countries (OPEC) increases in oil prices, and finally gold's renaissance as a store house of value will have a tremendous impact on the future of what it means to trade currencies.

This could be a fundamental shift in the next phase of currency development.

OTC Forex Contracts

OTC forex trading focuses primarily on the following movers: U.S. dollar (USD), British pound (GBP), Eurocurrency (EUR), Japanese yen (JPY), and Swiss franc (SFR). These currencies are the most actively traded in the world and are known as the "hard" currencies. Since currencies are traded in pairs, the following hard-currency pairs account for 80% of all OTC trading:

USD/EUR

USD/JPY

GBP/USD

USD/SFR

EUR/JPY

EUR/GBP

Other currencies that are not listed here are considered soft currencies. There are approximately 34 soft currencies traded around the world.

How Is the Spot Price Calculated?

Typical OTC spot leverage rules look like this:

There is a minimum margin of $1,000 per unit for accounts less than $25,000. Traders must maintain a balance $1,000 or 1% for each open unit. This policy permits you to trade foreign currencies on a highly leveraged basis (up to 100 times your investment). An investment of $1,000 would enable you to trade up to $100,000 of a particular currency. However, just a 50% drawdown in usable margin will generate a margin call.

Futures forex leverage is just as bad. If you traded one contract of the Eurocurrency (ECU), you effectively would be leveraging a total of 125,000 ECUs. The amount of margin you put up is US$3,240. As of this writing 1 ECU = US$1.20. The U.S. dollar value of this contract is effectively US$150,000. Your margin is only 2.16 % of the total value. Every point movement is the equivalent of $12.50.

The key difference between the OTC and futures market is the amount of money you must put up. In the faster OTC spot market, investors can get away with as little as 1% of the total currency value. In the futures forex market, the amounts are higher, more in the 5% to 10% range.

The high amounts of leverage available in the OTC forex market have created safeguards that automatically close trades when accounts drop below specific margin levels. This is designed so your account is never at a net deficit. This type of circuit breaker does not exist in any futures market, forex or otherwise.

OTC Participants

When investors trade stocks, there is typically a small universe of people involved. The market makers, the shareholders, and the mutual fund managers are the primary participants. When it comes to the OTC market, the list of people involved can be extensive. There are the central banks of every nation buying and selling currencies, as well as every major bank in the world, along with various importers and exporters. At the end of the day, it is the world that you are up against. Here is a short list of some of the participants.

Banks and dealers. Banks and dealers are the essential backbone of the OTC markets. Since there is no central marketplace, the banks and dealers provide the credibility, liquidity, credit, and the price quotes. Without these two groups, there is no forex market.

Insurers and corporations. Insurers and corporations are large users of forex to settle their annuity, import, and export transactions. Their businesses dictate that each transaction is customized. With this customization, they need the proper tools to protect themselves. The customized spot and forward contracts that forex can provide makes it convenient and flexible for their treasury departments to budget and plan.

Speculators. Forex has many famous speculators, from the most famous, George Soros, to the infamous, like the collapse of Long-Term Capital Management. The same banks and dealers that make markets for forex also trade for profit on their own account or on behalf of clients. Individuals now play a significant part in this 24-hour market.

Components of OTC Contracts

The language of the OTC markets is different from the futures market. There are some very specific meanings to particular concepts. For instance, a spot contract represents contracts that are settled within two days after the deal date. A few other concepts and definitions are discussed below.

The *currency pair* system is the normal way that currencies are priced. The first quoted currency is known as the base currency. The second quoted currency is known as the counter or quote currency. You buy or sell a currency in relationship to another currency.

There are hard currencies, such as the U.S. dollar, the euro, and the Japanese yen. There are also currencies known as soft currencies, such as the South African rand and the Romanian leu. Each currency price is listed in a five-number increment, of which only the last two numbers are quoted.

Currency spread is the difference between what the banks or dealers are willing to pay for a particular currency versus what they are willing to sell a particular currency at. This amount can have a range of anything. The typical amount is three to seven "pips."

Pips are the minimum one-unit increments in which currency instruments are measured. Depending on the currency, pips may have a value of approximately US$7 to $11.

Contract size is wholly customized by the trader. Depending on the size of the account, you will be able to trade contracts in the several hundred thousands or in the several millions. It depends solely on the amount of leverage you are willing to push for.

Interest rates play a crucial factor for holding long-term spot currency trades, known as rollovers. Since currencies are traded in pairs, the interest that you must pay to hold a currency minus the interest you receive when selling another currency is the interest you earn or are liable for past the two-day spot trading period.

TYPES OF POSITIONS AND ORDERS

There is common ground in the futures and forex markets. They share the same nomenclature when it comes to trading and the various orders that exist.

Positions

Long positions are the easiest to understand. They are the "buy low, sell high" philosophy. A trader initiates a trade by "buying" a contract. He offsets the trade by "selling" or shorting a contract.

Short positions are sometimes difficult for traditional stock traders to understand. In this scenario, the goal is to "sell high, buy low." A trader "sells" a contract and later offsets it by "buying" it back.

Although there are currency options on the OTC market, futures forex options play a more significant role for retail investors.

Types of Orders

Market order is used when you want to get the order done immediately at the market price.

Limit order is an order to buy at or better than your price, placed below the market or an order to sell at or above your price placed above the market. A limit order to buy will be filled at or below your price. A limit order to sell will be filled at or above your price. If the market is trading above a limit sell order when entered, it will act like a market order. If the market is trading below a limit buy order, it will act like a market order.

Stop order is used to buy above the market or to sell below the market. Unlike a limit order, you are not guaranteed that you will be filled at or better than your stop price. Stop fills are usually filled at worse than your stop price because the market is usually moving against you. Stop orders are commonly used to protect profits, attempt to limit losses, or to enter a market when the market is moving in that direction.

There are many more types of orders, but 90% of small speculators will only use one of these three.

OPTIONS

The third member of the daisy chain is the option. Options, futures, and spot trading all have similar objectives. However, they are fulfilled in vastly different ways. The primary objective of all of these financial instruments is to help you profit today based on the value of the product sometime in the future, whether that's 5 minutes from now or 10 years from now.

Option Rights vs. Obligations

Options fulfill their objective in three ways. The first is by separating "rights" from "obligations." When you hold an option, you have the "right" to purchase or sell the underlying product at any time before it expires, but in no way are you "obligated" to take delivery or make delivery of the product if you don't want to. In fact, you can simply let your option expire worthless without any repercussions, other than losing your premium.

Unlike options, futures are "obligations" to make or take delivery of the underlying product. This is a far cry from the noncommittal "rights" that options convey. Options also release you from the OTC requirement to constantly "roll over" your contract and pay interest rate differentials if you choose to hold on to the spot position.

Keep in mind that your futures obligation will only be enforced if a speculator holds on to the futures contract until expiration. Ninety-six percent of futures contracts are closed out before speculators are forced to honor these obligations. Speculators like you shouldn't expect to have 5,000 bushels of corn delivered to your doorstep. If you hold a corn futures contract, you fall in the 96% that offset the contract before obligations are enforced.

Premiums

The second way options fulfill their objective is through premiums. To obtain the option rights, you must pay a fixed up-front cost, called a *premium*. This premium guarantees that you are the holder of that option. The premium also sets the value of the option.

To determine the premium, you must first pick the exact price that you believe the product will reach or exceed. This is the *strike price*, which determines how expensive it will be to own the option rights today. This premium is also heavily influenced by how close your strike price is to the current value of the product and by the time it will take for your option rights to expire. All of these factors make the bid-ask spread on option premiums volatile.

It is important to realize that you never have to "buy" futures contracts. You simply put up the required margin amount to secure a trade. When you close out a trade, you receive your margin back, plus or minus any profits or losses and commissions.

Time

This brings us to the most important way options fulfill their objective— time. When you pick your strike price, you are forced to pick how long it will take before the underlying product reaches the strike price you have picked. This time component can be any duration.

Once your time is up, whether the underlying product has reached your strike price or not, your option will expire worthless. It's a wasting asset, similar to a car. As time goes on, the option becomes less and less valuable. In fact, 90% of options expire worthless solely because the time commitment cannot be fulfilled.

Options are highly erratic because of their time, price, and volatility. These three factors together make options unique.

Although futures contracts require delivery when they expire, less than 4% of contracts are ever held until expiration. Major corporations are typically the only ones that hold futures contracts until expiration. They either have a use for the goods or are attempting to liquidate their inventory.

Even these companies rarely use futures to transact business. The standardization of futures often makes it unrealistic for them. Either the type of commodity they need is not exactly represented by the futures contract, or the location where the items can be picked up is not feasible for their delivery and pickup system.

Types of Options

Options come in two varieties: *calls* and *puts.* You buy calls when you believe the value of the product is going up. You buy puts when you believe the value of the product is going down. Either way, you will never risk more than the premium you paid to gain the rights.

If you want to generate income immediately, you can sell calls and puts. You would sell a call when you believe the product is going to stay the same or if you expect the product's value to go down. You would sell a put when you believe the product's value is going to stay the same or if the product's value is going up. By selling the call or put, you gain immediate income, but you also have unlimited exposure to loss if the market moves against you.

UNDERSTANDING THE INTERRELATIONSHIP OF THE VARIOUS MARKETS

When would-be traders are introduced to futures, options, and spot market investments, they learn how to trade one section at a time. Sometimes they are even told that one type of investment is somehow superior to the others. This is simply not true! The spot market is designed to be protected by the futures market; the spot and futures market are designed to be protected by options.

Once you understand the interrelationship of each of these instruments, you begin to see trading opportunities that you never noticed before. These are just a few of the opportunities that you can take advantage of:

Spot and futures convergence. Watch the spot market as futures contracts expire. There may be opportunities to trade the narrowing spread between the two for arbitrage profits.

Trade spot and futures currencies together. In a spread position, similar to the hedgers, you can potentially benefit from the less expensive margins. There are also potential ways to use futures and options to protect your long-term spot positions.

Write options. You can write option futures against your OTC positions.

Contango and backwardation. The natural inclination of futures contracts is to be more expensive the further out they are. If you see near months that are more expensive, you are seeing backwardation, and there may be opportunities to trade spot, futures, and options against each other.

Take advantage of longer-term trending. Mixing and matching various vehicles together will help you catch the trend for as long as possible.

Beginning forex traders should start with the futures currency market. There is less leverage, volatility, and day-to-day pressure in the futures currency market. There is more margin for error and no need to day-trade.

CONCLUSION

Futures, forex, and options are not mysterious financial objects. Throughout the centuries, all types of people have learned how to use these contracts to their benefit. So, while the names may sound intimidating, they are no more difficult than stocks to learn how to use when you apply yourself.

CHAPTER 5

The Fallacy of Traditional Stock Investment Beliefs

I have come to expect a few things about "security investing": Bonds move opposite from stocks, the majority of investors are better off purchasing index funds, and stockbrokers just don't understand how futures work.

This is the typical dialogue of an investor and his stockbroker:

Stockbroker: Good morning, Bob! Glad to see you again. How may I help you today?

Investor: Well, Mr. Smith, I have squirreled away some extra money, and I want to invest in futures or forex.

Stockbroker: Why would you want to do that?

Investor: Well, I heard that there was a lot of opportunity, and I have seen gold triple in value over the last few years.

Stockbroker: Listen to me, Bob. Is it okay if I call you Bob? Listen, Bob, forget about it. Gold, schmold, what you need is some sound investment advice. Remember that gold stock I got you into last year?

Investor: Yeah, it's down 30%.

Stockbroker: Bob, remember, we're in it for the long haul. Buy and hold, buy and hold. In fact, since it's cheaper, we need to buy more. We buy more now, we can make up for that 30% loss that much quicker.

Investor: Well . . . I guess.

Stockbroker: Bob, let's look at the big picture. The price is cheap for this and a few other gold-mining companies. If the price of gold is going up, we need to get some more of these other companies in your portfolio while it's still low. Bob, are you listening to me?

Investor: I hear you. If you think this is the best way.

Stockbroker: Of course, I think this is the best way. Who in their right mind would want to buy and sell actual gold? It's too risky.

Investor: The gold-mining companies do it, right?

Stockbroker: Exactly, Bob, so don't waste your time.

This is the typical exchange between an investor and his stockbroker. While the investor may see the logic of skipping the middleman and buying the actual gold, the stockbroker can't or won't. Often, the reason they can't see the logic is that they are simply not licensed or trained to give their clients advice about futures and forex investing.

FUTURES AND FOREX INVESTING IS NOT NEW

In later chapters we will go in depth on the origins of futures and forex, but to suffice it to say that various forms of futures contracts have been around for hundreds of years. The current forex environment, while fairly new, is patterned, in many ways, after the futures market contracts.

So let's define a futures contract:

A financial contract obligating the buyer to purchase an asset (or the seller to sell an asset), such as a physical commodity or a financial instrument, at a predetermined future date and price. (Investopedia.com)

The forex market is defined as:

The foreign exchange (also known as "forex" or "FX") market is the place where currencies are traded. The overall forex market is the largest, most liquid market in the world with an average traded value that exceeds $1.9 trillion per day and includes all of the currencies in the world. (Investopedia.com)

Forex contracts are similar to futures contracts: You put up a small margin, and the currency contracts have a default standard size. The key difference between forex and futures is that forex has no centralized marketplace, and while futures contracts can be extended out months at a time, forex contracts are known as spot contracts and are on a 24-hour cycle.

Futures and forex investments are technically called *alternative investments*. They are outside the normal range of typical investor experience—stocks and bonds. The mistake that many investors make is that they feel as if they have to choose between their normal stock investing and these alternative investments. This is not the case. A simple approach to these investments can be taken that can incorporate them into your overall portfolio without threatening your overall portfolio security.

WHAT YOU DON'T KNOW CAN HURT YOU

After being involved with the futures business for the past 14 years, I have seen few stockbrokers who have known anything about investing in futures and forex. In fact, only a handful of stockbrokers hold the proper licensing required to sell or buy futures and forex investments in the first place. Of those few, even fewer build their practice around the actual selling of futures and forex investments. That being said, the majority of stockbrokers do have their client's best interest at heart. So they apply various platitudes that they have learned in developing a working set of rules to get thorough stock investing.

This working knowledge has helped them succeed and thrive over the years in helping their clients survive the stock market. The question becomes: Can the wisdom of stock market investing be applied to futures and forex investing? If it can, why haven't you been taught? If it can't, what is stopping it?

While there are numerous ideas and concepts about stock investing, there are five concepts that stick out like sore thumbs:

1. Buy and hold
2. Dollar cost averaging
3. Value investing
4. Portfolio diversification
5. Margin

We are going to look at these concepts and see how they can be beneficial when you invest in stocks but may not translate well into future and forex investing. We will also look at how these concepts may be reworked to apply to futures and forex investing.

EXPLAINING THE STRATEGIES

One of the best online web sites for financial terms and concepts is Investopedia.com. This web site is great at giving multiple definitions and links to related concepts. Investopedia was used in coming up with these definitions. While you may look elsewhere to find a more in-depth or thorough definition, these will suffice for our purposes.

Buy and Hold

Investopedia defines *buy and hold* as:

> *A passive investment strategy in which an investor buys stocks and holds them for a long period of time, regardless of fluctuations in the market. An investor who employs a buy-and-hold strategy actively selects stocks, but once in a position, is not concerned with short-term price movements and technical indicators.*

Why It Works for Stocks   Buying and holding on to a stock for the long haul is touted as a good idea. The amount of work necessary is all up front. You simply pick a halfway decent stock or market sector and forget about it. While picking the right stock may not be easy, once it's accomplished, the heavy lifting is done.

Time and time again we have seen the success of this stock-investing scenario play out. Investors who bought Coca-Cola 40 years ago or Microsoft 20 years ago have seen these investments increase tremendously, and they have been handsomely rewarded.

Conversely, major corporations that were once heralded, such as Piggly Wiggly, Toys 'R' Us, and Enron, are no longer around. Buying and holding these stocks may have not been the best strategy, particularly because they disappeared into oblivion. Nevertheless, more often than not, this strategy has worked for the average investor.

So the question becomes: Is "buying and holding" the perfect investment solution for everything?

Why It *Doesn't* Work for Futures and Forex   Can you buy and hold futures and forex investments?

Are you crazy! You could never buy and hold a futures contract.

Or can you?

The key reason why buying and holding futures and forex investments is difficult is not that they have any more inherent risk than stocks. In fact, the price movements of stocks can be more volatile on a one-for-one comparison. The weakness of futures and forex is the leverage.

When it comes to futures investing, you can easily find yourself with 20 to 50 times leverage on your account. So while a commodity such as corn may have an actual fluctuation of only 2% to 3%, because you only put up $1 for every $20 worth of value, when you make or lose profits on that 2% to 3% fluctuation, it is actually a loss or a gain of 40% to 60% of your total account equity.

In forex investing, the leverage is even worse. Many forex companies will allow you to leverage 400 to 1. Therefore a 2% to 3% fluctuation looks more like an 800% to 1,200% move. So while the price volatility may be small, leverage has exacerbated a potentially average-risk investment into an exceptionally risky endeavor. This is why spot forex traders are forced to be day traders. Fluctuations of 800% to 1,200% are tremendous and can be fatal for small accounts. Attempting to buy and hold on to trades through these types of swings can mean that the leverage can wipe them out at any time.

There are ways to manage or diminish the amount of leverage you are exposed to. Once you learn how to master how the leverage affects your account, then a buy-and-hold strategy in futures and forex is not only possible, but a sound idea. Commodities and currencies have a tendency to trend over the long run (look at gold, oil, interest rates, and the euro if you have any questions about that); it makes sense to buy and hold. You just have to be able to do it properly and in a way in which you can weather pullbacks and retracements and not be at the mercy of leverage.

Looking to the Future   Today's investor needs to take a more aggressive stance when it comes to managing his overall portfolio. Global warming, genetics research, and the growth of India and China, as well as many innovations that are on the horizon, have the ability to leave companies that are now darlings trailing behind the pack. This was seen clearly during the dot-com bubble burst of 2000 and the real estate bubble burst of 2006. Stockholders of the corporation New Century no doubt were blindsided by the sudden collapse and the subsequent delisting of this subprime lender.

Changing environment or changing investment landscape reflects only one reason why the buy-and-hold method is becoming more and more difficult to stick to. We also have to look at the inherent bias that a buy-and-hold strategy implies. Common sense dictates that what goes up must come down, but when it comes to stock investing, this is rarely advocated, if ever represented. When a stock is bought, the hope is that you are buying low to someday sell to someone else at a higher price. Unfortunately, this doesn't always work. Scandal, industry changes, and replacement products can have a significant impact on the long-term prospects of a company.

Dollar Cost Averaging

Investopedia defines dollar cost averaging as:

> *The technique of buying a fixed dollar amount of a particular investment on a regular schedule, regardless of the share price. More shares are purchased when prices are low, and fewer shares are bought when prices are high.*

Why It Works for Stocks   This is a great idea. This concept alone has allowed average Americans to become participants in the American dream of accumulated wealth. By investing a little at a time consistently and constantly, trillions of dollars have become concentrated in the 401(k)s and individual retirement accounts (IRAs) of an entire generation of Baby Boomers.

When prices are strong, there are benefits to dollar cost averaging. The old saying "The trend is your friend" definitely applies. You are constantly buying a stock that is getting stronger and stronger, with the added benefit of your overall portfolio lifting up in value. When prices are weak, or more importantly stagnant, but the company is still sound, you are able to buy shares at a flat or less expensive rate.

This is perfect for stocks. The market moves in only three directions: up, down, or sideways; most of the time, markets are moving sideways. Couple this with a buy-and-hold philosophy, and you can accumulate shares with little regard to where the price is. You own the shares, and there is no time limit on when they have to perform well.

Why It *Doesn't* Work for Futures and Forex   While this may be a great idea on the surface, dollar cost averaging is difficult to apply to futures and forex trading. In futures and forex trading, a similar activity is "pyramiding" your profits. You add on more leverage based on the profits from contracts that are successful. When it comes to "adding" more contracts to a leveraged position, you have to worry about how much capital you have, margin calls, and the fact that longs and shorts are treated equally.

Since the markets are leveraged, you have to keep in mind that by adding one more contract, you are doubling your losses and gains. If the volatility of the underlying market is at 2% to 3%, with leverage of 20 to 1, you are gaining and losing at 40% to 60% of your capital outlay on one contract. On two contracts, you are at 80% to 120%, and at three contracts, you are at 120% to 180%. This is why you can give back accumulated profits in no time. What took you X number of days to accumulate is given back $2X$ to $3X$ faster.

The same occurs if you are attempting to protect yourself against loss. If you are adding more contracts as the market moves against you, you must make sure that you have enough capital to cover the maintenance margin of the contracts you have, plus you must be able to put on the initial margin for each contract you add. With futures contracts having an initial margin of $2,000 to $5,000 and forex account contracts around $1,000, a small account of $10,000 would possibly have three to four chances at dollar cost averaging futures or forex contracts before the account runs out of steam in maintaining current contracts and adding on new contracts. All the while, you are losing cash at an accelerated rate.

This bumps up against the third problem. Stocks have an inherent bias—everything goes up. So even when the prices pull back, there are few that are actually actively driving the price downward; there is just an absence of buying activity at current levels. So the price moves down until a buyer is found at a level that is comfortable.

In futures and forex there are active participants who want to see the price drop or expect the price to drop. Either way, there is no one-sided bias, and this has tremendous impact on how low a market can go. If you are attempting to dollar cost average a significant drop in price, it's akin to catching a falling knife. The reality is that futures and forex are better traded with the trend, as opposed to attempting to build up a position while the market is strongly moving against you.

Value Investing

Investopedia defines value investing as:

> *The strategy of selecting stocks that trade for less than their intrinsic value. Value investors actively seek stocks of companies that they believe the market has undervalued. They believe the market overreacts to good and bad news, causing stock price movements that do not correspond with the company's long-term fundamentals. The result is an opportunity for value investors to profit by buying when the price is deflated. Typically, value investors select stocks with lower-than-average price-to-book or price-to-earnings ratios and/or high dividend yields.*

Why It Works for Stocks   What is the "intrinsic value" of a stock? Who determines it? What if you get it wrong?

The big problem to value investing is the "how" of estimating the intrinsic value. Determining the correct intrinsic value is difficult. Any number of investors are capable of looking at the facts and still coming to different conclusions, just like that round robin game. A lot of thought has to go into the potential price discrepancy. It definitely takes a lot of speculative prowess.

Whether you look at present assets/earnings or place value on future growth or cash flows, you are attempting to buy something for less than its worth. This can be a flawed investing methodology solely because you are buying into weakness. While our natural instinct is to constantly look for bargains, it may not be the best strategy when making investment decisions. However, value investors like Warren Buffett have turned this art into a science.

For the average stock investor, the benefit is that they have time on their side and can watch and wait to see if they made a good or bad decision. In futures and forex, time is of the essence.

Why It *Doesn't* Work in Futures and Forex   When buying clothes or food at a discount, there is a gratifying feeling of getting a bargain. That same feeling simply doesn't translate well when you are investing in fast-paced markets like futures and forex. I consider value investing on par with tarot reading or, worse, gambling.

When it comes to stocks, there is a natural upside bias. If a company's stock is priced low and there are clear indicators that no financial shenanigans are going on in the background, it's likely that it may eventually rebound. This same type of assumption cannot be made of currencies or commodities.

If a country is fixated on seeing the value of its currency go down, they will make it happen. For over a decade Japan's central bank has played a key part in forcing the yen down by consistently flooding the market with yen, just so they can maintain exports. On the other end of the spectrum, cotton prices can get as low as they need to because the government subsidizes cotton farmers so that they can compete on the world stage.

What is the true "intrinsic value" of the Japanese yen or cotton? Is there an upward bias? The answer to question one is "Who knows?" The answer to the second question is "No"! How do you deal with these kinds of markets—at what point do you invest in hopes that there will be a turnaround? This requires the ability to accurately pick tops and bottoms in the markets; if you can do it, I commend you.

For the most part, the whole reason why spot and futures trading exist in the first place is to discover the intrinsic value by the time of the contract's expiration. Any attempt at determining the intrinsic value by attempting to buy cheap has the potential to be disastrous because of the leverage that these markets employ. Couple that with the fact that there is constant pressure on both the up- and downsides, and we have a recipe for disaster.

Portfolio Diversification

According to Investopedia:

> *Studies and mathematical models have shown that maintaining a well-diversified portfolio of 25 to 30 stocks will yield the most cost-effective amount of risk reduction. Investing in more securities will still yield further diversification benefits, albeit at a drastically smaller rate.*

Why It Works for Stocks   Stock investing is a microeconomic view of the markets. Corporations specialize in creating or servicing various niche markets. As an investor, it makes sense that you don't place all of your eggs in one basket by being overly exposed to one sector. By having shares of various companies, you are able to gain the benefit of multiple sectors, and hopefully they do not correlate with each other.

There are tens of thousands of stocks out there, and for the lay investor it is difficult to pick and choose which ones are exactly right for your portfolio and to what degree you should be invested in them. The quick solution has been the mutual fund.

By allowing the mutual fund to set up the 25 to 30 essential stocks, an investor is able to get into the market with little thought. There are aggressive to hyperconservative mutual funds available. Each mutual fund has its own pros and cons. At the end of the day, it is far more accessible for the everyday investor. If you purchase one share of a mutual fund, you have full access to the 25 to 30 stocks in a fully diversified portfolio.

There is also a new trading investment called the exchange-traded funds (ETF). It basically operates like an index, but it is traded just like a stock. The price fluctuates daily and is often more accessible than mutual funds when it comes to price. ETFs are a revolutionary way to diversify investor accounts with little planning, but still have a big impact.

Between traditional mutual funds and ETFs, investors are able to take a microeconomic investment like stocks and have an immediate exposure to a macroeconomic-type diversification.

Why It *Doesn't* Work in Futures and Forex   There are two schools of thought when it comes to futures and forex investing: diversification and specialization. The proponents of diversification feel that contracts in various markets will increase your opportunity to profit. The problem with this theory is the too-often-ignored inherent dangers—varying leverage of markets and macroeconomics.

First, the various leverage amounts of different markets can have a significant impact on how you profit and lose in your trading. While the British pound may gain or lose at the rate of $6.25 per tick, gold gains and loses at $100 per $1 move. The speed at which you are gaining and losing in multiple markets can make it difficult for you to be "equally" diversified in various markets without having to significantly develop a weighing system that matches the gains and losses for each market.

This problem has often been found when companies develop various futures commodity indices. It is very difficult to attempting to give equal weighing to corn and oil, particularly when they move at different speeds and return different gains and losses at differing price movements.

The second problem is a bit more insidious and is a little more difficult to deal with. While each stock represents its own universe of corporate governance and success or failure in relation to the sector it is in, the opposite occurs in futures and forex. Each contract is an amalgamation of multiple factors that represent the macroeconomic definitive global feelings about that market. Couple that with the correlation and impact of substitute goods and the effects that currency plays on many of these markets, and it becomes quickly apparent that when you "buy gold," you are voting for and against multiple economies, products, and countries.

When you "buy gold," you are making a subtle or a not-so-subtle no-confidence vote against the U.S. economy, so you are effectively "short stock market (S&P or Dow)," meaning you believe the currency is weak so you are "short the dollar," which also implies you are "long silver and platinum," which are precious metals like gold. "Buying gold" also has a correlation to both oil and interest rates, not to mention the euro and the rand.

So by "buying gold," the macroeconomic influences will have a direct impact on how you diversify and whether or not you should. While you may want to invest in noncorrelative markets, the reality is that once you get past two or three different individual commodity markets, there is too much interrelationship to successfully reduce overexposure to the same set of macroeconomic factors.

The success of professional traders on the floor has always been specialization. For years, floor traders have succeeded by understanding the buy/sell rhythms of the specific pits that they trade in. When your leverage is 20 to 500 times greater than your initial investment, not specializing exposes you to "overleveraging" your account and not having the ability to weather small downturns in the market. Specialization gives you the ability to calculate and understand your risk at any given time.

As a specialist, you are able to become better equipped at the macroeconomic influences of global commodities such as oil, as well as globally interdependent currencies such as the euro or the Japanese yen. Import and export numbers, as well as central bank meanings, take on a life of their own.

If there is an overwhelming need to diversify when it comes to the commodities and currency markets, then look to the various commodity indices. The Commodity Research Bureau (CRB) puts out a Continuous Commodity Index (CCI) that tracks 17 different commodity markets. Then there is the Reuters/Jefferies CRB Index, which has tracked 19 different commodity markets since 1957.

There are also the Dow Jones Commodity Index (DJ AIG) and the Goldman Sachs Commodity Index (GSCI). While both indices are meant to give a well-rounded view of the markets, they both suffer from the macroeconomic factors discussed earlier. The GSCI has enjoyed much success over the past several years. This success has been largely due to its direct correlation with the oil commodity complex. At one point GSCI had a weighing of 80% in the oil markets and the DJ AIG had a weighing of 33%.

So while you are a trader who may want to be fully diversified, it is difficult to do on a macroeconomic scale, as evidenced by the major companies that have commodity indices yet have one third to four fifths of their assets concentrated in one area.

Margin

Investopedia defines margin as:

> *A brokerage account in which the broker lends the customer cash to purchase securities. The loan in the account is collateralized by the securities and cash. If the value of the stock drops sufficiently, the account holder will be required to deposit more cash or sell a portion of the stock.*

Why It *Doesn't* Work for Stocks October 24, 1929—Black Thursday—began a month-long drop in the stock market. It took 25 years, nearly a generation, before the stock market bounced back to pre-1929 levels. From October 25 to October 29, over $30 billion in wealth was loss. At the time, the U.S. government's annual budget was barely $3 billion. This was a disastrous event!

Many investors, because of a looser regulatory environment, had borrowed as little as 10% of the value of the stocks they were trading. Over $8.5 billion was on loan against stocks. This amount surpassed the total amount of currency circulating at the time.

The direct effect of the crash led to tighter rules on stock margin trading as well as the separation of commercial and investment banking. Today's reality when buying stocks on margin is very difficult. While there are a few exceptions in place for day traders, for the most part you are required to first be approved as a margin borrower; then, you must have at least 50% of the cash available of the stock's face value; and, finally, you must pay interest on the amount of cash you borrow to purchase stocks.

Combine that with onerous rules against shorting stocks, and you find that for a small stock investor it simply may not work using margin to buy and sell stock or to even bother shorting the markets.

Why It Works in Futures and Forex   The only thing the word *margin* for stocks and *margin* for futures and forex have in common is the spelling. Other than that, they are two completely different things.

While margin for stocks was intended to be a down payment to ownership of the underlying asset, margin for futures is not. Futures and forex margin represent "earnest" money—basically, a promise to pay. Since we know futures began with tangible products, we also know that the primary users of futures were the actual people buying and selling.

The exchanges were aware of this as well and came up with an elegant solution. Since the buyers and sellers are already heavily invested in their tangible commodities and the futures positions are designed to be a hedge—one side is making money while the other loses money—the exchanges allowed the hedgers to put up a small amount of money as collateral. This was done with implied intent that once the profitable side of the transaction was liquidated, the losses could be easily covered.

With the introduction of the speculator, the concept of margin as earnest money against true cash positions was put to the test. So those that were of sound financial standing were extended earnest money margin, but at higher rates than the true hedgers. Forex margins were developed on similar principals.

As a speculator, futures and forex margin can be very appealing on the surface, but since the margin represents only a fraction of the overall value, profit and losses can have wild fluctuations, and in the case of futures, you can actually lose more than your initial investment.

Don't Short the Market!

Investopedia defines shorting the market as:

> *[Selling a security] that the seller does not own, or any sale that is completed by the delivery of a security borrowed by the seller. Short sellers assume that they will be able to buy the stock at a lower amount than the price at which they sold short.*

This is an advanced and often risky strategy. Novice investors are advised to avoid it.

Why It *Doesn't* Work for Stocks   Shorting stocks is a difficult enterprise both mechanically and philosophically. Mechanically shorting stocks is not as easy as buying stocks. There are various rules and impedances against the average investor's shorting stocks, whether it is the one-uptick rule or the fact that you have to borrow stock to short, and there may be no stock available to borrow against to short. There is difficulty after difficulty.

All of these difficulties lead us back to the philosophical problem of shorting stocks. While common sense dictates that what goes up must come down, stocks, besides a few minor setbacks from time to time, are not meant to come down. There are no shareholders, board of directors, or management teams in their right minds hoping to go public just to see their stock collapse. Therefore, when investors purchase stocks, they expect them to go up, and everyone's hearts, minds, and souls are dedicated to the success of the stock market.

So, realistically, how do you short into an investment vehicle that is not designed for shorting and that also has an overwhelming majority of investors putting their hopes, dreams, and goals into seeing it go up in value? You can't. That's why the stock market has created exchange-traded funds to solve those problems. In the meantime, sophisticated investors are turning to the futures and forex markets.

Why It Works in Futures and Forex   Long, short, short, long—it really doesn't matter. The longs and shorts are treated equally. While there is an inherent long-side bias in the stock market based on expectations, in futures and forex, the attitude is about preparing for the inevitable. Crops can be strong just as easily as they can be weak. The dollar's value could increase because of economic growth just as it could easily collapse because of a mortgage default crisis.

The goal of the futures market is to act like a fulcrum and keep those who are truly vested in the actual products in an economic balance between long and short until one side prevails. Being able to short with little to no fanfare makes a world of difference in making the futures market function as an insurance vehicle.

This intent bleeds off into helping the speculators. There are no one uptick rules, no borrowing shares, and you don't have to worry about fighting the philosophy of an entire market.

Anyone new to futures and forex must embrace the short side as easily as the long side; otherwise, you will easily cut your opportunities in half when you initiate a trade. You will then cut your opportunities in half again when you attempt to hold on to a trade in the face of negative pressures, and by the time you realize you should take advantage of shorts, it will be too late. and you will then cut your opportunities in half by ignoring the longs. Long and short, yin and yang. You must be comfortable trading one as well as the other.

FEAR LEVERAGE!

The key problem that distinguishes the differences among stocks, futures, and forex lies between the application and usage of leverage. If you were to trade the futures and forex markets with no margin, your trading experience would be more on par with stock trading. Solely because of the use of margin do the potential problems with leverage arise, particularly with investors who come from a stock background.

The goal is not to fear margin/leverage, but to respect it. Once the everyday investor changes his attitude and begins to really respect leverage and learn how to incorporate it into his trading as a function of his activity, not solely as a financial savior, an entirely different approach to trading evolves.

Leverage is not an afterthought in the futures and forex market. It is the foundation of the entire industry. If it were not for the incredible amount of leverage available, sometimes 20 to 1 or as high as 500 to 1 in forex trading, we could never hear as many rags-to-riches or riches-to-ruins stories.

Leverage is defined by the Webster's dictionary as "the use of investment capital in a way that a relatively small amount of money enables the investor to manage a relatively large value." Leveraged investing is not to be taken lightly, though. While margin in futures is not strictly a form of borrowing, like stocks, it still can be looked at as a type of credit. And, like all credit, it comes in three forms: the good, the neutral, and the bad.

Good Use of Leverage

A good use of leverage is to purchase a home. A small down payment along with a loan is used to acquire the home. Yet the investment is well worth it because homeowners benefit from a home's increase in property value over time.

Using leverage to hedge your investments is beneficial. If your investments are tied to a stock index, you might find it difficult to adjust your portfolio quickly to coincide with the market's fluctuations. Index futures contracts allow an investor to protect his portfolio with just one investment vehicle. By using index futures, you can also avoid capital gains and unnecessary commissions, expenses that you would incur if you traded stocks or mutual funds alone.

Neutral Use of Leverage

Credit cards are a prime example of neutral leverage. You leverage your income in order to qualify for credit cards. This type of credit is neutral because you have the opportunity to purchase durable goods that can appreciate in value or goods that have no real value.

Like credit cards, leveraged investing is not inherently bad. It is up to the individual investor to devise strategies to protect him when the market moves against him. Often, this type of protection must take two forms: strategic and psychological.

The strategic form of protection involves planning. The psychological form of protection involves emotional discipline.

Bad Use of Leverage

Car purchases are the worst type of leverage. A down payment on a car typically just covers license, registration, and tax. After that, you get a loan on the balance of the car's price. Since a car is a depreciating asset, you immediately know that when you drive off the lot, you lose 50% of the purchase value.

The same can be said for an "options-only" leveraged investing style. Since you have to "buy" an option up front, you have a built-in loss from day one, plus you have to worry about the option's expiring before you can get a profit. Option sellers, however, have unlimited exposure to loss. Options are great tools as part of an overall investment strategy, but they are an inefficient use of leverage by themselves.

Leveraged investing does not have to be difficult. Approach it the same way you would approach personal credit—deliberately and cautiously. As markets become more volatile, investors will rely on leveraged investing in order to gain an edge. It will be important that the difference between good, neutral, and bad forms of leverage are understood. Once leveraged investing is understood, it can be an effective tool for any trader.

MYTH BUSTING

I take no pleasure in summarily knocking down each idea that may have successfully carried you in your stock investing. The goal is to help you open your eyes to the potentially harmful ideas that you can carry over into trading and to show you that investing and trading in futures and forex will take an entirely different skill set and way of thinking in order for you to succeed.

CHAPTER 6

How to Be Among the 5% Who Win at Trading

"Are you ready?" says the speaker.

"Yes, we're ready!" the crowd screams back weakly.

"I am going to show you the trading techniques that will make you a millionaire."

As he holds up his hand counting down with each finger, he barks, "No work. No studying the market. No money needed to get started. This is the last program you will ever need in order to beat the markets," with a sense of strong conviction in his voice.

"So I ask you again, are you ready!?" the speaker yells at the crowd.

"Yes, we're ready!" screams the crowd in unison.

THE REALITY

How many of you have attended events like this? They get you so excited, for that day or that hour or over the course of a few days, and you can't help but believe you will be successful in your trading.

In fact, didn't they just guarantee your success with their money-back guarantee?

Soon after you leave the event, though, something changes. You lose the euphoric feeling. The system is not as easy as you thought, and the daunting task of deciphering everything yourself quickly becomes frustrating. Couple all of this with your regular day-to-day stresses of work, family, and personal commitments, and it's easy to think of that seminar you went to as a faded dream that you may have imagined.

But what if you are one of the lucky few—you embraced the concepts fully and you committed to making this a success. You put your money where your mouth was and decided to execute a trade based on this system you just bought.

For the thrill seekers, this can be one of the most exciting times. You have money on the line, your palms are sweating, you are certain that trading is for you.

TRADING WITH EMOTIONS

Let's break down the timeline of emotions that you are taken through as a trader.

In the Beginning: Happiness

Nothing feels greater than successfully getting into a market in the right direction. Whether it's long or short, once you have picked a side and you see the market follow suit, you begin to feel smart. Trading is easy, and you begin to wonder what you were thinking. Heck, you didn't even need to buy the program.

It is often said that the worst thing that can happen to a new trader is to have successful trades in the beginning. This sets up unrealistic expectations for themselves and the market. It paves the way for future disappointment and frustration.

When I have dealt one on one with new traders and they have succeeded early on, their sense of euphoria quickly converts to arrogance, and they slide into the second phase.

Next Comes: Greed

Now that they have this "trading thing" licked, they begin to count how much money they can make off of this trade. They were pretty smart in picking the trade in the first place; they should be handsomely rewarded, right?

So a trade that was humbly believed could make a few hundred dollars at the initiation of the trade is now counted on to make thousands, possibly tens of thousands.

The fantasies roll in one after the other. They could quit their job—heck, they could pay off their mortgage, buy a brand new car, and live a life of ease. They start believing the hype that this is how the rich made all of their money, and they wonder why no one ever told them before.

Mind you, the first trade is still on, the profits are solely on paper, and they have not collected one red cent, but every last dime has already been spent from this trade and the next dozen trades.

Then something happens.

The market stops going in their direction.

At first it's a small pullback.

Okay, maybe you won't buy a Porsche; you'll stick to a Mercedes.

Then something else happens.

The market pulls back more. Then it starts to collapse.

Dreams of making thousands dissipate, and you wish you could get out of the trade with the few hundred you originally were hoping for.

That's when the third phase kicks in.

Followed Up by: Fear

Then it sets in. You really don't know what you are doing. You go grab your books and videos; you scramble around in your memory for everything they taught you in the seminar. You are looking for a way out.

Is your stop too tight, is it too far away?

What if this is just a temporary pullback—"a shake out"—how long can you hold on; what if this the real deal?

How could you have done this to yourself?

How could you have turned a winning trade into a loser?

Then the market hits your stop, and you are out of the market.

You give back your profits and you lose some of your principal, and more importantly, you see your fantasies die right in front of your eyes. The fourth emotion falls in place.

Which Leads to: Sorrow

Like the death of a beloved pet, you feel a sting in your chest as you watch your fantasies get walloped by the markets. You curse the seminar, the guy who told you about the seminar, and the alleged guru who was telling you his great secrets of trading.

You start second-guessing yourself, and you can't believe you lost money. You think about all of the things you could have done with money instead of chasing rabbit holes and pipe dreams. You wonder how you can tell your wife or family about what happened.

You decide you need to study a little more and find out exactly what you missed. As the acceptance of the loss sets in, you look at the screen one last time, just to see what the trade might be doing now.

Wouldn't you know it!

The market has turned around after all. It was a shakeout and your stop was just too close. That's when the fifth phase kicks in.

Next You Have: Frustration

What did you do wrong? You followed the program to the letter. You got in when they said, and you bought a stop at the right distance to protect yourself. What happened?

The market recovers your losses and gets back to where your original profits were and then some.

Had you just stayed in, your dreams would have been realized. You can't figure out what you did wrong, but you know that there is money in these markets. Maybe you just didn't understand how they told you to place the stops; maybe you misread or misinterpreted how to trade.

Next time, you won't use a stop. Next time, you will do things differently. You'll hold on to the loss a little longer and wait until the market turns around. Next time, you won't watch the market so closely. You'll just let your trade work itself out. But right now, you can't let the market get away from you anymore.

So you jump right back into the market again. You know how you'll do things differently now.

Wow! The market is going your direction again. Happiness tries to set in again. You picked the right market at the right time, and you didn't let the market get away from you.

Then it happens.

The market drops. Not a little bit like last time, but *all the way* down in one day. You lose everything by attempting the same trade twice. That's when the final phase kicks in.

Finally: Defeat

You will never figure trading out. What were you thinking? You've wasted money on a seminar, and you blew out your account—for what? Some fantasies, some pipe dreams, all based on some guy who probably makes all of his money just lecturing.

You are just going to give up trading for right now. You'll wait until you understand a little more or you've perfected your paper trading. Then you will try it again—you'll get it right.

Then one day a flyer comes in the mail. It's a new system, a better system, with a different guy, claiming even better results.

Maybe, just maybe, you can learn something new and the cycle starts all over again.

Anyone who's ever traded has cycled through these emotions when they lose money. The problem occurs when you don't learn from the cycle. Instead of looking internally at how the trader was reacting to the various emotions that were surfacing, it was a constant look back at what they didn't learn from the program or how the program failed them.

So a cycle develops: Every time something goes wrong, the solution is to find a newer program, a newer system, a better holy grail. The problem with this is that your own identity and desires get lost in the noise. Every program, seminar, video, or book should simply be an arrow in your knowledge base, to be applied to the money management, technical analysis, and risk management techniques and strategies that you are already comfortable with.

Nothing should ever be looked at as a holy grail, including the ideas in this book. The goal is to help you develop the same mind-set and approach to your trading that the professionals do and to teach you how to properly integrate new ideas into your framework.

WHAT THE OTHER 5% ARE DOING

Some people are afraid of success; others fear failure. Either way, the expression of the behavior is the same—not doing what is necessary and known in order to achieve success.

If you purchase a program that doesn't help you select trades and have clearly defined entry and exit points, it's incomplete. If you purchase a program that doesn't clearly separate risk management tools from money management tools, it's incomplete. If you don't have a clear way to create a trading plan from the core ideas presented to you in the program, then it's incomplete.

It is constantly said that 95% of traders lose money when it comes to trading. That means that 5% of the traders are collecting all of the profits. What are they doing differently?

There are four areas of a trade that have to be managed correctly in order for a trader to feel satisfied in his trading, whether he wins or loses. You have to know why you are selecting a trade, how to enter a trade, how to properly monitor the trade you are in, and, finally, how to exit the trade to the best of your ability.

If your decision-making process is faulty in any one of these key areas, you will start to cycle through the six emotions and become discouraged in your abilities as a trader.

Selecting Trades Properly

This is where so many traders go wrong. From the outset they don't know what type of trader that they want to be. The guru is a day trader or an option-only trader, so you should be, too. If the guru is trading a $50,000 account or recommends a $10,000 account, you should immediately follow suit.

Wrong!

You must trade to your strengths, interests, seed capital, time constraints, and abilities. Look at the experience of the program creator and realistically look at yourself. If you can't stomach day trading, don't do it. If position trading is too stressful for you, don't do it. Whatever the case, avoid putting on trades that simply don't match who you are as a person.

If you are looking to stretch your boundaries into new trading arenas, first use a demo account and apply, to the best of your ability, the same conditions that you would experience if you were actually trading that way. As we know, ideal conditions never set the rule—they prove exception.

A little self-knowledge can go a long way to diminishing or eliminating improper trades from your lifestyle.

Entering Trades Properly

This leads us into how to enter a trade. In order to make a trade successful, you have to know how you are going to get out and what you have at risk. By fixating on the profits, you set yourself up for failure. The reality of trading is that profits take care of themselves. If you have picked a good trade and the market is going in the right direction, there is little you can actively do to make that trade any better.

However, the question in the back of your mind should always revolve around: "What if I am wrong?" By entering a trade with that question on your mind, you can figure out if the trade is worth taking at all. Successful trade entry is based solely on what you will do to exit.

Often, this has to take into account what risk management tools you will use in order to make the trade successful.

Monitoring the Trade

If you are a position trader, why are you watching the market hour by hour? If you are a swing trader, why are you looking at end-of-day results? These are genuine questions I have had to ask clients over the years. The key reasons fall back on one of two answers.

They don't want to put a "stop order" in the market because they are afraid their stops will be run, so they keep mental stops and sit at their screen to get out fast; or they just like to "watch the market." They are actually letting every tick on the screen influence how they act or, more importantly, how they will react to the market.

Whatever the reason of how and why a trader monitors the market, the core reason is fear. They don't trust the judgment that they have used to get into the trade, and they really don't know how to protect themselves from losses besides either ignoring the market completely or watching tick by tick to anticipate what will happen next in the market.

Successful monitoring has to also have a back-up plan. Much like chess, you need to be three, five, maybe even seven moves ahead of your opponent. There is only one way to succeed in a trade: The market has to move in your direction. But there are at least two ways to lose: the market moves against you or the market does nothing.

If you prepare for these contingencies, your monitoring becomes a function of your preparation, not a crutch to rescue a trade that bad.

Exiting the Trade

Who determines how you get out of a trade, you or the market?

If it's you, then maybe your actions are reactionary or you simply don't have enough capital to be trading the markets that you are in. This is exactly why you have to know yourself when you execute a trade.

How you got in the market should be the exact reason why you get out of the market, if the markets fundamentally shift supply and demand in the opposite direction of your initial position.

When the market shifts, you should have targets in place to capture profits you have made or to protect your principal. These don't necessarily need to be monetary targets; they could be overbought/oversold indicators, Bollinger bands, and so on. The key point is that you have a reason for why you do what you do, coupled with a back-up plan that helps you reenter the market without being whipsawed or chasing the markets.

The exact way you get out of a trade will have a direct impact on how you get back into the market. It will determine if you can even get back in or if it's too late, or if you can double up on your contracts, or if it's time to find a new market altogether.

The exit, profits, and losses, should all be carefully prepared far in advance of ever putting your first dollar on the trade. This is the only way to prepare for an exit of a trade—leave a little room for unpleasant surprises.

BATTLING THE DEMONS OF FEAR AND GREED

There are two demons constantly nipping at the heels of every potentially successful trader: fear and greed. Our goal is to cut a path between these demons and help our traders gain control over their trading. This is what is meant by bringing security to speculative investing.

This is the motto of our company, and we live by it. We understand that no one can control the markets, but what we can control is how we react to the markets. This begins with the submission of the emotions of fear and greed. These two emotions can have a stranglehold over the unprepared trader, causing fatal mistakes that can and will blow out accounts.

Fear and greed can express themselves in a myriad of different ways. There are three common reactions that traders have when faced with unexpected market activity.

Holding Losing Trades

When you hold on to a "losing trade," you are doing yourself and the trade a disservice. If the market is going against you, you should be out of the trade. There are no ifs, ands, or buts. Let's look at some of the logic of why you would hold on to a losing trade.

Fear If fear is ruling your emotions, then you will hold on to a losing trade because you are afraid of missing a market rebound. As we all know, the markets are constantly moving up and down. So the theory is sound—if you can hold on just long enough, you may catch the market back on an upswing. The faultiness of this logic is that you are dealing with a finite amount of capital. So can you truly afford to wait it out?

Will you allow your fear of missing out on a rebound to dictate your losing all of the money in your account?

Greed If greed is ruling your emotions, then you will hold on to a losing trade because you want to get back to where you were. Giving back profits to the market can make you furious, so a little revenge trading sets in. Somehow, you believe the market owes you the profits you lost and then some. So when you have the opportunity to get out of a trade at a breakeven price, you still hold on, hoping the rebound will occur and give you back your profits. This greed will lead you to exiting the market only once all of your profits are gone and your principal has been tapped.

Chasing Markets

It's easy to get caught "chasing the markets." This can occur when you see an opportunity but you are too timid to take it the first time around, so you jump in once it gets moving. Then, immediately, the market doubles back on you and you start losing; you get out only to see the market start moving in your direction. So you go after it again, only to lose again. This is what is going on.

Fear The fear of missing out can be overwhelming. It will drive you to operate irrationally. The setup that gave you the position in the first place no longer exists. So you are operating on old information. The logical thing to do is to go ahead and reassess the market, see if the trade is still valid, put a risk management tool in place, then execute a trade. This doesn't happen; the fear gives you a false sense of urgency. If you don't get in now, you will never find another good trade.

Greed Chasing the markets when you are affected by greed is the worst ever. You have made money on the trade, the market stalls out, and you are patting yourself on the back. Then the market ramps up again and takes off. You got off the boat, it left the harbor, but you want back on. Don't do it!
　　This is a fatal mistake.
　　Greed is talking to you. The problem of trading is that we take our best educated guess on the information presented to us at the time. If the market says get out, you get out. Don't attempt to just jump on the bandwagon of the market without taking time to reassess. This is exactly how you end up buying the top or selling the bottom of a market only to give back all of your profits in a retracement.

Overleveraging Your Account

Overleveraging your account is simply putting on too many contracts for your account size. This is easy to do when you don't understand how leverage works in futures and forex, but it can also be a fatal mistake when a trader is "taking a chance." This is the equivalent of the "all in" in no-limit poker. If it works, you win big; if it doesn't work, you are out for the count.

Fear Those who overleverage because of fear are simply trying to get their accounts back to even money. Instead of being patient when they lose, they take an aggressive stance against the market to force it to cover their losses. The problem with this approach is that if you lose, you are losing twice or three times as fast as before. The fear of blowing out your account will come two or three times faster. The trick is to simply grind it out to recoup losses. Unfortunately, fear doesn't allow for a systematic recovery.

Greed Just because you made money with one contract doesn't mean you will make money with two contracts or three contracts. It's easy to look at your profits and calculate how much more you would have made with more contracts. This is the failure of 20/20 hindsight. You forget the agonizing when the market was moving against you, and you focus on the end result. Trading is a process. Have a plan and stick to it. Hold back your greed until you rewrite your trading plan based on your new capital amounts.

SO WHAT DOES IT TAKE TO BE A 5% TRADER?

It's flippant to say to just say do the opposite of the pitfalls mentioned in this chapter. I am a strong believer in the best offense being a good defense. Recognize what is going on with you emotionally and the fact that you are not alone; you can then open your mind to the possibility of there being another way to trade.

Can you get rid of your emotions?

No!

Can you get rid of your fear and greed?

No!

Can you stop being human?

Of course not.

Being aware of what can affect you and how it will affect you is a preparation tool. It will help you make an effective trading plan that is relevant for your reactions and how fear and greed manifest themselves in your life.

Throughout this book, I have developed tips and strategies that will put you ahead of the mistakes that 95% of traders make. I will show you how to think like a professional trader. I will teach you techniques on how to be proactive in the markets. In the end, what I can't teach you is how to eliminate emotions.

I don't believe that is necessary to be a good trader. By having a framework for how your emotions can express themselves, you are able to turn them to your advantage. "Fight or flight" is hardwired into our human DNA; it can make you the best hunter if you have the right tools.

Use your emotions to fuel your trading. Don't be a slave to them, and you will find that a consistently applied program can be liberating without trying to brainwash yourself into having a limited range of emotions and feeling.

CHAPTER 7

Becoming a Speculator

The future for today's investor is bleak—bleaker than it's ever been. While America enjoys a large middle class filled with prosperity, the system is unsustainable. More and more Baby Boomers are aging into retirement, and there simply is no money for an effective Social Security program. Couple that with the fact that America suffers the same problem that all thriving industrial nations are suffering from: low birth rates. There will be no Social Security for Generation X and beyond.

While the stock market is a great place to have your money, the reality is that it takes more real dollars today to buy food, shelter, and gas than it did just five years ago. So it is easy to extrapolate how much more expensive things can and will be 30 years from now. Today's retirees will outlive their money unless they can have a viable investment alternative or somehow profit from the real dollar increases themselves.

That's where speculation comes into play. Effective speculation puts you at the forefront of a move. It gets you buying Microsoft when IBM gave up on the personal computer. It gets you opening a hardware store at the beginning of a housing boom. It gets you buying an electric car at the first sign of oil prices rising. True speculation has you at the forefront of what will likely occur in the future based on the information we have today.

In order to succeed in these times, we need to make bold moves. Futures and forex speculation allow us to do just that. There is no real "investing" involved in these markets. They are fast paced, aggressive, and reflect the real world. There are only two ways to approach these markets—either you are speculating or you are gambling.

SPECULATION VS. GAMBLING

Investopedia.com defines *speculation* as "the process of selecting investments with higher risk in order to profit from an anticipated price movement."

Dictionary.com defines *gambling* as "to stake or risk money, or anything of value, on the outcome of something involving chance: to gamble on a toss of the dice."

The average investor gets confused when he hears the words *higher risk* and assumes that higher risk means "chance."

Dictionary.com defines *chance* as "the absence of any cause of events that can be predicted, understood, or controlled."

I am not advocating that you should ignore that the risk exists or that you should give up traditional investing altogether, but for your money to not only survive inflation and thrive in the future, it's a good idea to round out your investing style to incorporate speculation.

Gambling involves "chance," which has no cause and effect, cannot be controlled, and cannot be understood. Each instance is independent of the last. Speculation cannot be considered gambling because you are making an informed decision based on all of the current information available.

Unfortunately, in order to move your investment attitude from that of a gambler to being a speculator requires hard work. Not everyone that comes to futures and forex investing is ready to put in the hard work that true speculation requires. The holy grail is constantly being sought after by would-be speculators. By looking for the easy route to success and not understanding the underlying fundamentals of the markets that they trade or are talked into trading, they are leaving their success up to "chance" and therefore are gambling their money away.

The beginning speculator will typically lose his entire investment within six months. Ninety-five percent of traders lose money trading. Eighty percent of options expire worthless. Time and time again these statistics are tossed out, but what do they really mean?

Pareto's principle may hold true!

When it comes to options, the 80/20 rule can clearly be seen: 80% of the options are sold by a handful of companies, most likely 20% of the market's participants; they collect the bulk of the option profits available. The leftover 20% of options, while they may be profitable for the buyer, do not represent the same level of profit. The reality is that it is better to sell options as opposed to buying them.

A parallel can be drawn when it comes to trading in general. Eighty percent of traders will simply be on the wrong side of a trade. Therefore, as you meet people who have traded, you will come across more that have lost. They will have dire tales of buying gold when it reached $800 per ounce and seeing it tank all the way down to $300 for 20 years.

The fact that 80% to 95% of traders lose money trading may mean they are the gamblers; they leave their trading to chance. The remaining 5% are the true speculators. So just like the baby that crawls before he walks, walks before he runs, and runs before he drives, so must the investor learn to speculate before he trades.

Let's Define Gambling Addiction

Gambling addiction comes in two forms: action gambling and escape gambling. While I am no psychiatrist, I have never met a trader who was trading to get away from problems and emotional issues in their lives. I have a tendency to believe that "reckless" traders are exhibiting symptoms of the "action gambling" type of addiction. Only you know your motivations, though.

Action gambling is defined as gambling in which the gambler is addicted to the thrill of risk-taking as his or her "substance of choice." In trading, we know we can win big or lose big almost at the drop of a dime. This excitement can become like a drug. This "thrill-seeking" emotion has been likened to a cocaine or methamphetamine addiction. For the action gambler, the goal is to be recognized as the "winner." For a trader, there is nothing sweeter than making a profit. While that may not be a problem in and of itself, what you do with your profits afterward may make all the difference.

Addictive gambling has been referred to as the "hidden illness" solely because there are few physical symptoms. Nevertheless, it can cause major disruptions in your life—psychological, physical, or social. While gambling addiction is treatable, if left unchecked, it will progress. The American Psychological Association classifies compulsive gambling as a mental health disorder of impulse control. That is why it is so important for you to use a trading plan when it comes to entering and exiting trades. If you can reduce the number of random impulses, you help yourself step away from the potential of having your speculation turn into a type of gambling addiction.

Could Trading Represent a Form of "Gambling Addiction" for You?

The American Medical Association is currently reviewing the possibility of adding "video game addiction" to a handbook regarding mental illness. Depending on your personality and how you view trading overall, you may be battling an addiction as well. If the AMA is debating video game playing, then active or day trading may not be that far behind.

As we pointed out, gambling has a strong component rooted in "chance"; speculating involves more calculating based on cause and effects. Nevertheless, trading can be turned into a gambling game. In the past 14 years of my experience, I have seen traders time and time again drive themselves insane over trading, making wrong decision after wrong decision primarily because they became reactionary.

For whatever reason, the cycle was constant: Open an account; invest on a whim; at the first sign of trouble, hold on for too long. When they are profitable, they get out right away. Never let these guys have a big win right away—feelings of invulnerability kick in. Many of the losing traders end up looking like addicts, whether they are or not, solely because they do not know how to stay on track and be disciplined in their trading.

If you are gambling when it comes to your trading, then you need to stop trading—immediately. The highs and lows that come from winning and losing can create a false sense of excitement and enjoyment. While I am not an expert on addictions, I do want to put a spotlight on the possibility of your being addicted. I want to give you the tools that will help you and your family to have an enjoyable life. The definitions and diagnosis criteria are excerpted from Gambler's Anonymous. I suggest you visit their web site at www.gamblersanonymous.org.

I hope that none of you are gambling when it comes to futures. I hope that you all are striving to become or are currently speculators. In the event that you are not or are having difficulties, following are some questions excerpted from the Gamblers Anonymous web site.

Gamblers' Anonymous 20 Questions

1. Did you ever lose time from work or school due to gambling?
2. Has gambling ever made your home life unhappy?
3. Did gambling affect your reputation?
4. Have you ever felt remorse after gambling?
5. Did you ever gamble to get money with which to pay debts or otherwise solve financial difficulties?
6. Did gambling cause a decrease in your ambition or efficiency?
7. After losing did you feel you must return as soon as possible and win back your losses?
8. After a win did you have a strong urge to return and win more?
9. Did you often gamble until your last dollar was gone?
10. Did you ever borrow to finance your gambling?

11. Have you ever sold anything to finance gambling?

12. Were you reluctant to use "gambling money" for normal expenditures?

13. Did gambling make you careless of the welfare of yourself or your family?

14. Did you ever gamble longer than you had planned?

15. Have you ever gambled to escape worry or trouble?

16. Have you ever committed, or considered committing, an illegal act to finance gambling?

17. Did gambling cause you to have difficulty in sleeping?

18. Do arguments, disappointments, or frustrations create within you an urge to gamble?

19. Did you ever have an urge to celebrate any good fortune by a few hours of gambling?

20. Have you ever considered self-destruction or suicide as a result of your gambling?

Most compulsive gamblers will answer yes to at least seven of these questions.

10 Symptoms of Gambling Addiction

The American Psychological Association reports 10 diagnostic criteria for determining the extent of gambling addiction.

1. *Preoccupation.* Constantly reliving past gambling experiences or thinking of nothing but gambling. When trading, this may exhibit itself as talking about that one great trade over and over again, or investing too much money into educational products.

2. *Tolerance.* Needs to gamble with increasing amounts of money in order to achieve the desired excitement. This could be adding more contracts (i.e., overleveraging), trading too many markets, or holding on longer to losing trades than you would expect.

3. *Withdrawal.* Is restless or irritable when attempting to cut down or stop gambling/trading.

4. *Escape.* Gambles as a way of escape or to relieve helplessness, guilt, anxiety, or depression.

5. *Chasing.* After losing money gambling, often returns another day in order to get even ("chasing one's losses"). Chasing is a classical behavior pattern characterizing pathological gambling. One of the cardinal rules of trading the market is to not chase trades.

6. *Lying.* Lies to family members, therapists, or others to conceal the extent of involvement with gambling.

   Time and time again I meet traders who are afraid to tell their wives, friends, and family members that they are involved with futures or forex, or they have blown out their account and are secretly re-funding their trading accounts without the knowledge of their wife and family.

7. *Illegal acts.* Has committed illegal acts (e.g., forgery, fraud, theft, or embezzlement) in order to finance gambling.

8. *Risked significant relationship.* Has jeopardized or lost a significant relationship, job, or educational or career opportunity because of gambling.

9. *Bailout.* Has relied on others to provide money to relieve a desperate financial situation caused by gambling. For traders, this typically takes the form of chasing commission rates.

10. *Loss of control.* Has made repeated unsuccessful efforts to control, cut back, or stop gambling.

If you have five or more of these signs, you are considered a pathological gambler; if you exhibit three or four of these, you are considered a problem gambler; if you exhibit only one or two, you would be called an "at risk" gambler.

If there is a one-for-one correlation with trading, my hope is for you to recognize a problem within yourself and seek help if necessary. This information is provided to help, not to be a real psychological evaluation.

There are three phases to gambling addiction: the "winning phase," the "losing phase," and the "desperation phase." If you find that your trading behavior is only partially mirroring the behaviors associated with each phase, don't panic. This information is meant to inform and warn you against spiraling downward. If you completely recognize yourself in each phase, you may want to seek additional help.

1. Winning phase. *During the winning phase, gamblers experience a big win—or a series of wins—that leaves them with unreasonable optimism that their winning will continue. This leads them to feel great excitement when gambling, and they begin increasing the amounts of their bets.*

2. Losing phase. *During the losing phase, gamblers often begin bragging about wins they have had, start gambling alone, think more about gambling, and borrow money—legally or illegally. They start lying to family and friends and become more irritable, restless, and withdrawn. Their home life becomes unhappy, and*

they are unable to pay off debts. The gamblers begin to "chase" their losses, believing they must return as soon as possible to win back their losses.

3. Desperation phase. *During the desperation phase, there is a marked increase in the time spent gambling. This is accompanied by remorse, blaming others and alienating family and friends. Eventually, the gamblers may engage in illegal acts to finance their gambling. They may experience hopelessness, suicidal thoughts and attempts, arrests, divorce, alcohol and/or other drug abuse, or an emotional breakdown.*

Excerpted from: Pathological gambling: An addiction embracing the nation [Internet]. Illinois Institute for Addiction Recovery (Peoria, IL); 2005 [cited May 2006]. Available at www.addictionrecov.org/aboutgam.htm.

Seeking Assistance

Maybe if the American Psychological Association classifies certain forms of trading as an addiction, there will be support groups. Until then, there are many counseling and treatment programs for gamblers, and I suggest you follow up with them in order to improve the quality of your life.

www.gamblersanonymous.org. A 12-step program that assists people with gambling disorders.

http://gamblinghelper.com. An online support community with articles and forums for problem gamblers.

www.gamblingproblem.net. An institute that addresses the study, prevention, and treatment of gambling addictions.

THE ROLE OF A SPECULATOR

The futures industry has been around for 150 years in the United States. In other countries and around the world, it has existed even longer. Yet the average investor is still confused and dumbfounded at what it takes to properly succeed at trading and what their exact role is in the markets.

The futures market is an insurance game.

Remember that and half of your difficulties will disappear. The futures market was designed to protect the actual buyers and sellers of the real goods a way to protect themselves from the uncertainty of price change. Season to season, year to year, they had no idea if there would be a shortage, drought, or record crop, yet every year they had a fixed cost.

There will never be a Lloyd's of London that will insure companies against the normal cost of doing business. So the futures market was created to protect the spot market, and the idea of allowing price discovery to occur naturally was born. The thought was to allow hedgers to have the most efficient market in which to buy and sell their goods. Unfortunately, with two groups, actual buyers and sellers, fairly matched in their long term outlook, they needed to give room to a third player—the speculator.

Just as insurance companies collect small premiums, knowing that the majority of people will not make a claim, so do the exchanges entice speculators to provide the liquidity to pay off the "claims" that the hedgers make. This is why futures are a zero-sum game.

The money in your account gets directly deposited into someone else's when you lose; when you gain, the money from someone else's accounts gets dropped in your account. Yet the trading is rigged. The majority of the contract holders are buyers and sellers of the actual goods, and yet only 3% of contracts are ever delivered when a futures contract expires.

The buyers and sellers have better access to resources and knowledge about the marketplace, they have more capital than you, and they actually own the products, so even when they are losing money in their futures positions, they are still making money in their cash positions.

You have finite capital and finite time, and your abilities have to pit you against trillions of dollars. Couple this with all the psychological issues of discipline that the average trader battles, and it quickly becomes apparent why 80% of people are losing money when it comes to trading futures and forex. How do you compete?

ARE YOU A SUCKER OR A SPECULATOR?

"It's just like stealing candy from a baby." This is what a commodity trading adviser (CTA) told me when I interviewed him to be in the CTA Directory. "The average person that gets into leveraged investing tries to apply what he learned in stocks about buying and holding and we cream them every time."

Answer these three questions to the best of your ability. Write your answers down, take as long as you want, write as many sentences, paragraphs, pages as you need to articulate your feelings, theories, and ideas. Be thorough.

1. Where do you think oil is going?
2. What is the highest price for gold?
3. How will interest affect the direction of the dollar?

Okay, are you finished writing everything down? **Don't read further until you have completed the exercise.**

This exercise was a little unfair. It was a setup. It was to show you how hard the mind fights to keep hold of an idea. However you responded, I am sure you had a bias for the market. You either thought oil was going to continue going up or you thought the price was coming down. You felt gold had peaked or you assumed that the price had stabilized.

Regardless of what side you were on you had opinions, ideas, and feelings to support your assumptions, each point more valid than the last point, each concept you would defend to the grave—stubbornness that will take your account to its grave if you are not careful.

This stubbornness is why 80% of traders lose money, consistently and constantly, when it comes to futures and forex trading. As a human being, you have a natural inclination to pick a side or pick a team. Republican or Democrat, Yankees or Red Sox, rap or hard rock. There is little room to embrace both extremes simultaneously. It is the rare individual who can revel in both sides without conflict. Yet the most successful of us can and do both without hesitation.

As you read over your justifications on why you feel a certain way about a market, you will see that you are rationalizing your opinions. You will find those points that will support your point of view and ignore others that invalidate it. Your sense of ego will not allow any other possibility in and it will force you into a narrower and narrower set of choices until you arrive at the point where you no longer have any choices at all. Once you get to that point, you are no longer speculating—you leaving everything to chance, and you are gambling.

The trader who constantly sells himself on his position is a just the type of sucker that the hedgers are looking for. They want you to have an opinion, a bias in the market that you will defend until the end. Your bias is their profit. It's like betting on one horse in a two-horse race, knowing full well that either one can win.

To be a speculator, someone who takes on "higher risk in order to profit from an anticipated price movement," we have to disguise ourselves and our behavior. We must think and operate like our better-prepared, better-financed, better-man-powered competition, the hedgers, in order to eliminate the potential for being blindsided in our trading.

This is not easy, but it is simple. In order to start yourself on the right path, you have to ask the question: "Am I ready to be a 20 percenter?"

It takes more effort, it takes more preparation, and it forces you to take a hard look in the mirror about why you trade these markets, what your goals are, and what success means to you.

THE THREE KEYS TO SUCCESS

"If I could just pick the right market, I would be a better trader."

"If I could just predict where the market is going, I would make money."

"If I could just be disciplined enough, . . ."

"If I. . . ."

You fill in the blank. In search of the holy grail, would-be speculators are constantly telling themselves little lies that they think will somehow soothe their egos and will potentially boost their bank accounts. There are two secrets to trading futures and forex. The first secret is that you will have losing trades.

That's it.

No matter what you do, no matter how many books you read, no matter how many seminars you attend, you will have losing trades.

If you spend $2,000, $10,000, or $50 on the next great book, the next automated trading system, the best piece of software that shows you red and green arrows, you will have losing trades. Accept that you will have losing trades, and your life begins to change from would-be speculator to a true speculator.

The second part of the secret is that when you properly prepare for losses, the profits will take care of themselves. You will never need to force a trade. When the trade is properly set up, you can expect to enjoy the fruits of your labor, whether that's reduced losses or increased profits.

There is a bonus secret that we have talked about before, but we will reiterate it: Don't leave anything to "chance." Chance is the realm of the gambler, the realm of the 80 percenters. They plan for nothing, they prepare for nothing, and they expect everything. Leaving the wrong things to chance is what stops would-be speculators from ever becoming traders.

It is no secret that the forex market trades trillions of dollars daily. The futures market trades trillions of dollars monthly. No matter how much money you have to invest, it will never be enough to affect the markets. Ask Barings Bank or Amaranth if you don't believe me. Since we know that we cannot control the markets through sheer force of will or with capital, we turn our attention inward.

By focusing on ourselves, we begin to apply the right pressure in the right areas. Deciding when to get into markets is the easy part. Our success comes from the ability to integrate three aspects of trading together seamlessly:

1. Money management
2. Technical analysis
3. Risk management

The three steps to trading success revolve around how you are able to plan in advance on how you will react when you win, lose, or draw in each one of these areas. By mastering your reactions in each of these areas, you elevate yourself from speculator to trader. The goal is to be constantly in control of your actions and to diminish the amount of surprise that you may experience from the market or to at least be prepared by what the market throws your way. Having a good trading psychology is not enough, because when our willpower begins to fail us, it is good to have a set of rules to operate by.

Money Management

Money management and risk management are two different things. Money management involves what you do with your money in your account, how much money you will risk in a trade, how much money you hope to gain, how your account will earn you interest, commission rate, and so on. Anything that has to do with specific numbers or percentages involving the capital in your account that is what money management involves.

Technical Analysis

There are two schools of thought. One believes the market can be predicted, and another believes it's random. While both schools of thought have their place, in order to be fair, there is a cause and effect in the marketplace. Chance plays a small role in how the market moves from one tick to the next.

Yet when it comes to technical analysis, many investors go overboard. They will have dozens of indicators, many of them redundant, which only add to their confusion. There is a way to get the maximum benefit from it. You have to divide your technical indicators up into three parts:

1. Where is the market going?
2. How fast is it getting there?
3. When will it arrive?

One or two indicators that are capable of answering each of these three questions will improve how you trade overnight.

What about fundamental analysis? There are so many factors involved with fundamental analysis that the average speculator doesn't have the time to stay abreast of the information. Not to mention the fact that when the market news is distributed, many of the key players have already acted on it, whether because of foreknowledge or based on their own projections. So, for all intents and purposes, fundamental analysis is not as useful as one would hope.

Risk Management

When you purchase a car, there are a few key risks, for example, theft, damage, or car accident. You purchase insurance to protect you from the risk. When you purchase life insurance, you are protecting yourself against one risk—death. When you purchase an electronic product, you may get the extended warranty, which protects you from a myriad of potential problems/risks that could damage it.

Insurance and risk go hand in hand. When you trade futures and forex, you risk losing your money. When it comes to risk management, all you should be focused on is how not to lose money. The second thing you should be thinking of is insurance. Just when you are paid back or rewarded on protecting yourself from everyday risk, so should you be paid back or rewarded when you insure your trading. That's why, when it comes to risk management, using "stop losses" is not enough.

Stop losses are necessary, but they fail to reward you. They stop the pain but do nothing to counterbalance it. So when you get the initial position right, you are on cloud nine, but when you get it wrong, you are forced to make two decisions. The first decision is whether your stop was too close but your position was right. The second decision is whether you should now reverse your position and commit the cardinal sin of chasing the market.

USING THE KEYS TO MAP OUT YOUR JOURNEY

Money management, technical analysis, and risk management are moving parts, each feeding on the other until you are capable of trading with a level of success that borders on professional-level trading. While there are no right or wrong answers when developing your program revolving around these key areas, it is important that you incorporate all three. This is what will move you from the realm of gambler to speculator, and speculator to trader.

Now that you have all three pieces of the puzzle, you need the right tools that will keep moving you forward. There are three tools that will be essential for you to turn your trading professional. The first tool you will need is to develop a trading plan. A trading plan is designed to cover all contingencies and on paper to show your trading rules and how you will interact with the market. The second tool is a trade worksheet. The trade worksheet allows you to plan ahead. Before you execute any trade, you should know your risk-reward ratio and returns on margin and account. The final tool is the trading journal. Any journey worth taking is worth writing about. The trading journal is your teaching tool. The cliché that those who forget history are doomed to repeat is very appropriate in trading.

Trading Plan

Ask any successful trader how he became successful, and you will consistently hear that he had a trading plan. This plan guided him when he was making profits and, more importantly, when he was losing money. A useful trading plan covers three key areas. First, it determines what markets you should be trading based on your risk and volatility levels. Second, you should know the exact technical and fundamental tools you will use to enter trades. Finally, you must know how you will react during a losing streak as well as a winning streak.

Figure 7.1 on page 94 is a 30-question trading plan document that allows any trader, novice or advanced, to develop a customized trading plan for himself. The completed questionnaire will provide you with a blueprint for trading success that you can refer back to whenever necessary.

The rest of this section includes detailed discussions of some of these questions.

Know Your Account Balance   The money in your account is not "play" money. Just because it is risk capital doesn't mean it's not important. You must always know your account balance. If you don't know where you are, how are you going to know where you are going? Risk capital still has value if you intend to be successful. Many traders bring a gambler's philosophy to the markets: "house money versus my money."

For successful traders, there is no such thing as "house money." If you earned it, it is your money, no ifs, ands, or buts. By removing the gambler's philosophy from how you treat your money, you will begin to balance your account much like a checkbook. Be constantly vigilant of how you view your trading capital. Risk capital should not be treated as already lost.

Understand True Commission Costs   When you know your commission costs, that means you are also aware of all of the various other costs associated with your trades. As we all know, there always seem to be various "brokerage charges," "exchange fees," "NFA fees," and so on. If your bank tacked on fees here and there on every transaction you did, you would demand an explanation, and whatever the explanation was, you would make it a point to keep track of these fees and question them from time to time. No matter what a publicized commission rate is, you must understand that your true commission rate is inclusive of all ancillary fees, not exclusive of them. Be careful not to be fooled by low publicized rates.

Know Your Broker   If you don't know the name of your broker or have a contact at the brokerage, you don't have a broker. Make it a point to get the name of your broker and his manager, as well as an alternate broker to work with in the event your broker is not there. Often when we are trading, we are entrusting thousands if not tens of thousands of dollars to an institution we have never met. Regardless, if they are licensed with

Account Number:

Beginning Balance:

Commission:

Broker:

Return-on-Investment Goal:

1. What markets do I want to trade?

       Agricultural Metallurgical Interest-bearing Indices Foreign currency Energy

2. What am I trying to do with futures?

       Hedge Speculate

3. If I want to hedge, what am I trying to hedge against/for?

4. How many contracts would it take to accurately hedge part of my portfolio?

5. How many contracts would it take to accurately hedge my entire portfolio?

6. Am I satisfied with my overall investment portfolio's performance?

7. Why am I interested in speculating with futures?

8. Is there a viable alternative to futures?

9. What type of volatility do I want to trade?

       Volatile   Semivolatile   Low-volatility

10. What percentage of my account do I want to place on each trade?

       10%   30%   50%

11. Do I ever intend to hold a futures contract until expiration?

12. How many contracts do I want to put on at a time?

       1 contract   2 contracts   5 contracts

13. How long do I want to hold on to a trade?

       1–2 days   3–4 days   Week or more   Expiration

14. Why have I chosen this time frame?

15. How will I get out of a losing trade?

       At the market Stops   Margin call

16. How often do I want to take advantage of trade signals?

       Once a month 2–3 times/month   5 times/month

17. How will I determine trades?

       Broker Trading a system News Portfolio weakness

FIGURE 7.1   Trading Plan Questionnaire

18. What annual rate of return am I receiving in my stock portfolio?

19. What annual rate of return do I expect from futures or forex?

20. If I lose my initial investment before a year is complete, am I willing to invest more money to obtain the returns I am looking for?

21. Would a combination of managed futures and a self-directed account best suit my lifestyle?

22. What will my money management strategies be?

23. What are the rules of the system I'm trading?

24. Who can help me succeed with this new investment vehicle?

25. How long am I willing to trade futures?

   1 year   3–5 years   5–10 years   Part of diversification

26. What will I do to help me see every trade objectively?

27. What will I do with my profits?

28. How will I deal with losses I will have to take from time to time?

29. How will I deal with trades that I take profits early on?

30. Is it more important to be 100% right about market direction or profitable?

FIGURE 7.1 (*Continued*)

the Commodity Futures Trading Commission (CFTC) and members of the National Futures Association (NFA), it is important for you as a trader to feel in control of what is happening around your money as well as who is operating around your account. It is not the duty of the brokerage firm to make this information available; it is your duty to demand it.

What Is Your Investment Goal?   Time and time again traders make the mistake of not having a specific profit goal in mind. Unfortunately, too many traders simply want to make as much money as possible. If it were that easy, everyone would be doing it. To be successful in any endeavor, you have to know what your finish line is, so you can get geared up for the next race. For example, analysts say that over time the stock market has had a return of 10% to 12%. In that same long time frame, bonds have averaged 3% to 5%. If these are the normal returns, what really makes you believe that you can do a 10,000% return in six months to a year after reading one book or buying one set of software?

In order to create a sincere return-on-investment goal, look to the money managers of the futures and options industry. Find out what the top large and small CTA money managers are earning. From there, look at their experiences and the markets they trade, as well as their strategies. Compare all three of these things against what you are doing. From that point, you will be able to give yourself a reasonable profit expectation goal from your futures trading. This is not to say you might pick a stellar trade that will give you that amazing 10,000% return, but it does mean that you won't try to make every trade a stellar trade. This approach is not glamorous, but it gives you a sense of control over your "what if" daydreaming.

What Markets Should You Trade?   How you answer this question will ultimately determine your longevity in futures trading. There are many factors that determine which markets are best suited for you. Do you want to trade very volatile markets or low-volatility markets? Do you live on the West Coast where it's difficult to see the 5 AM opening bell for the currency and gold markets? Do you have a full-time job and you can't stare at your screen all day long? The market or markets you pick to trade should best suit your lifestyle.

It is also important to pick only two to three markets that you can potentially master. It is difficult to understand and trade the subtleties of every single market available. While technical analysis can be applied across the board, as a specialist you begin to understand what actually makes a particular market tick. You can then manage your money and your trades according to the rhythms in that market. By focusing on a handful of markets, you can become a specialist. Without a doubt, specialists in any field have a tendency to be more successful

What Am I Trying to Do with Futures Speculation?   Know why you are trading futures. Is it for fun, like a gambler, or is it a true desire to speculate? Or are you trying to "hedge" your overall investment portfolio? What many investors forget about futures is that there are two aspects to it. It can be both the riskiest investment and the least risky investment at the same time, if you let it.

For example, during the dot-com bubble, many investors had mutual funds and stocks that closely matched the Nasdaq 100. When the market began to slow down and investors found themselves in the precarious position of not knowing if they should liquidate their tech stock and investment portfolios, they could have simply used Nasdaq futures to protect themselves from any quick drops in value.

By looking at futures from both sides, speculating and hedging, you can come up with more versatile strategies of managing your money over the long haul.

How Will I Get Out of a Losing Trade?   While 80% of your time is spent trying to pick a trade, the most valuable part of your time, the remaining 20%, you have your cash on the line. The failure of most traders is not being able to manage that 20% of the time. Since the majority of trades end in a loss, it's important to be able to make a clean break.

There are several ways to do this—"at the market" with mental stops, hard stops (which have an option component to guarantee specific prices), soft stops (which are triggered into becoming market orders), or margin calls, to name just a few.

The level of volatility in a market will determine your reactive response to losing trades. Whatever you do, stick to a loss of no more than 2% to 5% on an individual trade.

What Type of Volatility Do I Want to Trade, and Why?
Investopedia.com defines *volatility* as ". . . the tendency of a market or security to rise or fall sharply within a period of time."

It stands to reason that the greater the market volatility, the sharper the rises and falls are. The lesser the market volatility, the less sharp the rises and falls are. Know your pain threshold. Know the daily ranges between the lows and highs of each market you would like to trade. Find the ones with tighter price ranges, in real dollars, if you like low volatility. Find the markets with the wider ranges, in real dollars, if you want high volatility. Doing this simple assessment can protect you from unhappy surprises when a market turns against you.

What Percentage of My Account Do I Want to Place on Each Trade?
Futures investing is simply "leveraged" investing. The amount you put in your account may represent only 5% to 10% of its total value in the marketplace. In order to be successful, you must be careful to expose yourself as "little" as possible to the total leverage available to you. For example, stock investors are used to investing a specific dollar amount and having it committed 100% to the market. This all-or-nothing attitude can quickly backfire in futures investing. The reality is that you are capable of putting up only 10% of the money necessary to profit from that same 100%.

So logic dictates that if you put up to 100% of your account on margin, you are actually 1,000% exposed to the markets. You are overleveraged. While it may be unusual for you to have cash sitting around in your stock investments, cash sitting in your futures account is a positive situation. Don't let it burn a hole in your pocket. It gives you the opportunity to bounce back from trades that don't work out.

How Many Contracts Do I Put On at a Time?
Definitely think about this. Too many traders overleverage their account. Keep in mind that your leverage in futures trading can be as high as 30 to 1. This means that every single contract you trade is like making 30 trades all at one time. So each contract that you add on to a position is the equivalent of another 30 trades. That means that if you trade 10 futures contracts with a 30-to-1 leverage, you have effectively done 300 trades.

Since so many traders come to futures trading with only a small amount of capital, it is best to learn how to trade 1 or 2 contracts at a time. I suggest that for your first 10 trades you stick to these contract sizes. You will be pleasantly surprised at how easy it is to manage your money and to track the success and failures of your trades. If you wish to increase the number of contracts that you trade, keep in mind that you should never have more than 30% of your total account value on margin at any given time. This way, you can weather any ups or downs.

How Long Do I Hold On to a Trade?   As a trader, it is important to know the rhythm of the market you are trading. If the market runs in 7- to 10-day cycles, then you should let your winning positions run in 7- to 10-day cycles when it comes to grabbing your profits.

Whether it's 2 days or 2 weeks, maintain your winning trades as long as possible. So many traders are fixated on being "active," "day," "swing," or "position" traders that they miss the fact that they really don't have a choice. The market dictates what kind of trading you will do.

How Will I Determine Trades?   Thoroughly understand the system you are trading. Make sure that, however you pick your trades, you are fully in control of the final decision. There are many "black box" systems out there that "never" fail. The problem is if something happened to the developer or if the program failed you, you would have no one to blame for your losses.

If you have your own system that you have developed, document it. It is important to clearly know the rules of the system and to force yourself to stick to it with little to no deviation.

Getting Started in Technical Analysis by Jack D. Schwager is a great tool in understanding how each technical indicator works and the parameters that trigger buy and sell signals.

If I Lose My Investment, Am I Willing to Invest Again?   If you cannot answer this question honestly, then you should not be trading. The CFTC statistics state that 90% of all futures speculators lose money. No other investment touts such high losing ratios.

Therefore, there is a high likelihood of blowing out your account before you reach your profit goals. Be psychologically prepared for that possible event, and be financially prepared to make a second go of it if you are determined to succeed.

What Will Be My Money Management Strategies?   Clearly understand how and why you lost money in the past. Define those financial mistakes and rein them in. Here are some cash rules to protect against losses:

- Don't risk more than 2% to 5% of your total account value on one trade.
- Don't risk more than 10% of your total account value on all of your trades for the month.
- If an expected move in a market does not occur within two to three days, exit the trade immediately.
- When you make profits in excess of your beginning balance, put them in a separate account.

Please use these suggestions as a guideline to your own trading. If you can take more or less risk than I have suggested above, please adjust the parameters according to your risk thresholds. At the end of the day, the name of the game is capital preservation.

Is It More Important for Me to Be 100% Right about the Market's Direction or to Be Profitable? How you answer this question will determine your success in the markets. If you allow your ego to constantly cloud your vision, no system, no holy grail, no market guru can help you. As a student of the markets, it is important to truly listen to the one thing that matters—the markets.

Dissecting the Trading Plan Prequestions When I sat down to design the trading plan questionnaire, I wanted to have one simple tool that clearly outlined the risk-reward levels of the novice and intermediate trader. It was important for me to help them define realistic goals as well as help them figure out the true level of volatility they could accept based on their risk profile. More importantly, I wanted them to think about why futures trading was right for them and what strategies they would use, physically and emotionally, in order to get themselves over the guaranteed losses they knew would occur when they traded.

The questionnaire itself is broken down into 30 numbered questions and 5 "prequestions." These are the first 5 prequestions:

1. *Account number.* This is simple enough to answer. Unfortunately, too many traders do not know this information. At our brokerage firm, we will have people who want to transfer their accounts over, but they do not know what their account number is, much less where their statements are. This negligence is all tied together. If you are not currently maintaining your statements in some sort of binder, you are making a grave mistake. When you open a futures trading account, it belongs to you. It is no one else's responsibility, so treat it as such. In the event of an emergency of any type, being organized in this regard is essential. Also, by knowing your account number or having it at your fingertips, you are capable of executing your trades at your brokerage firm's trade

desk in the event of a technology meltdown. This can be important if you are in a trade and want to exit it early because the market signals have changed.

2. *Beginning balance.* Know the exact amount you have in your account at all times. Everyone comes to speculative trading with risk capital. That doesn't change the fact that the money you bring to the table has a real value. There is no "house money" when it comes to speculating. All the money is yours, your profits and your seed capital. Establishing your beginning balance helps you balance your account much like a checkbook. Notice I didn't say "your" checkbook—because some of us aren't very good at that. Simply put, be conscious at all times of how you view this money. Risk capital should not be treated as already lost.

3. *Commission.* When I say know your commission rate, I mean not just the publicized rate. It is easy to be fooled by low publicized rates only to get hit by various trading and account fees. Every clearing firm has these extra fees, know what your fees are so you can compare apples to apples when selecting where you intend to trade.

4. *Broker.* If you don't know the name of your broker, you don't have a broker. Make it a point to get the name of your broker and his manager, as well as an alternate broker to work with in the event your broker is not there. The current trend among discount brokerages is to keep no licensed people on staff. Beware! The only help you can receive is technical and it can be difficult to get anyone on the phone for simple account adjustments. Do your best to find out their emergency phone numbers and maintain a second account somewhere else if you want to talk to a live person from time to time to help you solve your problems..

5. *Return-on-investment goal.* Profits don't just happen, they take a lot of time and preparation. By designing realistic "return-on-investment" goals you make the trading process easier on yourself. Professional futures and forex money managers can help you know the difference between what is possible versus what is probable. Various reports are distributed online and in major publications pointing out the best and worst money managers. Reviewing these lists will help you in both your expectations and market approach. This is not to say you won't pick a stellar trade that will give you that amazing return, but it does mean that you won't try to make "every" trade a stellar trade. This approach is not glamorous, but it gives you a sense of control over your "what if" daydreaming.

These 5 "prequestions" are just the beginning of a well-rounded trading plan. Once you have answered and done the suggestions surrounding just these 5 questions, you will quickly find yourself ahead of 90% of all other futures and options traders.

Trigger Event (news, approvals, underperforming fund manager, too much stock in employer, etc.): _____

Trade (circle one):   Hedge Scenario   Speculation Scenario

Type of Trade:

Agricultural   Metallurgical   Interest-bearing   Indices   Foreign currency

Hedge Scenario (How many contracts needed to hedge, entrypoint, exitpoint, stop, margin,+/– % return on margin, +/- % return on account) _____

_____

Speculation Scenario (entrypoint, exit point, stop, margin, +/– % return on margin, +/– % return on account): _____

_____

FIGURE 7.2   Trade Worksheet

Trade Worksheet

Do the math!

If you are not willing to do the math, do you really deserve the profits? When you are investing in such a highly leveraged investment, it's important that you understand the basics of the trade, the value of what you are putting into it, what you are getting out of it, and all of your potential loss scenarios. You are also able to figure out risk management scenarios while using it.

The trade worksheet (see Figure 7.2) helps to narrow down your focus and gives you a level of comfort on what can and might happen regardless of the outcome. You design hedge scenarios along with speculation scenarios together to make it work to the best of your account's ability.

The trade worksheet helps put you in control of your trading. Calculating your profits and losses ahead of time lets you know if the risk you are taking is a risk worth taking. This is how you gain control of your trading. You become prescient on whether the opportunity you are taking is a good one or not.

This puts you ahead of the majority of traders who simply fly by the seat of their pants.

Trade Journal

A journey of 1,000 miles begins with the first step. A trade journal is the key to long-term success. It is simple to maintain and perfect to use for improving your skill. The trick is to print a copy of the chart you use to enter a trade and a copy of the chart you use to exit the trade. Once this is accomplished, you take your notes directly on the chart. By writing on the chart, you diminish your paperwork.

Maintaining this information lets you know what you are thinking and feeling when you enter and exit trades and lets you know if your trading tools are working properly. It also shows you if you are exiting too quickly or if you are going against your trading plan.

Trading is an art. By being aware of your intuition and your feelings, you may find that you are able to trade in unique and different ways. The only way to discover that is by documenting it. The information can be maintained separately or right on the charts that you use to execute trades. The key is to document your emotions, logic, and reasoning for entering and exiting trades. Through the accumulation of 10, 30, or 100 journal entries, you are able to reasonably determine how well you are doing.

If you are a swing trader or a position trader, it is easier to maintain a trade-by-trade trading journal. However, a day trader or active trader may find it difficult to document each trade, so a general sentiment of how he is maintaining his system and the overall sentiment on the day may be more appropriate. As you learn some of the various risk management techniques, it will be come simpler to use a trading journal on a per-trade basis. Until then, let's take our time.

See Figure 7.3 for an example of a trading journal.

Entry date:

Long or Short:

Type of commodity:

Number of contracts:

Month and year:

Fill price:

Exit date:

Exit price:

Profit/loss:

Profit/loss as a percentage of margin:

Profit/loss as a percentage of equity:

Thoughts and feelings of trade:

Entry date:

Exit date:

FIGURE 7.3 Trading Journal

PULLING IT ALL TOGETHER

Transitioning from your everyday investor to a true speculator can be a difficult road. There is no magic word that instantly transforms you. It is a task fraught with its own dangers and perils. To be successful at it, you need the right set of tools and the proper mind-set with a healthy dose of desire to make it work.

Once you lay the foundation with a strong trading plan; an understanding of the interrelationship among money management, technical analysis, and risk management; plus a knowledge of the difference between speculation and gambling, you will find that you can have an enjoyable trading experience, whether you are winning or losing.

PART III

Seven Lessons for Trading Success

When I wrote my first set of books, *Futures for Small Speculators and Forex for Small Speculators*, my goal was to write for traders who already had experience in trading and who had, from time to time, for whatever reason, had a difficult time protecting themselves from everyday trader mistakes.

The problem arose when new traders, who had no trading system or experience, would pick up my book because of its title and would confuse the ideas of "small speculator" with "new speculator." That's when I sat down and began to keep track of my trading, keeping notes on how I thought, how I trained the guys in my office, and what emotions and thoughts had impacted me in my trading career. That's how I came up with the simple one-hour seminar entitled "Seven Steps to Trading Success."

For the first time, it broke down my holistic approach to trading and gave traders insight into not just the how of trading, but the why as well. The next seven lessons will put you through the paces. Some information you may know, some you may not know, and other information is twisted in such a way that you can see a new perspective. Whatever the case may be, the tools in the upcoming chapters are meant to open up the world of trading to you in an exciting new way. Read them, review, and, most importantly, use each chapter to its fullest capability in order to help you succeed in all of your trading endeavors.

CHAPTER 8

Lesson 1: Developing a Trading Plan

It is stupid to fight a battle that you cannot win, and you cannot win unless you have properly planned for it.

—Sun Tzu, *The Art of War*

We took the roundabout way to get to the actual seven steps to trading success. Nevertheless, it is important that you are able to understand the dire problems with retirement and the expansion of the world economy, be able to distinguish between speculation and gambling, and be able to determine why you are involved in this type of investment as opposed to stocks and bonds.

Now that you have evolved from the investor's mentality, it is time to take you from being a speculator to becoming a trader. In order to do that, we have to address the reality that every trader faces. No matter who you are, no matter where you are from, traders have three things staring them in the face: time, capital, and opportunity.

The difference between an average trader and a successful trader is subtle but important. We know that the markets are measured in the trillions of dollars. The forex market at any given time has anywhere from $1 to $2 trillion dollars in capital floating around daily. The commodity exchanges have as much as $1 trillion dollars floating through them monthly. So no matter what size account you are starting off with, $200 or $200 million, you will never have enough money to move the markets. Ask Amaranth or Barings Bank if you don't believe me. So all traders have to accept the simple fact that they have "finite capital" in relationship to the markets they trade.

The second handicap is time. No matter who you are, no matter where you live, we all have the same 24 hours in a day. The majority of people divide their life between sleeping, eating, family time, working, hobbies, and commuting. Therefore, the development of 24 hour trading was never meant to encourage normal everyday traders. With all that we do in a day, the only people who can truly benefit from a 24-hour market trading place are the major corporations with the automated computer systems and scores of employees working around the clock to monitor them. So the average trader squeezes his trading in where it can fit—a few hours in the morning; a few hours in the evening; or, if they are retired, they schedule their trading around their golf schedule. The bottom line is that they are dealing with "finite time."

So all traders are on equal footing with having "finite capital" and "finite time." What makes the difference between the average trader and the successful trader?

Opportunity.

More importantly, the preparation of opportunity.

While the average trader is struggling with finite time and finite capital, he also struggles with one more problem—he is overwhelmed by opportunity. The trader knows that there are opportunities and potential money to be made, but he cannot overcome his emotions of fear and greed. He is overwhelmed at the possibilities and does not have a handle on how to narrow them down.

Therefore, his fear emotion will stop him from getting into trades that might be profitable, or his fear emotion will convince him not to take a loss just in case the market rebounds. However, the greed emotion can kick in and force you to buy too many contracts or to hold on to your winning trades too long. Whatever the reaction, the opportunities of the average trader become overwhelming. They can become overwhelming to the point of paralyzing.

Successful traders, however, embrace their opportunities. They see that their opportunities are unlimited solely because they are prepared for their emotions acting up. They know what to do, when to do it, and, more importantly, why they are doing it. All of this puts them in control of their fear and greed.

Twice a year, I read the book *The Art of War* by Sun Tzu. It is both motivating and insightful, particularly for traders. The quote "It is stupid to fight a battle that you cannot win, and you cannot win unless you have properly planned for it" sticks out when it comes to teaching traders how to trade. Trading cannot be won if you do not properly prepare for it.

In the Liverpool trading system, there are three components that we work with to properly prepare you: money management, technical analysis, and risk management. Each component is broken into two parts. In this chapter and the next, we will tackle money management. The first part will involve how to gain control of your trading. In this chapter we will learn how to create a realistic trading plan. We will determine the markets you can and should trade to maximize your account.

In Chapter 7, I showed you the tools that can help you succeed in trading: trading plan questionnaire, trade worksheet, and trading journal. While each of these tools is important in and of itself, the most important first step is to develop a trading plan. For the past decade every book and seminar I have attended has talked about this mythical beast. They recommend it and encourage it; they also give you the impression that you can't live without one. I have yet to find a succinct way to develop a trading plan that doesn't revolve around technical analysis.

Like a business plan, a trading plan is a living document. It will evolve and change around who you are and what you want at the time. There is no one trading plan that fits all types of traders. Every individual brings his or her own desire and expectations to bear on the market. While it is not easy to design a trading plan, you will be left at the random mercy of the markets without it.

With all of the capital and people involved in the markets, it is more of a force of nature than anything else. Therefore, since there is no way to control a force of nature, we need to focus on what we can control, which is our reactions to this force of nature.

While the trading plan you write up today may look nothing like the trading plan you are using a year from now, there are three main purposes of every trading plan you design:

1. It gives a clarification of your purpose.
2. It helps you set your goals.
3. It gives you the necessary preparation steps to help you deal with the inevitable.

How you approach your trading will depend on how much capital you have and your risk tolerance levels. Too often, the capital you have doesn't match your risk level. Whether you have a little capital or a lot of capital, your risk tolerance will dictate how you will succeed. Like any business, you have to make sure you are neither under- nor overcapitalized. If you are facing either scenario, your likelihood of success begins to diminish.

MYTHS OF TRADING

There are many trading myths that affect both novice and experienced traders. Typically, these myths force traders into a narrow belief that they have to be perfect or nearly perfect in order to succeed. This myth, along with a few others, holds traders back from achieving their true mission—making profits.

Myth 1

It's easy to trade if you can just pick the direction the market is going.

Reality

Ninety-five percent of traders lose money when they trade futures and forex.

If all it takes is the ability to pick the market direction, why are people still not succeeding? There are many great advisory services and newsletter services out there, but in order to succeed in trading, you must have more versatility. Picking a market's direction does not match up with its timing, nor does it indicate you will succeed in exiting the market with a profit.

Myth 2

If I could just be a day trader/swing trader/position trader like person X, I would be able to make money.

Reality

In order to succeed in trading, you must trade to your own needs, desires, capital, wants, goals, risk, reward, volatility levels, and so on.

No two traders are alike. Customize your trading for your life! A study was conducted in which sports scientists wanted to do their best to figure out what made the best quarterbacks in the world great. After reviewing video after video, they came to one conclusion: Every quarterback had one thing in common—nothing. Everyone approached the snap and release differently. Some could run, others stayed in the pocket well, others played a short game, and still others played a long game.

Once you learn the basics of our trading method, you will be able to find your personal style as well.

Myth 3

If I don't see success in X time, futures/forex are impossible to invest in.

Reality

Any undue pressure you put on any new endeavor makes it more difficult to succeed.

One trade should never make or break you. Too many beginners come to futures and forex trading betting the farm on one trade. They pick some seasonal opportunity, or they read something in the papers, or a broker will call and hype them up on the *biggest* investment since sliced bread. Whatever the case, when that one opportunity fails, they give up. These same one-time investors will then come back to the markets 18 months later and do the exact same thing all over again, buying a trade as opposed to learning how to trade. Step out of the box. I recommend that you invest at least 100 hours paper/demo trading and real trading in order to become successful.

Also, before you decide on any new business venture, you have to carefully prepare and plan to decide on the exact type of business you will be in. It is very easy to get caught up in the hype of the markets. One of the most prolific promotions during the dot-com bubble was day trading. This day-trading phenomenon encompassed e-mini S&P, the Dow Jones, and the e-mini Nasdaq. While very exciting, it became clear that not everyone was suited for this type of trading.

Whether their lifestyle didn't make it conducive, they were holding down full-time jobs, or their stomachs couldn't handle the constant flip-flopping that's required of successful day traders, the hype led them to participate in a type of trading that in the long run worked against their overall personality.

The same thing occurred when forex trading was first introduced—it became heavily promoted. While some have found success in this marketplace, the numbers play out just as dismally. Ninety-five percent of the traders are simply not succeeding in their trading. To add insult to injury, the number one corporate player in the forex investing arena, Refco, ended up closing its doors and being delisted from the New York Stock Exchange.

Now that you have laid a few myths to rest, I hope that you are beginning to see it is very important that you become your own trader. No one else can determine for you what type of trading is best. The quicker you come to that realization, the less frustration you will experience. The first step in taking control comes through the process of picking the right market that fits you and your goals.

WHAT MARKETS SHOULD YOU TRADE?

Late night infomercials may not be the best way to get involved in a new investment no matter how attractive the hostess is. Be wary of gurus that say they have the *only* guaranteed way to succeed. There are so many factors influencing your potential success that everything has to be customized. Don't let anyone tell you otherwise. In this chapter we will figure out what markets you can trade and we will go through the seven-point checklist that will give us the best insight into how you should be picking the best possible market for you.

Seven-Point Checklist in Finding Futures Markets That Work for You

1. Get a margin sheet of all of the tradable markets.
2. Understand initial margin and maintenance margin.
3. Figure out which markets have margins less than your account.
4. Learn minimum tick or point values of those markets.
5. Determine average true range to choose acceptable volatility.
6. Organize "short-listed" markets from least to most volatile.
7. Check the "open interest" for each market to find the most liquid.

Seven-Point Checklist for Narrowing Down Forex Markets That Work for You

1. Get a list of tradable spot markets.
2. Determine if you will be a full-size or micro trader.
3. Figure that you want to have three times the amount of margin necessary to control one contract. If you are a micro trader on a $250 account, make sure you have $750 backing each contract that you intend to trade in the spot market. This strategy gears your margin down in your account three times, which gives greater control in your account.
4. Understand the pip movement of the markets you trade.
5. Use average true range to determine volatility of the corresponding futures market.
6. Organize short-listed markets.
7. Check the open interest for each market to find the most liquid futures option contracts.

The following section explains step by step the seven-point checklist in finding futures markets that work for you. By going through this process, you will gain insight into both futures and options. It will also make it easier for you to do the less intensive research, if you prefer forex, of picking the right currency markets as well.

1. Get a Margin Sheet of All of the Tradable Markets

There are a little over 60 tradable markets in the United States. While the universe of futures and commodity contracts may reach into the hundreds around the world, they do not come anywhere close to the tens of thousands of stocks out there. That virtue alone makes it easier to wrap your mind around these markets—not as much information to sift through.

At the same time, it is vital to understand what you are up against. While stock prices can be clearly seen on their ticker symbol, the prices for commodities have no correlation to the amount of margin that is charged. A secondary problem is the fact that margins fluctuate based on volatility. The more active a market becomes, margins will fluctuate higher as a safeguard against speculation. The less active a market is, margins will fluctuate down in order to make them more appealing to trade.

Therefore, the only way to determine if you can trade one of the 60 tradable markets is to get an updated margin sheet. You can find an updated margin sheet on our web site at www.liverpoolgroup.com. Each market is listed, along with its margin and symbol. Every market is customized, and it's important that you learn the details of the market you want to trade. Following is a list of the 60 tradable markets.

Tradable Markets

Australian dollar (Pit)	Gold (Pit)	Orange juice
British pound (Pit)	Goldman Sachs Index	Palladium (Pit)
Canadian dollar (Pit)	Heating oil (Pit)	Platinum (Pit)
CCI Index	High-grade copper	Pork bellies
Cocoa	Japanese yen (Pit)	RBOB gasoline
Coffee "C"	Kansas City wheat	Rough rice
Corn	Lean hogs	S&P 500 (Pit)
Cotton	Live cattle	Silver (eCBOT)
Crude oil (e-miNY)	Lumber	Silver (Pit)
Crude oil (Pit)	Mini corn	Soybean meal
Dollar index	Mini Dow Jones	Soybean oil (Pit)
Dow Jones	Mini gold	Soybeans (Pit)
E-mini Nasdaq 100	Mini silver	Sugar #11
Emini Russell 2000	Mini soybeans	Swiss franc (Pit)

E-mini S&P 500	Mini wheat	Treasury bonds (Pit)
Eurocurrency (Pit)	Nasdaq 100 (Pit)	Treasury note—10-year (Pit)
Eurodollar (Pit)	Natural gas (e-miNY)	Treasury note—2-year (Pit)
Federal funds (Pit)	Natural gas (Pit)	Treasury note—5-year (Pit)
Feeder cattle	Nikkei 225	Unleaded gasoline (Pit)
Gold (eCBOT)	Oats	Wheat (Pit)

There are six categories that the markets fall under:

1. Agricultural
2. Metallurgical
3. Interest Bearing
4. Indices
5. Foreign Currency
6. Energy

Pick a category, and then narrow your trading experience down to one or maybe two markets within that category. Often, I hear from stock investors that they don't know where to begin when it comes to futures and commodities trading. These investors may have 15 or 20 years of stock experience, and all of a sudden they think they need to throw all of their experience out of the window.

The simplest way to pick a category is to look back at various types of stocks you have invested in over the years. If you found yourself in the tech sector a lot, look to the Nasdaq. If you enjoy mining companies, look to the metals or the energy sector. If you have a firm grasp of stock market dynamics, maybe you will follow the Dow Jones.

When all is said and done, focus on markets that already pique your interest. As long as they hold your interest, you will follow them and want to learn more. If you are the type of trader who is picking markets just for the markets' sake or because of some technical indicators, when the market does something you don't expect, you will be ill prepared to deal with it.

Where our interests lie is where we will find our most joy. So even if you have never invested in stocks before, as long as you pick markets that you are interested in, your joy is what will sustain you when you're losing in your trading. You will know how and want to figure out and research what is going on in the markets you have chosen. Like all human beings, when we know where to find answers, it reduces our frustration and adds to our ability to learn dynamically.

As I said before, futures are not new. They have been around in some form or another for hundreds of years. So, while they may be new to you, there is no excuse to ignore the tremendous amount of historical data and information that is available to help you learn from your mistakes. This becomes easier when you are looking at only a handful of markets that you are trading.

Futures Month Codes

F = January

G = February

H = March

J = April

K = May

M = June

N = July

Q = August

U = September

V = October

X = November

Z = December

Full-Size Markets When it comes to trading, it is important to know what your capital can do for you. Unlike the stock market where it is common to fully invest all of your capital in the markets, this is an ill-advised strategy in the futures market.

Margin means leverage in futures—they are synonymous. The amount of margin a contract requires you to put is simply a reflection of your ability to pay back in case you need to take delivery. Unfortunately, all of your profits and losses are what is known as *marked to market*. As someone gains money, it is withdrawn directly from someone else's account. When you make money, it is automatically deposited into your account. This is what is meant by a zero-sum game.

The closer your total account value is to the contract margin value, the more difficult it will be to sustain the account when the market is moving against you. I singled out various different markets that work for varying account levels. Each large account size can have an impact on the markets preceding it. A $20,000 account can trade markets that are good with a $10,000 or $5,000 account. Trading in the other direction is not allowed.

In the next chapter we will be examining a little more in-depth the money rules of margin. Suffice it to say that the recommended contract charts are designed to make sure you have enough capital left over to effect another trade or to set up a risk management strategy. The goal is to avoid over-leverage at all costs.

All accounts are traded differently as well. A $10,000 account is traded differently from a $15,000 account, from a $25,000 account, from a $50,000 account, and from a $100,000 account. Each account size has a different set of objectives, goals, purchasing power, and volatility tolerance. You are just as capable of underleveraging your account as you are of overleveraging—find a balance. Avoid trading too small a contract for your account size.

The majority of new traders begin a futures and commodity account with $5,000. While this is not the most expensive way to start, it can get your feet wet in understanding how to trade. There is still a large breadth of markets to choose from. There are commodities, currencies, interest-bearing products, and livestock. Look at Table 8.1 for all of your choices.

Depending on how much seed capital you have, more markets will open up to you. In Tables 8.2, 8.3, and 8.4, we can see the various markets that you can get involved with, without worrying if you are overleveraged or not.

E-mini Trading   It has become increasingly popular to trade e-mini markets. Many stock companies are offering these electronic markets to their clients with little to no instruction (see Table 8.5). While on the surface they may seem new and exciting, there is little to no difference between the e-minis and the pit-traded markets. In fact, whether you are trading the electronic markets or the pit-traded markets, the way the symbol is quoted doesn't change. Table 8.6 shows the layout of the typical futures market symbol; market, month, and year. The primary differences between the two different types of markets, e-mini versus pit, revolve around reduced commissions and margins.

When the e-mini margin is significantly cheaper than the pit margin, this is known as *gearing*. Gearing is the ability of the Futures Commission Merchant to essentially vouch for you at the exchange. They extend you even more credit than the standard margin because they want you to have the ability to trade more contracts than you normally would in your account.

This gearing comes with two costs, though. The first cost is position control. When you gear your trading, you are allowed only to be a day trader. They offer you the reduced trading margin only during the day or evening session, depending on which one you pick. You must be out of your trade by the end of the day or you will be otherwise penalized for holding

TABLE 8.1 Recommended Markets for Accounts with $5,000 or Less

Contract	Exchange	Symbol	Initial Margin	Maint. Margin
Australian dollar (Pit)	CME	AD	1,148	850
British pound (Pit)	CME	BP	1,485	1,100
Canadian dollar (Pit)	CME	CD	1,148	850
Cocoa	NYBOT	CC	1,260	900
Corn	CBOT	C	1,350	1,000
Cotton	NYBOT	CT	1,260	900
Dollar index	NYBOT	DX	1,131	850
Eurodollar (Pit)	CME	ED	743	550
Federal funds (Pit)	CBOT	FF	338	250
Feeder cattle	CME	FC	1,350	1,000
Kansas City wheat	KCBOT	KW	1,250	1,000
Lean hogs	CME	LH	945	700
Live cattle	CME	LC	1013	750
Lumber	CME	LB	1,650	1,100
Oats	CBOT	O	743	550
Pork bellies	CME	PB	1,620	1,200
Rough rice	CBOT	RR	810	600
Soybean meal	CBOT	SM	945	700
Soybean oil (Pit)	CBOT	BO	608	450
Soybeans (Pit)	CBOT	S	1,215	900
Sugar #11	NYBOT	SB	910	650
Swiss franc (Pit)	CME	SF	1,215	900
Treasury bonds (Pit)	CBOT	US	1,620	1,200
Treasury note—10-year (Pit)	CBOT	TY	945	700
Treasury note—2-year (Pit)	CBOT	TU	608	450
Treasury note—5-year (Pit)	CBOT	FV	608	450
Wheat (Pit)	CBOT	W	1,688	1,250

TABLE 8.2 Recommended Markets for Accounts with $6,000 to $10,000

Contract	Exchange	Symbol	Initial Margin	Maint. Margin
Coffee "C"	NYBOT	KC	2,240	1,600
Eurocurrency (Pit)	CME	EC	2,025	1,500
Gold (eCBOT)	CBOT	ZG	2,349	1,740
Gold (Pit)	COMEX	GC	2,700	2,000
Japanese yen (Pit)	CME	JY	2,430	1,800
Orange juice	NYBOT	OJ	2,240	1,600
Palladium (Pit)	NYME	PA	2,025	1,500
Platinum (Pit)	NYME	PL	3,375	2,500
Silver (eCBOT)	CBOT	ZI	3,375	2,500
Silver (Pit)	COMEX	SI	3,375	2,500

TABLE 8.3 Recommended Markets for Accounts with $12,000 to $20,000

Contract	Exchange	Symbol	Initial Margin	Maint. Margin
CCI Index	NYBOT	CI	3,500	3,500
Crude oil (Pit)	NYME	CL	4,050	3,000
Dow Jones	CBOT	DJ	5,625	4,500
Goldman Sachs Index	CME	GI	6,000	4,000
Heating oil (Pit)	NYME	HO	5,400	4,000
High-grade copper	COMEX	HG	6,413	4,750
Nikkei 225	CME	NK	5,000	4,000
Unleaded gasoline (Pit)	NYME	HU	5,400	4,000

TABLE 8.4 Recommended Markets for Accounts with $21,000 Plus

Contract	Exchange	Symbol	Initial Margin	Maint. Margin
Nasdaq 100 (Pit)	CME	ND	16,250	13,000
Natural gas (Pit)	NYME	NG	7,425	5,500
RBOB gasoline	NYME	RB	7,088	5,250
S&P 500 (Pit)	CME	SP	17,500	14,000

TABLE 8.5 Mini Contracts

Contract	Exchange	Symbol	Initial Margin	Maint. Margin
Crude oil (e-miNY)	NYME	QM	2,025	1,500
E-mini NASDAQ 100	CME	NQ	3,250	2,600
E-mini Russell 2000	CME	ER	4,000	3,200
E-mini S&P 500	CME	ES	3,500	2,800
Mini corn	CBOT	YC	270	200
Mini Dow Jones	CBOT	YM	2,813	2,250
Mini gold	CBOT	YG	783	580
Mini silver	CBOT	YI	675	500
Mini soybeans	CBOT	YK	243	180
Mini wheat	CBOT	YW	338	250
Natural gas (e-miNY)	NYME	QG	1,856	1,375

TABLE 8.6 Futures Ticker Symbol

Market	Month	Year
GC	Z	7
Gold	December	2007

a position overnight. This can mean increased margin requirements or liquidated trading positions.

Whatever the case, it is important that you understand the responsibility that comes along with deep discounted commissions. The second cost of gearing and trading in the electronic markets period is the inability to accurately hedge your trading with options. There are few options on the electronic markets, and the level of their liquidity is suspect. So while you may have the added convenience of utilizing the electronic markets, there are velvet handcuffs that can inhibit your risk management techniques if you are not careful.

2. Understand Initial Margin and Maintenance Margin

There are two types of margin: initial margin and maintenance margin. Initial margin is the amount to get into a trade, and maintenance margin is what you need to stay in the trade. Knowing both numbers gives you a clear picture of where you stand. For those with a stock background, futures margin is nothing like stock margin. Your profits and losses are added or subtracted from your margin in real time. The margin that you put up to hold on to a contract is considered a part of your account equity and is treated as such.

Margin is based on volatility and can adjust according to the amount of risk you have in a trade or in your account. As a speculator, you will have to put up the maximum margin required. As you learn more about the Liverpool Trading Method, you will begin to enjoy the benefits that the classification of "hedger" enjoys.

For instance, if you were to trade the British pound, the initial margin would be 1,480, and the maintenance margin would be 1,100.

Maintenance margin is slightly trickier. Maintenance margin is designed to let your trade have breathing room if the market moves against you. You don't have to act when your account drops below the initial margin just when the maintenance margin is penetrated. That's when you have to bring your account back up to initial margin level. This is called a *margin call*. The easiest way to avoid a margin call is to pick the right trade! In lieu of that, don't be overleveraged. This is why I advocate trading one contract at a time and establishing a large enough account reserve.

At all costs, you want to avoid a margin call. In fact, you should never put additional money into your account to cover a losing trade. If you feel compelled to do so, you are acting out of desperation and not in your own best interest. In no universe does it make sense to throw good money after bad.

3. Figure Out Which Markets Have Margins Less Than Your Account

I did half the work for you by breaking down the markets for the various-size accounts. Now you have to take it one step further. It's not good enough to just pick markets that have a margin you can afford. You must categorize margins according to three values: 10%, 15%, and 30% of your total account size. By breaking it down in this fashion, you can determine the level of exposure to the markets. As an added bonus, you can calculate, to an extent, the number of opportunities you will have when it comes to trading.

The less capital you have to put up for a trade, the less likely that market is going to significantly affect you when there are losses. However, the fact that a market has a very low margin doesn't mean you want to trade it. There are other factors to consider: option liquidity, volatility, and open interest.

You also have to be careful that you don't get involved with a market just because it is popular in the media. Too many traders tell me that they are just learning on this or that market, but they really want to trade another market. I say you should learn on the markets you want to eventually trade semiprofessionally. Your learning curve will be reduced, and if you paper trade with them, you will already have established a trading journal that could start you on your way to developing your own trading style.

4. Learn Minimum Tick or Point Values of Those Markets

This is a self-explanatory step, but you would be surprised at the number of futures and commodities traders who are clueless as to how they actually make and lose money in a trade. It is important that you stay on top of the minimum point value movement and the minimum tick value. The two do not always match.

By knowing these numbers, you can calculate your potential losses or potential gains before you ever commit a dime. Planning ahead is the greatest gift you can give yourself in transitioning from investor to speculator, speculator to Hawaii.

For example:

"British pound" market has a minimum point value of $625. "British pound" market has a minimum tick value of $6.25.

See Figure 8.1.

FIGURE 8.1   British Pound Example
Source: Genesis Financial Technologies, Inc. (www.tradenavigator.com).

5. Determine Average True Range to Choose Acceptable Volatility

Now you have narrowed down a few markets you are interested in, but you are still not sure if the market you picked will have an unacceptable amount of volatility for you. Volatility is what makes commodities prone to gaps up and lock limit moves. Often, there is a fundamental shift in the underlying factors that is keeping the actual buyers and sellers at a happy equilibrium.

A limit move occurs when a commodity opens up or down its maximum allowed move and does not trade again until the next session.

The way I prefer to measure volatility is through J. Welles Wilder's average true range (ATR) indicator. ATR does an excellent job of measuring volatility. It factors in gaps, limit moves, and small high/low ranges. By measuring volatility for yourself you may realize that the market you were eyeballing with the super-small margin just doesn't fit your risk-reward profile.

The worst thing you can do is get into a new trade not knowing what the fluctuations are. Some markets may have an ATR, the distance from its high to its low, of a few thousand dollars; others may be a few hundred dollars. Ideally, what you are looking for is how much you would risk if you

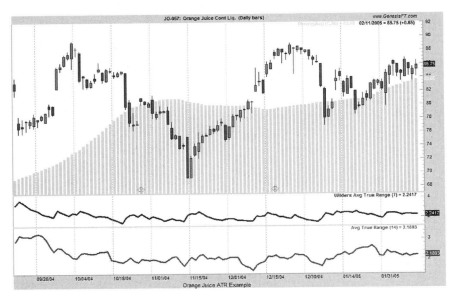

FIGURE 8.2 Orange Juice Average True Range Example
Source: Genesis Financial Technologies, Inc. (www.tradenavigator.com).

were 100% completely wrong on the trade. You accidentally buy at the top and sell it at the bottom, or vice versa.

For example, see Figure 8.2, where orange juice margin is $700, one point move = $1.50, and average true range is 2.21 or $331.50.

6. Organize "Short-Listed" Markets from Least to Most Volatile

Now comes the organizing. Basically, your infamous short list is developing. Your list may or not be shared by other traders. Most likely, your short list will carry your thumbprint of experiences and how you see the world. This gives you a realistic assessment of what markets you can trade and the level of confidence you will trade them with.

So what do you do with the markets that have a high volatility rating? You paper trade them, of course!

While you may not feel comfortable trading them with real cash because the potential loss exceeds 10% or greater of your account value, you can demo trade with various strategies to your heart's content. This gives you trading practice and helps build up your tolerance levels to risk as you boost your confidence.

Now with your short list, you can fully customize your trading plan and focus your energy where you can get the most results. You also solidify your foray into the world of fundamental analysis. You have a narrow set of markets that you have to view and follow up on. This puts you one step closer to being a professional trader.

7. Check the "Open Interest" for Each Market to Find the Most Liquid

The seventh and final tool you put your short list through is open interest. Open interest can be viewed several ways. The secret to open interest is that it represents liquidity. In much the same way that stocks are observed along with their volume, the open interest gives us clear insight into the actual number of contracts outstanding, both long and short.

When we approach open interest, we are looking to discover the answers to three questions:

1. Am I trading the right month?
2. Is the corresponding option market liquid?
3. What is the momentum of this market?

We will address two out of the three questions first.

When it comes to futures and options trading particularly, you need concentrate your efforts in the months where you can get out. It is easy to get into to trades; you just want to make sure there is enough liquidity. You will typically want to trade in the front months. You will purchase your risk management tools, options, around key front-month prices that have enough liquidity to exit.

There are a few different ways to determine the open interest. I prefer using the Commitments of Traders report. This report is released weekly by the Commodities Futures Trading Commission. In it, they document the number of outstanding long-short positions based on multiple categories: large speculators, small speculators, and hedgers. It gives insight into what their motivations are and how long they have been accumulating or distributing their inventory.

A second way to view open interest is to overlay it on the charts. What you would be looking for are declining and inclining slopes on the open interest and how they affect or do not affect pricing. It's a little more art than science when interpreting the open interest slope, but it can be done.

Figures 8.3 and 8.4 show examples of two different markets with varying levels of open interest and volume. Figure 8.3 is an example of the high

FIGURE 8.3 S&P E-mini S&P Open Interest and Volume (Open Interest: 921,020; Volume: 810,953)
Source: Genesis Financial Technologies, Inc. (www.tradenavigator.com).

level of open interest in the E-mini S&P, almost reaching a million contracts. In Figure 8.4, lumber's open interest is barely past 5,000 contracts.

Regardless of the level of open interest and volume for these markets, the declining and inclining slopes are used in the same way.

There are two demons that are constantly nipping at the heels of every potentially successful trader: fear and greed. My job is to use education as a way to cut a path between these demons to help lead you toward your investment and trading goals.

Brokerage Accounts Should you operate as a corporation or a sole proprietorship for purposes of deducting your trading on your taxes? I cannot say. I suggest you work with a competent tax professional in order to discover what works best for you. Many allowances that were passed through when day trading was a new phenomenon are no longer passing muster with the IRS, and you may find yourself in deep trouble if you don't handle your situation properly from the outset.

As a trader dedicated to success, at any given time you will have three different types of accounts: a style account, a sweep account, and an interest-bearing account.

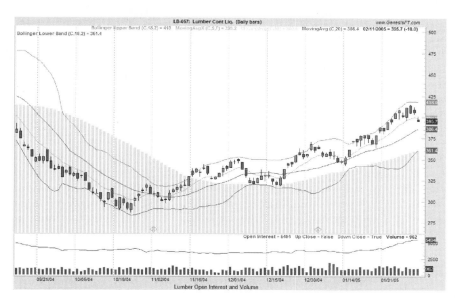

FIGURE 8.4 Lumber Open Interest and Volume (Open Interest: 5,494 Volume: 962)
Source: Genesis Financial Technologies, Inc. (www.tradenavigator.com).

Style Account   As a trader, you will go through many phases of learning and experimentation. Sometimes you will want to be a day or active trader; other times, you will want to swing trade or position trade. Do not do this experimentation and manipulation in one account.

To be successful, you must document what you do. By keeping different types of trading in separate accounts, it becomes easier to monitor. If you want to trade new markets with which you are not familiar, trade them in a separate account. They are simple to set up. Based on your original paperwork, many commodities brokerages will give you a simple one-sheet authorization form. Filling out the form takes all of five minutes, but it makes a world of difference to your trading.

Sweep Accounts/Interest-Bearing Accounts   If you have $10,000 or more in your trading account, you qualify to purchase a T-bill. Current T-bill interest rates are earning 4.82% to 5.012%, depending on the length of time you are holding on to the T-bill. A T-bill will cost you $35 to $50 to purchase, depending on the brokerages administrative fees. Every brokerage varies, but you will be able to trade anywhere from 70% to 95% of the face value of the T-bill.

Another recommendation is to move your profits into a sweep account. As part of your trading discipline, it simply makes sense to learn to trade with the money you started with. By trading in this fashion, you will be able to determine if the system you are using really works or if it's a fluke. I know many of you will be saying, "What about compound interest and trading with my profits?" We'll get into the hard numbers in the next chapter. Just keep in mind that a sweep account should be set up at the same time as your regular account.

Trading for Retirement   Don't do it!

If you can avoid using your 401(k) or individual retirement account (IRA) to trade futures and forex, then definitely do it. The average trader simply doesn't have the intestinal fortitude to weather fluctuations in his retirement account, particularly when he is the one managing it. I suggest you put the problem on someone else if at all possible.

If you have an IRA or 401(k) that is valued at 100,000 plus, you can effectively hire a commodity trading adviser (CTA) with a track record that can help you. A great publication to read is *The CTA Directory*. It showcases CTAs of all different styles and types. You can get your free subscription at www.thectadirectory.com.

If your IRA is new or you have had a bad experience with a CTA, there is a simple strategy anyone with a decent-sized retirement account can do. It's called the *10% solution*. You take 90% of your capital in bonds or T-bills; the remaining 10% you put in an S&P futures contract, mini or large, depending on what your account can hold.

On a $100,000 account you would have $90,000 in a T-bill earning as much as 4.98%. You would put the remaining $10,000 in a buy-and-hold strategy for the S&P 500 mini contract or a Dow Jones contract. Current YTD for the S&P 500 is 5.26%, and for the Dow Jones is 7.02%.

A mini S&P 500 contract is $3,500 in margin, and a Dow Jones mini contract is $2,813.

In either market you can have two to three contracts. The true value of each contract would be:

S&P 500 mini contract: $75,362.50

Dow Jones $5 mini contract: $67,140

Buying and holding one e-mini S&P 500 would have netted you $5,075. See Figure 8.5.

Buying and holding one $5 mini Dow would have netted you $5,045. See Figure 8.6.

So 90% of your account would have been safe in T-bills, and you would have earned $4,482 at a 4.98% rate of interest.

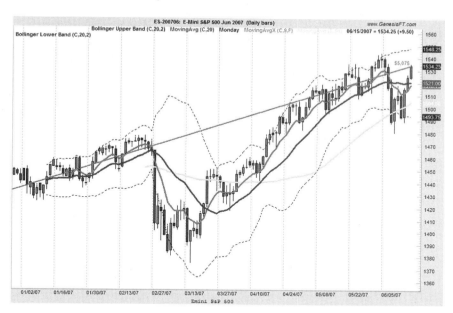

FIGURE 8.5 E-mini S&P Potential Profits
Source: Genesis Financial Technologies, Inc. (www.tradenavigator.com).

FIGURE 8.6 Mini-Sized Dow Potential Profits
Source: Genesis Financial Technologies, Inc. (www.tradenavigator.com).

Had you taken 10% of your account and only purchased one S&P 500 or Dow Jones contract, you would have potentially made an additional $5,000 on your account, giving your account an effective overall return of $9,482 and an effective yield of 9.48%.

The *20% solution* takes the same scenario one step further. You still retain the bulk of your portfolio, 80%, in Treasury bills, but this time you add a commodity index on top of the stock index—one of each. The profit breakdown now looks like this:

80,000 T-bills @ 4.98%: $3,984

10,000 mini S&P or DJIA (one contract): $5,075 or $5,045

10,000 CRB Commodity Index (one contract): $10,350

Total return: $19,334

So your return on a $100,000 account would be 19.33%.

Keep in mind that all of these calculations are hypothetical and are based on buying the contracts on January 1 and holding them throughout all of their fluctuations. Nevertheless, there are possibilities in buying and holding the indices as opposed to attempting to market time or cherry pick stocks or hot commodity markets.

The Yale International Center for finance released a white paper entitled "Facts and Fantasies about Commodity Futures," in which they came to this conclusion:

> *In addition to offering high returns, the historical risk of an investment in commodity futures has been relatively low—especially if evaluated in terms of its contribution to a portfolio of stocks and bonds. A diversified investment in commodity futures has slightly lower risk than stocks—as measured by standard deviation. And because the distribution of commodity returns is positively skewed relative to equity returns, commodities have less downside risk.*

So when it comes to your retirement portfolio, look more toward a diversified strategy that will encompass both stocks and commodities. If done properly, the leverage will allow you to take 10% to 20% of your account and gain as much exposure to the markets as necessary while you hold the bulk of your capital in cash.

One way to gain exposure in the commodities market without attempting to "cherry pick" is to purchase a contract in one of the various commodity futures indices (Table 8.7). One of the most historic and well-known commodity indices is the CRB Commodity Index (see Figure 8.7). The data for the Commodity Index has been compiled since 1967.

TABLE 8.7 Various Commodity Indices (Central Time)

Commodity Contract	Trading Hours	Point Value	Initial Margin
CRB Index Futures	10:00A–2:30P	5 Points = $25	$2,250
DJ AIG Com. Index	8:15A–1:30P	1 Point = $10	$1,688
Goldman Sachs CI	8:45A–1:40P	5 Points = $12.50	$3,150

WHAT YOU HAVE ACCOMPLISHED

Picking the markets you want to trade or, more importantly, you should trade is not a task to be taken lightly. It is simple to have someone tell you what you should trade and how you should trade it. In your development to becoming a true trader, you must be able to think and act for yourself.

There are many markets you could potentially trade; the question is which of these markets rings true for you. Not only must these markets fit with the amount of risk capital you have, but they must also match your personal risk, reward, and volatility levels. Only then does trading in futures and forex have relevance for you.

FIGURE 8.7 CRB Commodity Index Potential Profit
Source: Genesis Financial Technologies, Inc. (www.tradenavigator.com).

Attempting to simply trade based on what someone else likes or what works for them in the end will lead you down a path of disappointment. Go through this chapter and really search for the markets that make sense to you. Once this is accomplished, the task of integrating your overall portfolio of stocks and bonds with this alternative investing approach becomes easier.

CHAPTER 9

Lesson 2: Preparing to Speculate

There are a great number of speculators turned traders. They purchase courses and attend seminars, and they all maintain fantasies of becoming the next George Soros or the next "oracle of Omaha," Warren Buffett. While these dreams are important to have, they also become an impediment to traders forming their own opinion and view of the markets. It also lays the foundation for reckless behavior and inability to grind it out.

Although trading can be exciting and rewarding on a day-to-day basis, the truth is that it is not a sprint. There are few times in a trader's history that he will make all of his profits on one trade. It takes consistent effort over long periods of time, a marathon approach that will help traders even come close to possibly replicating the great feats of Soros and Buffett.

With this fact in mind, it is no wonder that 95% of traders fail. Whether they fail on an individual trade or blow their account out in six months, it all stems from a rush to action, a false sense of urgency that if they miss this opportunity, it will be a long time before another one comes or another one may never come. History tells us that life moves in cycles and that what was once new will be old and what was once old will become new.

As traders, we must believe that with all of our being; if we don't, we are doomed to be reactionary pawns based on the whims of the market. This moves us from general to foot soldier. In order to be a general, we must take a step back and look strategically at the opportunities around us and prepare accordingly.

In this chapter we will tackle two things: emotions and actions. We will first look at our reactionary feelings toward the insidious emotions of fear and greed. Second, we will look at the importance of managing and preserving capital. Finally, we will talk about how we manage the trade.

This is the second chapter dealing with money management. As we continue, I hope to impart to you the fact that money management has nothing to do with trading except for the fact that you have incentive to protect/preserve your capital. It has everything to do with self-preservation and your desire to make sure that the grub stake you have accumulated can last as long as possible.

Can you lose money using money management techniques? Of course, you can!

Money management has nothing to do with risk management techniques or technical analysis. It is solely about preserving your capital to the best of your ability. If you lose money because of a bad trade, money management will help you lose less. When you make money, it will help you preserve your wins and prepare for losing. It generates income from your capital when you need it, and it sets the stage on how you will behave with your money when you are right and when you are wrong.

While I have done my best to separate money management, risk management, and technical analysis into independent explanations, the reality is that each item is interconnected and there will be overlap of ideas and concepts. I hope that this will serve as a constant reminder that you will have to use all aspects together if you choose to succeed as a holistic trader.

Can money management techniques backfire? Of course, they can!

The approaches I recommend tend to be very conservative. This makes it difficult for a good number of people when they see an opportunity to trade but feel like they are being held back by arbitrary rules. Remember, this book is designed to help, not hurt. If you are already doing things a certain way and they work for you, don't abandon them. What works for you works for you; we only look to modify or enhance those activities that are not working.

Rules are rules because there are exceptions. Without rules, we cannot assess whether something has deviated from the norm. Use my rules as guideposts; if your gut tells you something else, for whatever reason, follow your gut. If you keep losing by following your gut, then you may want to come back and learn a few basic rules.

I thought "stops" were my money management tool—what gives?

Stops deal with one concept alone: losing in a trade. While we never want to lose money, the potential loss of money while we are in a trade is a function of the risk of the trade. This risk has little to no effect on our overall account unless manifested, and until we know what has occurred—gaining or losing value—it has no effect on our seed capital.

So *money management* would be defined as the specific actions we take to preserve or enhance our seed capital, and *risk management* would be defined as the actions we take specifically in a trade to diminish our potential risk of loss.

Preserving seed capital and protecting from risk of loss, while capable of complimenting each other, are not the same thing. Near the end of the book we will get more in-depth into how to protect yourself from the risk of a trade. In the meantime, I felt it was important to help distinguish the two so you could improve your trading with a greater degree of efficiency.

YOUR MONEY, YOUR EMOTIONS

No matter who you are or your length of trading experience, there is a consistent set of demons nipping at your heels: fear and greed. These two psychological pressures tear into you and make it difficult for you to find equilibrium in your trading.

There are many great books that talk about how to improve your psychology. A trader philosophy of "Think better, be better" is being promoted. Somehow through the sheer force of will and discipline, maybe even some form of self-hypnosis, you can undo nature's evolutionary handiwork of "fight or flight" and become an emotionless super trader!

While this is a lofty ambition shared by many and promoted by many, the truth remains that you are not an automaton. While I have no doubt that there are the "Michael Jordans" of trading who are so in control of their emotions that fear doesn't bother them, greed never affects them, and everyday is Christmas, I have met few traders who exhibited those characteristics. Of the few that I have seen, even fewer have been able to sustain that sterile approach to trading.

So let's embrace the fact that you have emotions: You love your spouse, you hate broccoli, and you wish every day could be like that day you won your favorite trophy. Since we cannot beat our emotions, we have to join them; we have to recognize fear and greed and be prepared in how we will react when we see them rearing their ugly twin heads.

Defining Fear

An unpleasant often strong emotion caused by anticipation or awareness of danger and accompanied by increased autonomic activity.

Dictionary.com, October 31, 2006

Fear is important—it is crucial to your survival. In ancient times, if you did not fear walking into dark caves, you may have accidentally stumbled on a bear. If you didn't fear drinking water in strange countries, you could end up with diarrhea or dysentery. If you didn't fear heights, you wouldn't wear a parachute when skydiving.

Fear preserves our life. The "awareness" of danger protects us and others from harm while giving us opportunities for survival. The problem with fear and trading is not that we have it, but how it is applied. In the definition, fear is stated as "an unpleasant often strong emotion caused by anticipation . . . of danger. . . ." This is where the problem lies.

Whether the danger is real or not, it is the anticipation of a perceived danger that disrupts the life of the average trader. By anticipating that something could go wrong and not having the necessary tools to build the confidence that you know what to do if things go wrong, fear takes root.

Fear will force you to do the opposite of what you know to be true. Acting on pure emotions confuses how you should act and makes it difficult to succeed because you are operating in a reactionary mode. This is why traders are whipsawed in and out of trades. This is why you miss the trade you know you should have taken but didn't. This is why you blow out your account.

Fear doesn't affect just the individual; it affects en masse. There are several expressions of fear that constantly have potentially successful traders not succeeding. By recognizing these expressions of fear, you will be able to monitor your behavior, and that is the first step to modifying the behavior.

Regret Theory   Regret theory says that people anticipate regret if they make a wrong choice, and take this anticipation into consideration when making decisions. Fear of regret can play a large role in dissuading or motivating someone to do something. By anticipating you may make the wrong choice, you can end up paralyzing yourself from making sound trading decisions. It has its deepest impact when you are on a losing streak in your trades. Depending on how and why you lost in the trade, two things will occur: constant replaying of what you did wrong and your inability to act on the current information you have from the market because of a desire to "get back at the markets."

Regret will drive you to cherry pick trades or look for the holy grail of trading, both of which you know is irrational in the face of so much information that trading success is a numbers game. Depending on how often you trade, "optimal" opportunities as opposed to "perfect" opportunities will be the true determiner of your long-term success. This is a frustrating concept to adhere to, but nevertheless is known to be true by anyone who has ever traded before.

When it comes to battling regret theory, it is important to realize from the outset that you will be wrong. You do not have a crystal ball, so the "anticipation of making the wrong choice" is eliminated by the reality that you *will* make the wrong choice. This is comforting. Once you know what will happen, you can plan accordingly.

Trading is about *speculation*: taking the best of the information that we have and acting on it. There is no need to regret your choices if they have been based on the best possible information at the time. So while all of your choices will be wrong, by default all of your choices will be right because you will be prepared ahead of time in case you lose money.

Panic Selling   Panic selling is widescale selling of an investment, causing a sharp decline in price. In most instances of panic selling, investors just want to get out of the investment, with little regard for the price at which they sell.

It's always darkest before the dawn. This is what panic selling typically represents. This is very typical when there has been a big run-up in a market. The market hits new highs, and at the first sign of a pullback someone pulls out, which triggers stop orders and limit orders, which adds to the downward pressure. This is all reactionary. Panic selling will occur particularly when there is no fundamental shift in the underlying factors that move the market in the first place.

Typically, after this panic selling, the market will rebound and the average trader is caught chasing the market on its upswing. This usually involves a lot of cussing about why you didn't stay in the trade.

Panic selling is avoidable. As with anything we understand, we fear it less. There is no need to fear panic selling. In many respects it can be your friend, depending on what has preceded it.

If the market has dropped significantly but the trend is intact, you have stumbled upon two excellent opportunities. First, you are afforded the opportunity to jump on the bandwagon and catch the downward momentum, regardless of your initial position.

You can add to your short position or exit your long and get short as quickly as possible. The second opportunity arises out of your ability to wait for the turnaround. No market ever goes straight up or straight down. So as the corrections occur, you can participate once the corrections have passed, particularly when there has been a market correction based on a panic selling rooted in fiction as opposed to facts.

Preparation is the key when avoiding panic selling. Don't get suckered into the moment if the fundamentals are intact.

Sell-off   Sell-off is the rapid selling of securities, such as stocks, bonds, and commodities. The increase in supply leads to a decline in the value of the security.

A sell-off is something different. There has been a fundamental shift in supply and demand. It can be disguised as panic selling, or panic selling can turn into a genuine sell-off. It occurs after a big run-up but the trend converts from being a long trend to a short trend.

This can happen quickly and without warning. Traders who are long will misinterpret the data and will be afraid to get out of their current trade lest they miss out. This fear leads to average traders' giving back their profits and turning winners into losers—a most disheartening phenomenon.

Yet it is avoidable. As with all behaviors, it is a learned response to a stimulus. We learn fear in the same way we learn to avoid fire. Touch it, you get burned. Leveraged trading, futures, and forex trading do the same to us. The first time you mistake a sell-off for simple panic selling, you become hesitant to trade either sell-offs or panic sells, or you overreact to these phenomena and your fear in your mental universe becomes amplified and muddied.

Both of these tie right back into regret theory, in which you cannot trust your judgment on anything and you give up altogether.

Overcoming Fear

Everyone's first reaction is to look for the holy grail, whether to control their emotions or to pick the optimal trades where they will never be fooled again.

The holy grail does not exist. The book you hold in your hand is a philosophy, a way to look at the markets to increase your control of yourself and make your actions proactive. I cannot tell you with 100% certainty when a panic sell is a true sell-off, nor can I force you to not regret your past trading actions.

What I can do is give you the tools that will give the ability to diminish your regret and not to get caught up in the emotional activities of the masses—panic selling and sell-offs. It is faith and confidence in the tools that will help mitigate your fear.

There is nothing that will eliminate your fear, it's directly connected your fight-or-flight response. By having money management rules and a fixation on preserving your capital at all costs, you will change how the fear impacts your trading. That's the best you can hope for and still stay functional in your trading day to day.

Defining Greed

"Greed is good," Gordon Gecko said in the movie *Wall Street*. Isn't that why you trade futures instead of bonds? You want the maximum returns. You want the biggest payoffs. You want the best possible opportunities. The problem is that greed can cloud our judgment. It can make us take risks that are unnecessary. It can force us into situations we wish we had never gotten involved in, and it can make us squander our success.

Of the emotions that plague every trader, fear and greed, I believe that greed may actually be worse. While fear may stop us from doing anything and thus we may simply preserve our capital through passivity, greed forces us to do something—to act when we should be doing nothing.

> *An excessive desire to acquire or possess more than what one needs or deserves, especially with respect to material wealth: "Many . . . attach to competition the stigma of selfish greed" (Henry Fawcett).*
> **Dictionary.com, October 31, 2006, Greed. (n.d.). WordNet® 2.0**

In this definition, the words that stick out are *excessive desire*. So while it is okay to want to be successful, there is a point where it becomes unhealthy. How do you determine that point? Who decides that you have an excessive desire? Where does the feeling come from?

There are several expressions of greed when it comes to trading. We will tackle three of the most common expressions and how to emotionally prepare for them. These definitions are based on the explanations from Investopedia.

Overstay   *Overstay* is the act of holding an investment for too long. It often occurs when traders attempt to time the market by identifying the end of a price trend and the beginning of a new one, but, due to greed and fear, tend to overstay their positions. This usually results in reduced gains or, worse, further losses.

The worst thing that can happen to a trader is early-on success. The feeling of invulnerability kicks in and the belief goes from your being a good trader to your being able to predict how the market operates. There is an old traders' saying: "I'd rather be lucky than good."

There is much truth to that statement. Too often, we are forced to live up to our own reputation when we profess how good we are. It is so much better for the psyche, not necessarily the ego, to chalk our success up to luck, being at the right place at the right time.

It diminishes our need to prove something. This is why overstay is so common. Somehow, success is confused with market timing. The reality is that you can make a profit getting in the market too late and exiting too early. It's more difficult to make a profit in the market getting in too early and exiting too late. This goes back to the fact that we have finite capital.

Whether it's the fear of missing out or the greed of making more, there are warning signs that get ignored in trading, particularly if you are making a profit and you begin to realize that the market is pulling back. This is where rationalizing becomes a problem. The trader wants the home run and is not satisfied with the double or triple, and immediately the profits become "house" money.

For some reason profits are not as valid because they came from the markets, so if you lose them, you are not as worried.

This is *greed* talking. The moment your internal dialogue comes up for reasons why you should stay in the trade or you start fantasizing about how much money you could make if this trade goes to X, *get out*. This is the litmus test for "excessive." Will you leave money on the table? Yes. Does it matter? No. One trade does not make or break a true speculator. This trade you are in is one of many. Take your profits and move to the next. While fear is easier to manage, greed should come with a warning label. It will disguise itself as happiness or logic, and then it will abandon you when things are not working. Remember what happened to Charlie Sheen in the movie *Wall Street?*

Chasing the Market   *Chasing the market* is entering or exiting a trend after the trend has already been well established. Investors are often unaware of the fact that they are chasing the market, which can dent the value of a portfolio. This type of investing is often seen as irrational, as decisions are often based on emotion instead of careful analysis of the value of the investment.

It is easier to see a price go from 1 to 2 as opposed to going from 6 to 12. Both are a 100% return. Why is one easier than the other?

The old cliché is "The trend is your friend—until the trend ends." If you pick a market at the beginning of its trend and you capture profits, and your indicators say the trend has ended, there is no shame in taking profits. The problem arises when you decide, after you have taken your profits, that they are not enough.

The market has continued in the direction you expected, and you are out of the market now. You have a profit, but the profit isn't good enough. You get bitter and resentful that all of the money you should have made is going to someone else. This is the most difficult emotion to subdue. You were right about the market, which happens so rarely, and now you aren't getting your just desserts.

You want the thrill of "getting it right" back and that's when you succumb to greed. You reenter the market, and then it happens—the panic selling or buying, the big sell-off or "buy-back, and you are giving your profits back. All of the careful preparation you used to get into the trade in the first place is squandered in a matter of minutes, and you find yourself wishing you had the profits you originally started off with.

While there are ways to lock in your profits and hold on to trades that are doing well, moving stops or moving options, if you exit the trade, the amount of effort you put into getting into the trade in the first place should be used to reenter. No impulses, no assumptions that what worked before will continue to work. You have to redo your analysis and treat this need to jump back into the market as an all new trade. Only then will you be able to avoid the demon of greed.

Chasing the markets is so dangerous because at the time it makes so much sense. It's hard to believe that greed is what is motivating you. Learn to appreciate what you have and you will find that, although you took your profits early, you are not going to let one trade—one mistake—make or break you.

Hog   A *hog* is an investor who is often seen as greedy, having forgotten his or her original investment strategy to focus on securing unrealistic future gains. After experiencing a gain, these investors often have very high expectations about the future prospects of the investment and, therefore, do not sell their position to realize the gain.

> *"Bulls and bears make money; hogs get slaughtered."*

Unrealistic trading expectations are not entirely your fault. Late night infomercials; radio advertisements; and a recent 25-year high in oil, gold, and the British pound color how much and fast you can make money in futures and forex. They give you a feeling of invincibility and abundance.

That's the hype.

I hope by now you are beginning to get the picture that trading successfully requires preparation, planning, and consistent execution. This is not the Wild West. These investments have been around for hundreds of years. In the past 30 years, we have seen the level of financial sophistication in currency trading and in options and futures trading grow exponentially, particularly because of the advancement of computers.

The "small speculator," the trader working on his own with finite time and finite capital, cannot afford to give up his most valuable asset—flexibility. While corporations, agribusiness, and farmers go toe to toe in the markets, you cannot afford not to be humble.

Too often, a trader attempts to make *all* of the money by overleveraging, overstaying his position, chasing the markets, and a myriad of other greedy habits. Without fail, he will blow up his account and come back to the markets believing he did nothing wrong. Being a hog is a personality flaw stemming from ego.

Until you can relinquish the belief that you are the direct result of your success—"I'd rather be lucky than smart"—you will continue to attempt to make grand slams on legitimate singles and doubles. It's like attempting to steal a base with the pitcher staring right at you.

As I have said before, there is opportunity, in fact, unlimited opportunity. The only way to enjoy it is to be methodical in picking a side and picking your trades. Be bullish or be bearish. Don't try to do everything—that's being "excessive." It will only come back to haunt you.

Overcoming Greed

As I said earlier, this emotion is actually worse than the demon of fear. While fear has the ability to protect you from getting involved in trading in the first place, greed forces you to push the envelope. Greed makes you act irrationally, it will force you to hold on to winners long after you should have gotten out and add on positions you can't afford.

Quelling the demon of greed requires a lot of energy and discipline. The question is whether your capital will survive long enough for you to gain control. There is no easy answer to fixing the greed problem. You may be good at picking the market, so your ego will play a large role in whether or not you can accept leaving money on the table.

The quicker you can subsume your ego and humble yourself to the idea that the market is bigger than you, the less opportunity there is for greed to take root and stay. Accept that you won't be right about everything; sometimes you will get out too early, sometimes you will not have enough contracts on, sometimes the market will simply get the best of you. So instead of focusing on being right, focus on being profitable.

SETTING TRADING GOALS FOR YOURSELF

The first step in battling the demons of fear and greed is setting your trading goals. By developing a road map of where you want to go, you can begin to temper your reactionary behavior and make it proactive. Goal setting is the most effective but least used technique in improving a trader's chance at success.

When a trader is new to trading, he typically states that his goal is to make money. The amount is unknown, the how is unknown, and the real reasons why are unknown. So is it any wonder that he loses money or the emotions of fear and greed take root and limit his opportunity for success?

The trading plan we discussed earlier is designed to help ground the desire for success with the reality of what it takes. At the end of the day, it may be discovered that you simply don't have what it takes to make your dreams come true by yourself, whether it's a lack of discipline or an inability to understand the markets. That's where your goals come in handy in helping you find someone who can.

So to begin, you need to ask yourself three questions and use the answers to hone or temper your approach to trading:

1. Why am I investing in futures/forex?
2. What percentage return am I looking for?
3. When will I know if I have succeeded?

By answering these three questions *truthfully*, you can make it easier to set your trading goals and achieve them. There are no right or wrong answers, nor do you have to stick to your answers if you determine a different route would be better later on.

Why Am I Investing in Futures/Forex?

In a nutshell:

Beat historical stock market returns.
Beat historical bond market returns.

Why invest in futures or forex? These investments are risky. If you invest in futures the wrong way, you can lose your entire investment and more. By all accounts, 75% to 90% of options purchased expire worthless. The spot forex market is so aggressive that even during peak announcement times it is difficult to execute an order in the trillion dollars a day marketplace.

When done right, according to the Yale study, there are advantages to investing and trading in futures and commodities. They don't correlate to stock and bond investments, so when there are opportunities to profit in stocks, there are opportunities to profit in futures, and when there are losses mounting in stocks, there are still opportunities to profit in futures and commodities. This is a big difference from the negative correlation that stocks and bonds have from one another.

The trick is in understanding what is the right way to invest. If your goal is to beat the stock market's average annual performance of 12% and the bond market's average annual return of 6%, the potential is there. In order to do it and not have to deal with a learning curve, your best bet is to find someone with a performance history and invest in him; at the very least, you have the peace of mind of knowing that there is someone to blame if things go horribly wrong.

If you choose to trade on your own, then I would suggest that you don't fall into the greed trap and expect results greater than your experience. Be disciplined in your trading. Focus on not losing, and let the profits take care of themselves. Even a top money manager listed with the Barclays Group as of this writing has a monthly return of 21%, but a year-to-date of −2.98%.

Their top currency trader program has a monthly return of 10.05%, but a year-to-date loss of −4.07%.

What Percentage Return Am I Looking For?

Many new traders are just looking to make an extra few thousand a month, and they are expecting that futures and forex trading is the way to go. The mistake that is too often made is thinking that anyone gets started with as little as possible and begins making millions right away. Often, there are unrealistic expectations placed on the amount of capital to get started with. Couple that with the way profits are typically treated, and you have a recipe for disaster.

Are you looking to make $1,000, $2,000, or $5,000 per month, or are you looking to make $500 per day based on your active trading? Then, like any business, you get out what you put in. If you have a few thousand to start with, don't expect to make several thousand per month. If you had $2,000 in your account and you were able to consistently make 10% returns a month (i.e., $200), at the end of the year you would have a 120% return on your money. No bank in the world could beat that. While $200 a month is not glamorous and doesn't come near to significantly changing your lifestyle, you could not find those returns anywhere else!

This is typically where greed sets in: 10% is not enough. You need 100% every month or 200% every month. You need to turn over your money three or four times per month in order to appear successful. Yet if someone came to you and said they could make you a 1,200% return on your money, you would laugh him out of the room.

Too often, the failure of traders is due to their lack of willingness to apply the standards of reasonability to themselves as they would to others. This is not to say there aren't people making phenomenal returns, but every industry has its superstars. I hope you are one of them. Just in case you are not, take a realistic look at the amount of capital you are committing and look to make returns that are both reasonable and don't put undue pressure on you to succeed.

Instead of attempting to make $500 a day, how about making $500 a month on a $10,000 account. That's a 5% monthly return, a 60% annual return. Set a realistic expectation of how much you want to supplement your income, then multiply that number by 10 or 20, and you will have a reasonable idea of the amount of capital with which you could feel comfortable without stressing that each trade could be your last.

Trading for a Living   The forex spot market trades 24 hours per day. The futures and commodities markets trade at various times in Chicago and New York, with overnight activity having a significant impact on what happens on the opening. For every commodity, there are multiple trade associations, clubs, journals, conferences, and trade shows disseminating new information about the players and products. Every currency is affected by every country on the globe—employment rates, inflation, interest rates, import/export numbers, and so on.

To trade for a living requires a dedication that goes beyond just reading technical analysis books and attending seminars. It requires that you become a student of the markets you want to trade. It requires that for longevity you become an insider. You may not trade on the fundamentals, but you understand how the fundamentals work and how they impact the small universe of markets that you have decided to trade.

The capital requirements are also greater. In much the same way that we multiplied our monthly supplement by 10 or 20, so should you do your bills. If you have bills that equal $3,000-plus per month, you should have at least 10 times that amount in your trading account. This way, you give yourself as many opportunities as possible to succeed without overleveraging or burning out your account.

Can you trade with less?

Of course you can, but the amount you trade with will be in proportion to the level of aggressiveness you will need to take in your account, along with the level of stress you will have to endure.

To Bolster Tax-Free Retirement Savings   I have said it before and I will say it again: *Don't* trade your 401(k) or individual retirement account (IRA) money yourself. You can bolster your returns, but at what cost? You are playing Russian roulette with your retirement. There are professionals that can do it for you. You will have to commit more capital, but it also gives you greater peace of mind. They have track records and performances.

When Will I Know If I Have Succeeded?

If you do not have well-defined goals on how much money you hope to make, when do you stop risking it all? Time and time again I have seen traders put themselves on automatic pilot. No matter how much money they have made, they take the same risk and chances as when they started. This is the core reason why there can be huge fluctuations in the value of the typical trader's account.

By setting short-term, midterm, and long-term profit goals, you are able to stabilize your market participation and have concrete profit-and-loss targets that tell you when you are on or off track. Knowing this information is essential to your achieving the success you want in your trading.

MONEY MANAGEMENT RULES

It is said that the game of golf is not played on the green but between your two ears. The same can be said of trading. Your mind-set and the preparation of your mind are all important. You must be focused on the who, what, when, where, why, and how of a situation in order to formulate your course of action. While it is not easy, it is simple.

There are three areas that you must focus on in your money management to be effective: your capital, your account, and your trades. These are rules that you utilize when you are making money, losing money, or doing nothing. These rules are benchmarks of how you should be thinking. Apply them to how you feel most comfortable. The goal is for you to modify your thinking, which will put you ahead of the 95% of traders who are losing money and don't know why.

These rules were developed from my observations of commodity trading advisers (CTAs) and the treasury departments of corporations and how they treat their money and their clients' money based on their fiduciary responsibilities.

The following are the money management rules laid out in clear, concise language for you to refer back to at any time.

Have "Capital" Money Rules

1. When the market isn't going in your direction, you must decide when and how to exit, whether that's based on a fixed percentage of your account size or a set of rules based on technical analysis.

2. We use a combination of horizontal resistance and support, Fibonacci retracements, candlestick charts, and moving averages. We will discuss this further in our next chapter.

3. Any tools that you use must comply with your own personal trading plan.

Have "Account" Money Rules

1. Have a commitment to a tradable market—pay attention to the volume while looking at the open interest as well.

2. Trade what you know. If you work in textiles, look into cotton; if you buy primarily small-cap stocks, look at the Nasdaq index. Focus on what you know, and your interest will not wane.

3. Use no more than one third of your account in any one market. This is a net figure minus purchasing an option as a risk management strategy.

Have "Trade" Money Rules

1. Never risk more than one to gain two.
2. At the outset of your trading, maintain that the "one" you are risking is the equivalent of 10% or less of your total account value.
3. The less of your account you leave up to leverage the better—CTAs maintain a max 2% loss because of the sheer size of their holdings.
4. Your maximum monthly loss should not exceed 25% of your account value; otherwise, halt your trading and come back the following month.
5. Ideal trading loss should not be greater than 10%, account size permitting, not accounting for huge spikes; limit up or down days.
6. A 50% halt rule is used by CTAs. It should also be considered for individual traders. If you lose 50% of your account value, you should stop trading. Determine if you have lost money because of your mistakes or if there is a fundamental shift in the supply and demand in the market you are trading.

Option Rules

1. When using an option as a trading tool, have a maximum loss rule—50% of its value or better.
2. When using an option as a stop, use the value of it as maximum built-in loss for your futures position.
3. Be willing to sell options as part of a strategy to decrease your expenses in either getting in a trade or recouping losses.

Trend versus Countertrend

1. Know which one you are trading.
2. Have rules to determine which is which.
3. Set realistic expectations for where your potential profits and losses lie, depending on the trend you have picked.
4. Moving stops have limitations on trend trades.
5. Moving options have limitations on countertrend trades.

Your Capital

The amount of capital you are putting into your futures or forex account is supposed to be risk capital. But just because it is risk capital doesn't mean you treat it as if it is disposable. This is not Vegas (refer back to Chapter 4 if you need a refresher). There is no house money, there are no acceptable losses, and we never let our capital ride! When it comes to trading, it is a business. You calculate your profits and losses, return on investment, return on capital, and maximum potential loss (look to the trade worksheet) in order to gain the optimum opportunity before you ever put your first dime on the table.

Can you lose your entire investment after doing all that work? Certainly. That's the difference between taking a calculated risk and throwing your money at chance. When you take a calculated risk, losing your capital is one of many possible outcomes. When you throw your money at chance, losing all of your capital is the most likely outcome, with all other outcomes being a pleasant surprise.

How we treat that precious seed called "operating capital" is important. In George S. Clason's *The Richest Man in Babylon* (Signet, 2004; first published in 1926), it was when the main character took his hard-earned savings and placed it with a partner who knew what gems were all about that he began to prosper. So must you be your own conscientious and trustworthy partner when it comes to watching the books.

Preserving Operating Capital   Preserve your capital, and at all times do your best to maintain a consistent operating capital amount. It's one thing to lose money in your trading—that's unavoidable. The key, though, is not to do the opposite: Don't add to your account without first redoing your trading plan and goals.

How a man with $5,000 operates and the markets available to him are completely different from how a man with $10,000 operates. Couple that with the fact that futures trading has built-in leverage, sometimes 50 to 1, and forex has leverage as high as 400 to 1, and you have to ask yourself if the additional capital is worth the additional risk. It may or may not be, but you have to do the math to make sure you are not overleveraged or underleveraged for your investment goals and capital in your account.

Your Account

One of the most overlooked aspects of trading is the trading account itself. Just like bank accounts, there are a variety of different flavors and opportunities available. With particular minimum amounts met, you can earn interest on your account. Various brokerage firms let you work with your IRA and 401(k). Other times, you can open up multiple brokerage accounts, with the same paper work, to try out new ideas or to place your profits. Knowing what your account features are is essential to being able to manage your money.

T-Bills   We touched on T-bills in Chapter 8. If you can make money on your futures account, why aren't you? If you can afford to open a $10,000 account to gain the interest, do it. Trade the account as if it were a $5,000 account. In CTA language, this is the difference of the "notional value," the 10,000, and the "nominal value," the $5,000 that you actually use.

T-bills are typically purchased in $10,000 increments. Sometimes after the first $10,000, the Futures Commission Merchant will allow you to purchase in $5,000 increments. You can trade at as much as 95% of their face value, while earning the prevailing interest rate. One year is currently about 4.98%, with a purchase fee of $15 to $50

Sweep Accounts   Why are you trading? For profits! Yet time and time again I see traders achieve their goal only to squander it and give their profits back to the market. This ties in with the fact that you should not let your operating capital fluctuate. If you have $10,000 and you make $73, don't leave the $73 in the trading account—"sweep" it to a profit account.

Every time you book a profit, "sweep" it to your side account. *Do not trade* your profits. Separate any profits you book from your principal, and move them to a completely separate account.

Your Trades

While it's believed that compound interest is the most powerful force in the universe, the concept rarely translates well to the world of leveraged investing. It is easy to see people make profits over a lengthy period of time, increase their trading volume because of their account size, and give it all back in one bad trade.

There are great books that talk about the risk of ruin and optimal contracts to account value. One of my favorite books is *The Trading Game* by Ryan Jones (John Wiley & Sons, 1999). It's an in-depth book on the numbers and how to arrive at the right equation for any size account.

I am a more basic guy and I like to do what makes sense. One of the rules that I have is that you should never risk more than one third of your account value on one market. Simple enough to follow—few of us need a calculator to figure out that one third is approximately $3,333 of a $10,000 account. So let's run through a scenario:

If you have a $10,000 account and you trade one third of it, you have only $3,333 at risk in the market. Let's say you make $5,000 in profits. That's great, but if you trade your new account size of $15,000, you now have $4,500 at risk. Trading with $3,333 is not too much different than trading with $4,500. (Look back at the markets that different account sizes can trade.)

So in order to gain an extra $1,177 in purchasing power, you are risking your entire $5,000 in profits. Basically, you are risking four times as much money as you are gaining in extra purchasing power—not a good investment.

Taking Profits   Take your profits off the table. If you are going to focus on your goal of making returns, I would suggest in the beginning that you forget about reinvesting your profits or ideas of compound interest—these are all greed-induced fantasies.

Look at interest in futures, forex, and options investing as "simple" interest. If you can risk one to make two, you are ahead of most. You risk your operating capital in leveraged investments in order to gain unusually big potential returns compared to other alternatives. I am sure there is some special mathematical formula, but suffice it to say that leveraged investing, more so than any other investment, does not take kindly to compounding. Take your profits home.

Trading Options Only   A lot of speculators-turned-traders attempt to start off with options trading. They feel comfortable because they know their risk up front and feel more in control. Just because you know your risk up front doesn't mean that it's a risk worth taking, though.

The statistics say anywhere from 70% to 90% of options expire worthless. It goes back to the chance-versus-calculation argument. You can take a chance that you bought the right option, but your opportunity for success is a very narrow window of 10% to 30%. Options were never really meant to be traded alone. Therefore, as a trader, you need to be able to incorporate options as a part of your risk management strategy, but not over rely on them.

As an alternative to an option-only strategy, CTAs, the money managers of the futures and forex world, rely on specific loss amounts to dictate their actions. If they lose 25% of their client's account equity, they halt trading and reevaluate their strategy. If they lose 50% of their client's account equity, they shut down their program altogether and refund the money that is left. Since these policies are good enough for CTAs, then they are good enough for you as well.

CONCLUSION

If you take nothing away from this chapter, I want you to remember these four pillars to help you preserve your capital and have it thrive:

Pillar 1: Limit the maximum leverage exposure of your account to 30% in any one market.

Pillar 2: Limit your maximum account risk to 10% on one trade.

Pillar 3: Limit your monthly maximum account risk to 25%.

Pillar 4: Be willing to halt your trading.

Trading, as opposed to investing, is an inherently greedy endeavor. As traders, we are attempting to find the small discrepancies in price in order to make a profit. The problem is not the action, but the all-consuming emotion that can blind us in our trading. Greedy emotions will make it impossible to see a 100% return as good, solely because a 105% return would be better.

When it comes to futures and forex trading, the temptation to lose perspective is not only easy but insidiously pervasive. A distortion in what success, and even failure, means is lost. You must constantly ground yourself by comparing what you make against various other investments around you. By taking a critical look, you will hopefully curb your desires to push for more in a trade when it isn't necessary.

The emotion of fear is just as distorting and crippling as greed. What you risk must be weighed against what you had hoped to gain. Just because you lost doesn't mean you should not try again. The emotion of fear must be put in context. If not, it will run rampant and drive you from trading altogether.

Every successful trader is constantly battling it out between these two emotions. The success comes from finding some middle ground that makes sense just for you. This is the only way to keep perspective, or at least to realize that trading may not be meant for you.

CHAPTER 10

Lesson 3: Choosing Your Technical Indicators

The wrong weapons placed in the hands of un-
trained soldiers will result in defeat.

—Sun Tzu, *The Art of War*

N o matter what you may think about trading, the first myth we have to dispel is that trading is technical analysis. The thrust to create a pseudo-scientific face to trading has led many people to look at technical analysis as the end all–be all of trading. Somehow, it is believed that if you can figure out the right combination of indicators, then you will become the best trader ever. I am sorry to disappoint you, but that is not how it works.

Technical analysis is one aspect of trading. Every indicator that you use is being used by somebody else. There was a time when there was a competitive advantage in using technical analysis. Computers weren't prolific, and many nonprofessional traders were keeping hand charts. Therefore, when you stumbled upon a piece of knowledge, it became a game of early adoption. Your trading was bolstered because you knew what was going on before anyone else.

This is no longer the case. Free services such as Futuresource provide more than enough technical indicators for you to make an educated decision on whether to buy or sell in a market. Many of the common market patterns—double tops, head and shoulders, flags, saucers—have been talked about and rehashed. I am not sure if that is "technical analysis" as much as it is pattern recognition. Whatever it is, some traders feel comfortable with it. I am not here to refute or support any type of technical analysis, just to point out that everyone knows them.

This chapter is meant to focus on what is important—"price." As a speculator, your profit potential comes from the price discrepancy—the distance between where you get in and where you get out is what goes into your pocket. If you don't benefit from the price discrepancy, then you have failed. As we know, all of the actual buyers and sellers are using futures and the spot market in order to find the optimum price for the goods and currencies they are buying and selling.

This price discovery takes into account supply, demand, and multiple factors—known and unknown. The price reflects the best information at that time and thus the best price at that time. Our goal as the speculator is to find the arbitrage. We have to assume that the pricing is out of whack and that through our trading we will discover exactly where that price discrepancy is.

Technical analysis is our best tool at quickly assessing price by answering "what has happened," "what is happening," and "what might happen," all at a glance. The trick is to use technical analysis efficiently and apply it effectively to an overall trading plan that incorporates money management and risk management. This is not to say that fundamental analysis doesn't have a place in the scheme of things. The goal is to make your trading simpler, and by narrowing down your trading to a few key technical analysis indicators, you give yourself an efficiency edge over the majority of traders.

FUNDAMENTAL VERSUS TECHNICAL ANALYSIS

Ever since I started trading, there has been a constant debate between whether fundamental analysis was superior to technical analysis or vice versa. As a trader, I am concerned only with price and accurate information. While fundamental analysis may have accurate information, it fails to give up that information easily or quickly. At the end of the day, the nonprofessional trader can find the information more confusing than helpful.

In order to be effective at fundamental analysis you have to be able to understand and interpret a lot of information. Unless you make a conscious decision to become a specialist in only one market, it becomes difficult to stay abreast and understand the domino effects of every action and reaction.

Here is a sample list of just a little information that goes into the fundamentals of market:

- Consumption
- Production
- Future availability of current product (change in stocks)

- Actual quantity available
- Exports
- Non-U.S. demands
- Disposable income
- Supply of substitute goods
- Marketing
- Wholesale price
- Weather
- Interdependent commodities
- Profit margin
- By-product market factors

Accurately knowing, let alone understanding, a few of these factors, much less all 14, would drive anyone insane. Couple that with attempting to understand the true value of the commodity and then attempting to decipher if there is an arbitrage opportunity and determining if the opportunity is worthwhile, and it can be overwhelming for one market—let alone 3 or 4 markets.

The task of sifting through fundamental analysis data becomes Herculean. Even if you decide to pick just a handful of points to use as your foundation, you will still be at a loss because you will still fail to have the big picture. So when deciding on whether to use fundamental or technical analysis, I have to point out that technical analysis is simply more efficient. While fundamental analysis has its place, it should be considered as a supplement and not as a trading style of its own.

WHY TECHNICAL ANALYSIS WORKS

When it comes to market behavior, there are two schools of thought. The first is the "random walk theory" and "market efficiency theory." While both are convincing ideas, only one supports technical analysis.

> *Random walk theory: The theory that stock [commodity] price changes have the same distribution and are independent of each other, so the past movement or trend of a stock price or market cannot be used to predict its future movement.*
> **Investopedia.com, October 31, 2006**

The random walk theory states that each price is independent of the last price. In futures and forex trading we know this not to be true. Since we deal in real commodities and actual currencies that reflect the economies of entire nations, it is easy to realize that price has a memory.

Whether it's last year's orange crop freeze or Iran's refusing to accept U.S. dollars to purchase oil—whatever the case, it is difficult to believe in hard assets that have or lack a memory of what transactions have occurred in the past and the influences those memories have in the present.

Market efficiency theory: The degree to which stock [commodity] prices reflect all available, relevant information. Market efficiency has varying degrees: strong, semi-strong, and weak. Stock prices in a perfectly efficient market reflect all available information. These differing levels, however, suggest that the responsiveness of stock prices to relevant information may vary.
                                        Investopedia.com, October 31, 2006

Technical analysis trading doesn't have at least 14 different ideas to research in order to make a decision. Technical analysis involves three simple components:

1. Price action
2. Volume
3. Open interest

With these three bits of information, plus the underlying influence of time, you are able to know what is going on whether or not you know what the underlying fundamental factors influencing them are. This plays well with the second theory, "market efficiency."

This theory is elegant in its definition, yet makes the utmost sense. It states that prices reflect all available relevant information. From insiders to commercials to speculators, every tidbit of information that they know is reflected in the market price. The only time that price drastically changes is when there is a monumental shift in supply and demand. Then the market compensates, and attitudes shift accordingly.

While this concept may seem stifling at first, it can also be liberating. It can give the off-the-floor trader the confidence necessary to trust his technical analysis tools without second-guessing their voracity or his lack of insider knowledge. What is on the screen is what you trade, no more no less.

The failure that can be easily made with technical analysis is to attempt to use it as a predictor of what will happen as opposed to a snapshot of what is happening. There are no crystal balls or holy grails of trading that I know of. While many systems and black box programs claim that they are accurate at predicting the market if you just spend X dollars, it is difficult for me to advocate on their behalf or condone that type of thinking.

If you know where the market is and you use probability combined with common sense to determine "multiple" outcomes, you put yourself in control of your technical tools as opposed to being controlled by them.

There was an old *Twilight Zone* episode with William Shatner in which he and his fiancé are in a little backwoods town when their car breaks down. They decide to stop at a diner to grab a bite to eat while their car is being repaired. Shatner spies a "predicting" machine with a little devil bobblehead that bounces up and down, left and right. In the beginning he asks the machine small, innocuous questions, then escalates to more serious and important questions, and finally he asks the bobblehead whether he and his fiancé can ever leave the town.

Shatner becomes so gripped with fear and belief that he loses sight of the fact that this machine is destroying his budding family. Eventually, with the help of his fiancé, he leaves the machine alone and he and his fiancé leave the town. Not more than 30 seconds later, a disheveled couple comes into the diner, rushes to the same bobblehead machine, and asks, "Can we leave now?," to which the response is "No."

Too many traders are like the second couple—they feel that technical analysis is the panacea of trading and that if they simply look at the right tools or charts, all of their decisions will be made for them. While the novice traders will take time to understand this, the experienced traders already know that technical analysis is just a tool. It is meant to aid you, not think for you. The moment you confuse the two. you are doomed to follow the path of those who want to be right about the markets, as opposed to being profitable in the markets.

Do not rely on technical analysis to be your only trading plan—it will fail you.

TECHNICAL ANALYSIS STRENGTHS AND WEAKNESSES

Technical analysis has many strengths and weaknesses. Each strength gives it a sense of reliability, while each weakness puts you one step closer to making a fatal mistake. By becoming adept at knowing the weaknesses, you are able to shore them up with the proper money management and risk management techniques.

Strengths

Minimal Reliance on Fundamental Info   Practically every day there is some report coming out in the United States or overseas, whether it's regarding job numbers, import numbers, or interest rate increases or decreases. Each bit of news has already been factored into the market's activity in some form or fashion.

At one time, the concept of seasonal trading was "hot." Every TV and radio guru talked about gasoline prices increasing in the summer, heating oil going through the roof in the winter, or oranges being wiped out by hurricanes. While these seasonal opportunities may have been tradable in the past, because they are so well known now, the level of impact that the seasons have on the markets has changed. Oftentimes the actual movement in the market occurs far in advance of the actual seasonal problems themselves.

So instead of waiting for these seasonal trades to occur, it is far simpler to watch these markets and see the technical analysis movement now. If it's heating up, get into the market; if it's cooling down, get into the market; if nothing is happening, keep waiting and watching—don't just follow fundamental analysis blindly.

Quick Snapshot of Data   Price, volume, and open interest all on one chart. With the right set of technical analysis tools and asking the right questions, you are capable of looking at a chart and within a few minutes being able to determine if a trade is worthwhile or not. You should also be able to determine your profit targets, loss risk, and risk management parameters as well. There is no comparable way to glean this much information from one piece of fundamental news.

A Sense of Immediate Control and Understanding   "What we don't understand, we fear."

As traders, we strive to be in control of the situation. The market itself is a beast. It moves up and down, left and right, for however long it wants and however violently it wants. There is little we can do with our finite amount of capital to truly move it. Therefore, the goal is to put the market in a context you can understand.

Since the mind enjoys creating patterns, we give ourselves the opportunity to look at daily, monthly, and weekly charts. We analyze minute-to-minute charts and focus on giving ourselves the best opportunity possible. Technical analysis does just that for us. It gives us the window to take a mass of information and to place it on the screen and feel like we can ride the wave as opposed to being crushed by it.

Weaknesses

Lagging Indicators Aren't Always Appropriate   Don't misplace your faith. Technical analysis is a wonderful tool to be used; at the same time, you have to be careful when attempting to use it for predictive features. Elliot Wave, Gann, and Fibonacci can tell you only what happened and what is happening, but they cannot reliably tell the future.

Once you begin to rely on the predictions to the point of where you believe they are absolute and you fail to prepare for contingencies, you give yourself few outs. This goes back to the difference between gambling and speculating. Predictions cause us to make assumptions about what will happen that leaves little room for what is happening.

Since the information for technical indicators revolves around price and time movements that have already occurred, it is best to temper your reliance with common sense, which means that you will use technical analysis, not let it use you.

Tools Are Available to Everyone   Bollinger bands, candlesticks, and William's %R, are on all charting software. From the newbie just opening an account to the professional trader working for a hedge fund, the information is readily available. The calculations are known, the setups are known, as well as common market wisdom, and gaps are filled.

Using off-the-shelf information gives you little to no competitive advantage over fellow traders. In fact, how you operate plays into the hands of self-fulfilling prophecies, which leads to predictable stop placements and whipsawing in the market.

Putting your own custom spin on the tools will be to your advantage as well as immunizing your predictability in following conventional forms of money management and risk management. At every turn, customize either your reactions or your interpretation of the information in order to refine your opportunities for a competitive advantage.

Interpretation Is More Art Than Science   No one can guarantee that every time you see a "cup and saucer" the market will behave with 100% predictability. No one will claim that every time the price of a market hits the upper Bollinger, it will collapse in price. Technical analysis is an art masquerading as science.

While the numbers themselves may accurately calculate deviation, accumulation, and distribution, as well as relative strength, the interpretation of this data is the key. What does it mean this time, and how will I react to it? Everyone has their own spin on the function of their technical analysis tools. There is no wrong way.

This is the reason why many commodity trading advisers (CTAs) may have a mechanical trading program, but they still leave the final decisions up to discretion. They know full well that there are patterns and various activities that cannot be left to chance and solely for a robot to determine.

This is the tailspin that too many traders take when they believe that technical tools are the gospel.

QUESTIONS FOR TECHNICAL INDICATORS

So we beat up technical analysis pretty well. We realize that it's a lagging indicator, we understand that there is no holy grail, and at the same time we understand that it is a lot easier to approach technical analysis as opposed to fundamental analysis.

What gives?

For traders, both novices and the experienced, I developed three questions that clarify the role that technical analysis plays in helping us make a trading decision:

1. Where is the market going?
2. How fast is it getting there?
3. When will it arrive?

By using technical analysis to answer each of these three questions, we can begin to create a framework that will allow us to trade with confidence. We also are capable of narrowing down our technical indicators from a field of 30 or 40 to just the essential 1 or 2 necessary to answer the question presented to it.

This chapter is chock-full of charts that I looked at as well as the tools I use when going about answering the three questions above. There are so many good indicators out there that you have to effectively pick the ones that work for you. My focus is not so much on which ones you use, but that you find the tools that will help you successfully answer each of the three questions to your satisfaction.

Keep in mind when choosing your technical indicators that you want to have a built-in redundancy. In order to answer each question with confidence, develop a backup set of tools that will have the capability to back up or counteract your trade assessment. In all, you should have no more than six to nine indicators that you use on a consistent basis.

Now let's answer some questions!

Where Is the Market Going?

This is the most important question you must ask yourself when it comes to trading. Regardless of whether you are a day trader, swing trader, or position trader, you need to know the tone of the market. There are only two answers: bullish or bearish. Within those two answers the market can move in one of three directions: up, down, or sideways.

If the tone of the market is bullish and the prices are moving up, then the market is moving with the trend. If the tone of the market is bullish and the prices are moving down, then market is moving "countertrend" to the tone.

If the tone of the market is bearish and the prices are moving down, then the market is moving with the trend. If the tone of the market is bearish and the prices are moving up, then the market is moving "countertrend" to the tone.

Knowing the tone of the market and understanding if you are following or entering on the trend or the countertrend is essential to your success as a trader and the use of your money management and risk management. The problem with traders is that the assumption is you can go long or short solely based on the price activity with little forethought to the trend and countertrend.

If you are trading the countertrend and the market abruptly stops, but you are unaware that you are trading the countertrend, you may find yourself holding on to a trade that ends up giving up all of your profits and later turns into a loss. This is the most common way that traders hold on to their losers—the expectation of the turnaround.

If you are trading the trend and the market abruptly stops, but you are unaware that you are trading the trend, you may cut your losses short only to see the market collapse and you miss out on gaining the bulk of your potential profits. This is the most common way that traders cut their profits short.

Know the market's tone and you can unlock how you will actually interact with it. This is a step above just being long or short. Since hedgers and professionals are constantly both long and short the market at the same time, it is essential that there is an understanding of what the market is doing or to have a market bias. Once you have that, you are capable of setting up a risk management strategy that makes sense for the goals that you wish to accomplish.

Determining Trend Sentiment   None of the trading that I do is particularly fancy. I use everyday indicators to determine how I will interact with the markets. Sometimes I will modify them or tweak their parameters to refine my entry and exit; other times, it's not necessary. When it comes to determining trend sentiment, it isn't necessary to get fancy with your indicators.

You can use various types of tools to determine the tone/trend; just make sure you determine the trend before you ever enter the market.

Three tools that help me determine the tone of the market:

Primary

1. 50-day moving average

Redundant

2. Higher lows
3. Lower lows

Primary Trend Indicator: 50-Day Moving Average

The market can be only one of two things, regardless of the price action: bullish or bearish. When it comes to the stock market, many stock investors will use the 50-day moving average (MA) to determine short-term trend and the 200-day MA to determine the long-term trend. Since futures and forex typically have tighter expiration cycles, 60 to 90 days, I opted to use the 50-day MA as my litmus test.

As seen in the gold example, whenever the market price is above the 50-day MA, it's bullish; whenever it is below the 50-day MA, it's bearish. This gives me the ability to look at any market and determine if the tone is bullish or bearish.

In the chart we see that there are various times where the price will cross the 50-day MA or ride along the 50-day MA and then go the opposite way after several days. This is the reason why I do not trade MA crossovers at all. In order for the tone to be established, the price needs to have three successive down days reinforced by a proper candlestick.

At the same time, it is rare to suddenly execute or initiate a trade right when the market is crossing the 50-day moving average. More likely, you will be starting up your trading out of the blue and you will need to quickly establish what the tone is.

If the price is running sideways along the 50-day moving average, do not initiate a trade. In fact, *stay out of the market when it is sideways* unless you have the proper risk management tool in place to take advantage of it.

Bulls and bears make money; pigs get slaughtered. Trading when there is no ambiguity is the best possible way to be involved; if you have to wait until a tone is established, then wait. It is a far simpler feat than assuming you know where the market will go and then be steamrolled as the market goes the opposite way—hard.

Recently, many traders were bullish on corn because of the news on ethanol. Once news came out that there was the potential for a bumper

FIGURE 10.1 Gold Comex Pit Higher Lows
Source: Genesis Financial Technologies, Inc. (www.tradenavigator.com).

crop, corn collapsed from its sideways action on the 50-day MA. The same thing occurred on the chart in Figure 10.1 when gold was strong.

The only time the market tone shifts from bullish to bearish is when there is a fundamental shift in supply and demand. Once this occurs, the establishment of the new tone is rapid and swift.

Redundant Trend Indicators: Higher Lows, Lower Lows

Trading one type of indicator can lead to disaster, particularly if you don't have complete faith in what you are using or understanding. So as a backup, I look for higher lows and lower lows to confirm that the market tone is bullish or bearish. You can use the inverse higher highs and lower highs, just as long as you are able to connect the trend with three points or more.

In Figure 10.2, we see an example of the gold market. In this chart we measure the higher lows starting from November 2, 2005, until March 16, 2006. In Figure 10.3, we look at gold again, this time zoning in on the lower lows from August 18, 2006, until October 2, 2006. As a redundant indicator, it gives us a clear view on the direction of the market.

FIGURE 10.2 Gold Comex Pit Lower Lows
Source: Genesis Financial Technologies, Inc. (www.tradenavigator.com).

FIGURE 10.3 Gold Comex Pit 50-Day Moving Average
Source: Genesis Financial Technologies, Inc. (www.tradenavigator.com).

I cannot emphasize it enough—this information is not meant to be used on its own. It is designed to give you a quick snapshot of where the market is and to help you establish your decision-making process. Will you trade the trend or countertrend, and why?

Trading the Trend versus Countertrend Why is it important to know the trend versus the countertrend?

When we trade, it is easy to see that markets fall faster than they move up. We may be in a trade for weeks, riding the profits up, only to see it wiped out within a matter of days. In Figure 10.1, around August 23, 2006, we see the gold market has penetrated the 50-day MA on the bearish side, following one of the redundant patterns of lower lows, and has turned around on the horizontal support found around the $620 price level. The market moves up for four days only to give it all back in one long down day and for the market to finally "establish" its bearish tone downward.

While the tone of the trend had not fully established itself as bearish, the constant testing of the 50-day MA and the lower lows was hinting at a force that was attempting to establish a new bearish trend.

The true tone of the market was a "very" weak bull or, better yet, the "beginning" of a bear market. Therefore, any moves in the "long" or bullish direction were "countertrends" that did not have a likelihood of sustaining themselves. The best course of action if you took the long trades was to exit at any signs of the countertrend's ending. This occurred on the first "red spinning top" that came at the end of the four-day run-up.

The market finally collapsed and showed its true stripes as the bear it wanted to be, and the trend became your friend. A second countertrend developed around September 21, 2006, and after seven days of moving upward collapsed and set a new low around October 5, 2006.

Trend versus countertrend will constantly establish how you interact with the markets and what you will do if the market fails your expectations. Forearmed is forewarned.

How Quickly Is It Getting There?

Now that we have established where the market is going, we have to find out how quickly it is getting there. There are three phases of a market's movement: beginning, middle, and end. The first two phases are the most desirable; the last phase carries the most risk. The last phase, the end, is the riskiest because it makes us unsure if the trend is ending and countertrend is establishing itself or whether the trend is reasserting itself.

So to make sure we are not getting in on the tail-end of the run, we need to find out how much momentum is behind the current move and if we will be pushed forward or if we are getting in at the extremes of the activity.

Determining Momentum   There are key concepts that you want to identify when it comes to momentum: Are there more longs than shorts? Has either increased over the last week or two? Are the new contracts being added in accordance with the price movement, or is it early? Has the market reached extremes in contract purchases or sells? Is it overbought or oversold, and by how much?

In order to determine momentum, you can use accumulation distribution, the market sentiment index, the Commitments of Traders report, or a myriad of other tools that show you if the market has just started to be on the move or if it's late in the cycle.

The tool that I prefer to use is the relative strength index (RSI). While there is a classic way to use the RSI—30% or below represents oversold, 70% or above represents overbought—frankly, I have found few opportunities where this actually applies. I use a more fluid application of RSI and apply overbought and oversold activity based on the past performance of the market and when it turned around on its own self-contained extremes.

For redundancy, I use the increases and decreases in open interest for the futures market and I use the moving average convergence/divergence (MACD) for the forex markets.

Primary

1. RSI

Redundant

2. Open interest (OI)
3. MACD

Primary Momentum Indicator: Relative Strength Index

Figure 10.4 shows a Gold Comex pit contract. Over a five-day period the market has aggressively moved upward in a countertrend direction. Yet RSI has not penetrated the 30% oversold number—what gives?

If you look back on gold's four-month RSI activity, has it penetrated the 30% level? In fact, the lowest it has ever fallen has been exactly 30%. More often than not, it turns itself around from the oversold bottom in and around the 40% to 50% mark. To wait for it to get to 30% would prove disastrous.

FIGURE 10.4   Gold Comex Pit RSI
Source: Genesis Financial Technologies, Inc. (www.tradenavigator.com).

On the other hand, gold has never penetrated the 75% mark in being overbought, no matter how extreme the price levels were. So the tradable overbought–oversold range for the gold market is between 30% and 75%, with a more prominent alert system between 40% and 75%.

Every market has its own adaptation of the RSI. Some will follow the classic patterns of oversold–overbought, others may be in a narrower or wider range. The goal is to look back over a four- to six-month time frame in order to understand the self-contained extremes that the market has. Even within a market, the extremes of overbought and oversold will change over time. The trick is to match up the price action with the extremes and trade accordingly.

By monitoring the momentum, you can make a conscious decision on whether you will initiate a new trade for the trend or the countertrend or if you would prefer to wait until the market's current price movement has burned itself out.

In Figure 10.4, you could buy into the countertrend and with strong money management rules ride the market up until it reached 75% or until the market had a down day. However, you would want to be careful in attempting to initiate a purchase if it were close to the 75% market; nor would you want to initiate a new short until it was evident, usually two to three down, days, that the market price was pulling back and the RSI was coming off the 75% extreme.

By combining the 50-day MA, knowing the tone of the market, looking at the price action to see if it is moving with or against the tone, and then adding overbought or oversold extremes to get a feel for entering the market, you have now established a visual parameter on whether the trade is good or not.

Redundant Momentum Indicators: Open Interest and MACD
Open Interest

Figure 10.5 shows one of the redundant momentum indicators, open interest. In the chart we can easily see the OI declining off of the sideways movement that occurs. This shows a lack of faith by the longs and represents their exodus from oil contracts.

The way that OI operates is to show a balance of longs and shorts. One new buy plus one new sell equals an addition of OI. If either the new buy

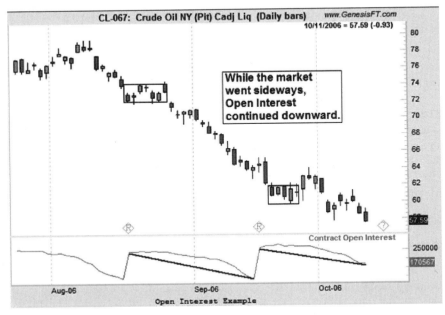

FIGURE 10.5 Crude Oil Open Interest
Source: Genesis Financial Technologies, Inc. (www.tradenavigator.com).

or new sell offsets his position to a new trader, then OI does not decrease. If two current contract holders offset each other, then OI declines.

This is a big difference from volume, which measures all activity.

OI and price work in tandem to give us a clue as to the underlying activity of the market and to help us determine momentum. If the price is up and OI is up, expect the market to be strong. If price is up, but OI is down, this typically represents that shorts are getting out of the market, and this is a technically weak bull.

If price is down and OI is down, the bulls/longs are leaving the market and driving the price down. If price is down and OI is up, then new shorts are coming into the market and a real bearish drop.

While volume and OI are independent of each other, the truth is that it is difficult to interpret OI on low volume. So while it is a great redundant indicator, there has to be volatility and volume in the market you are watching to make it worthwhile to interpret.

Rules of Open Interest Activity

1. Price = up Open interest = up	Technically strong
2. Price = up Open interest = down	Technically weak bull
3. Price = down Open interest = down	Longs are exiting, temporary pullback—bearish
4. Price = down Open interest = up	Potentially more selling ahead—very bearish

Moving Average Convergence/Divergence

A trend-following momentum indicator that shows the relationship between two moving averages of prices. The MACD is calculated by subtracting the 26-day exponential moving average (EMA) from the 12-day EMA. A nine-day EMA of the MACD, called the "signal line," is then plotted on top of the MACD, functioning as a trigger for buy and sell signals.

www.investopedia.com

When it comes to trading the forex market, there is no OI data to follow. While you can use futures and options by proxy to give you an idea of the potential momentum activity that is occurring in the spot market, it is also just as common to use the MACD to determine momentum.

As a redundant confirmation tool to the RSI, it is excellent. It measures extremes. When the price "diverges" from the MACD, it signals the end of the current trend or when the 9-day exponential moving average (EMA) moves sharply against the MACD, it represents being overbought. Combine these two interpretations with "zero line" activity, above upward momentum, below downward momentum, and you have an indicator that can help you determine your entry into the market once you determine if you are trading the trend or countertrend.

When Has It Arrived?

Finally, you have to know "when the price has arrived"/"when the price will arrive?" If you don't know where you are going, how will you know when you get there? Trading is based on probability and speculation. When you trade, you must be willing and able to set profit targets as well as loss thresholds.

Establishing your targets makes it easier to know if you are entering a trade at the beginning, middle, or end of a cycle and whether you should wait before you enter your trade. It also helps you establish your risk-reward ratio parameters and gives you an idea of what you are willing to give up in order to gain.

Of the three areas, knowing where you are headed and where the market may potentially stall or reverse, this may be the most important because what you know can also help prepare you to use the proper risk management techniques that will either keep you in or get you out of the trade.

Over the years, I have used several different types of target parameters. The one that has been the most reliable for me is horizontal resistance and support. As redundant tools, I will use Fibonacci retracement and Bollinger bands. They give me potential targets when deciding on profit goals.

Primary
1. Horizontal resistance and support

Redundant:
2. Fibonacci retracement
3. Bollinger bands

Primary Turnaround Indicator: Horizontal Resistance and Support There are three ways that the markets can move: up, down, and sideways. While the most exciting times occur when the markets move up and down—that's where all the big money is—most of the time the market spends its time sideways.

There can be a myriad of reasons why, but I would like to believe it comes down to simple economics. While the traders and speculators thrive on volatility, the actual producers and buyers have to present some form of stability to their shareholders and board of directors. So when they find an equilibrium in price, they tend to stick with it plus or minus a few percent. Only when there is a fundamental shift in supply and demand do we see activity.

It is no secret that the majority of futures and spot contracts are held by major corporations, banks, and governments. That being the case, they move the markets, and understanding and following the guidance of these horizontal resistance and support lines can go a long way to giving you an idea on where a market will end up.

Determining horizontal resistance and support is a twofold process. In Figure 10.6, two points have been marked as resistance levels. The first horizontal resistance point is at 260. It is based on the classic candlestick "spinning top" almost creating an "island reversal pattern" that occurred around mid-May.

The second horizontal resistance point is at 272, where the market moved sideways a lot around the end of May until early June, before finally collapsing downward.

Every time I am looking to establish horizontal resistance and support I am looking for those telltale signs, island reversal or as near as possible and heavily congested sideways price movement, with or without a breakout history.

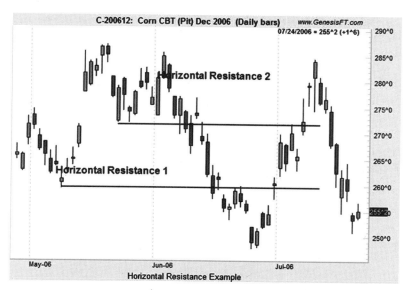

FIGURE 10.6 Corn Horizontal Resistance
Source: Genesis Financial Technologies, Inc. (www.tradenavigator.com).

FIGURE 10.7 Corn Horizontal Support
Source: Genesis Financial Technologies, Inc. (www.tradenavigator.com).

As we look at Figure 10.7, we can see that there is heavy congestion in corn around the 235 to 250 trading area. Support is established around the 235 area and any break below would bode disaster for the long traders.

Understanding horizontal resistance and support gives you clear numerical targets to shoot for when it comes to profits as well as setting up the proper risk management techniques, like stops, that will keep you from losing all of your account on one trade.

Redundant Turnaround Indicator: Fibonacci Retracement and Bollinger Bands

Fibonacci Retracement

The belief is that a market will retrace its tracks at various levels before continuing on in the direction it was headed. What makes Fibonacci retracements so special is that key Fibonacci ratios are used to determine various points of resistance and support.

When using any type of retracement system, it is important to trade the market first and the target second. It is easy to get wrapped up in the idea that the market should be doing X or it should be doing Y as opposed to paying attention to what the market is doing right now.

FIGURE 10.8 Corn Fibonacci Retracement
Source: Genesis Financial Technologies, Inc. (www.tradenavigator.com).

When utilizing the Fibonacci ratios, set up one or two profit targets as your goal and be willing to exit at the first sign of weakness. If you choose not to exit, make sure what you are risking is worth what you could potentially gain; if it is not, walk away from it.

In Figure 10.8, we take the same corn chart and measure out the 50-cent gap between 285 and 235. Along the way, the Fibonacci tool that we use marks various prices that match up with the ratios 253, 259, 264'6, and 284. Each number is a potential long profit target. If the market hits any one of these numbers and fails to break through, then we have the turnaround.

The turnaround is the setup for us to take the opposite position, in this instance to short or to look for a shorting opportunity.

Bollinger Bands

Bollinger bands are a simple indicator that measures volatility along with the extremes of being overbought and oversold. The indicator uses a simple MA anywhere from 20 to 26 days and adds a 2% to 5% standard deviation. Where the deviation lies, the markets have a tendency to reach yet rarely exceed them.

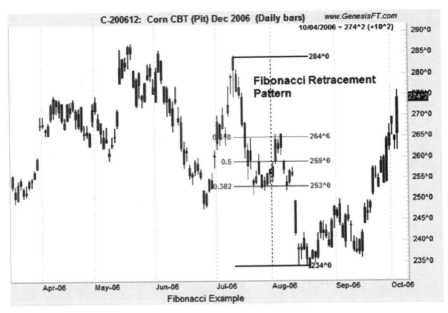

FIGURE 10.9 Corn Bollinger Bands
Source: Genesis Financial Technologies, Inc. (www.tradenavigator.com).

By itself the Bollinger bands cannot be used as a trading tool. It can be inaccurate in determining when the market is ready to turn around. Markets can ride the tops and bottoms of their standard deviation for weeks before there is any break in sight.

As a back-up tool, it's excellent. It will give you an idea of where the market is heading at a glance and help you prepare for the potential turnaround. In Figure 10.9, it does just that.

On the third horizontal resistance in Figure 10.6, we found a top resistance of 284, which was later confirmed using the Fibonacci in Figure 10.8; this is later confirmed by the upper Bollinger band riding the tops of the market in Figure 10.9 all the way as corn makes new highs.

While this is an extreme example of how in sync the Bollinger bands can be with the overall market, it does become difficult to use as a predictive tool for exiting the market.

LIVERPOOL TRADER CHECKLIST

There you have it! We have narrowed down our technical indicators to be capable of answering one of the three questions: "Where is the market going?," "How quickly is it getting there?," and "When will it arrive?" By mixing and matching technical analysis tools to make you feel comfortable, you will be able to answer these questions in no time.

If you find technical indicators that don't answer any one of these questions, dump them. If you have more than two or three technical indicators to answer any one of these questions, dump them. If you find yourself attempting to trade from fundamentals only, dump them.

Here are the key technical analysis indicators and the questions that they answer:

"Where is the market going?"	50-day MA	Higher lows, lower lows
"How fast is it getting there?"	RSI	Volume, OI
"When will it arrive?"	Horizontal support, resistance	Fibonacci retracement, Bollinger bands

BLACK BOX AND SYSTEMS TRADING

When speaking of technical analysis, I could not leave out black box and systems trading. Time and time again there will be talk of 90% accuracy or a program that tells you what trades to pick. While the program may be successful at picking trades, the art of making money in leveraged investing is still based on how well you get out of trade.

Don't be fooled by high-accuracy percentages that may or may not reflect money made. If trading were that simple, why would multinational corporations still be hiring specialists and brokers to help them make money? If it sounds too good to be true, it usually is. Develop and use your own technical tools first before you turn to an off-the-shelf product that may cost you thousands when all you really needed was the ability to answer the three main questions.

CHAPTER 11

Lesson 4: Developing Tactics for Entering and Exiting the Market

The last chapter was all about the setup. You learned how to understand the market's overall tone. You were able to determine trend versus the countertrend, plus you were able to formulate an opinion on how you would interact with the market based on where the market is going, how fast it is getting there, and when it will arrive. This is what I call the "macro technical analysis"; it gives you the big-picture base for your trading.

No matter what type of trader you are, day, position, or swing, it is essential that you can look at the market and within a few minutes be able to understand what is going on. The macro technical analysis tools do that for you. These tools are not designed to get you in the market; they simply give you the road map just in case you decide to get on the road.

Once you know that the market's overall tone is bullish, the momentum is still in its infancy, and you are midway to the second potential profit target, what do you do? How do you enter the market and, more importantly, how do you protect yourself from risk?

In this chapter we will answer the question of how you enter the market. In the next two chapters we will discuss how to protect yourself with risk management techniques. Formulating your opinion is more essential than getting the absolutely perfect entry price. We are not attempting to picks tops and bottoms. The objective is to enter the trade as best as possible as soon as you have a solid opinion. You want to simply participate in the potential activity going on.

While technical analysis is important, it is simply one part of a holistic approach to trading. Therefore, it is important to understand the

175

differences between strategies and tactics. Knowing when to apply tactics and understanding how tactics are just a part of an overall strategy is essential.

By breaking up entries and exits into five distinct opportunities, we will introduce some of the relevant candlesticks that indicate market turnaround. We will also explore the Bollinger bands some more and distinguish between false "overbought" and "oversold" signals. We will explore horizontal support and resistance as well as diagonal support and resistance. We then take a more in-depth look at moving averages (MAs): 9-day EMA, 20-day-MA, 50-day MA, and 200-day MA. The intent is to learn how to enter the market based on price and its penetration of these key MAs.

Where the last chapter was a focus on a macro use of technical analysis, this chapter is about micro technical analysis, with the core emphasis on entry and exit. This is the technical analysis that you use when you have made a decision to execute the trade.

Do not trade any technical analysis by itself!

If you have skipped straight to this chapter, you have missed the message. Technical analysis is just one component of a successful trading plan; it is not a trading plan in and of itself. Without money management and risk management, you have limited your potential for success.

This leads me to help you understand that there are key differences between strategies and tactics:

Strategy
An elaborate and systematic plan of action.
                              WordNet 2.0, 2003, Princeton University

Long-term action plan for achieving a goal.
                                            Investorwords.com

Tactics
The branch of military science dealing with detailed maneuvers to achieve objectives set by "strategy."
                              WordNet 2.0, 2003, Princeton University

Near-term actions taken to solve specific problems or accomplish specific goals.
                                            Investorwords.com

This entire book educates you on how to trade. It gives you the necessary strategy that you can use to improve your trading. Technical analysis is just one of the tactics; just like the definition of *tactic*, it gives you the detailed maneuvers you need to help you achieve your goals.

When it comes to developing your trading plan, it takes the tactics of money management, technical analysis, and risk management to succeed. In much the same way I would not suggest that wars are won by frontal assaults alone, I don't suggest you take the technical analysis ideas below and use them by themselves.

What follows are five separate entry/exit tactics that will give you an ability to exploit the market opportunities that you find.

FIVE TOOLS FOR ENTRY/EXIT

You are already familiar with some of the five tools for entry/exit. We covered some of this ground when we discussed macro technical analysis, particularly when we answered the question "When will it arrive?"

Resistance and Support

There are many different ways to determine resistance and support. I prefer horizontal lines/trading ranges. You can also use diagonal lines/trend lines and internal trend lines to determine specific prices.

There are many ways to determine resistance and support. The key is to use it in conjunction with price. When I first got involved with trading, I was introduced to a charting service called Commodity Price Charts. On the front page would be a write-up of several different markets. Each market would have a projection and a list of support and resistance numbers.

Each week, I would plot those support and resistance numbers (Commodity Price Charts came to you in the mail on a weekly basis), and see if the market came close to reaching them or not. As I plotted, I began to notice a pattern of the market's reaching these numbers and breaking out or the market's reaching these numbers and collapsing. After each subsequent breakthrough or collapse, the market itself would stage a massive move.

The relevance of resistance and support targets became apparent for me. If I were right, I could be in for a big reward. If I were wrong, I could get steamrolled. At the time, I believed in stops and felt that was the best way to go in protecting myself. Unfortunately, with each subsequent market failure, my stops would be run—hard. That's when I realized I wasn't at the racetrack. I didn't have to pick a horse named "long" or a horse named "short." I could box it and play both sides.

This is what knowing horizontal support and resistance numbers does for you. They allow you to set up a trade, plan for the probability of the

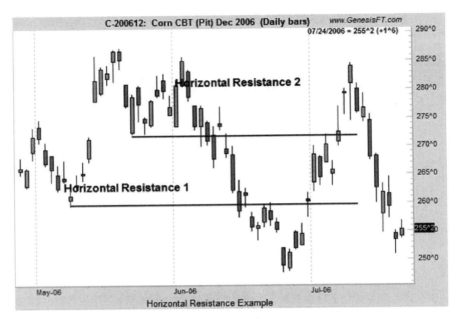

FIGURE 11.1 Horizontal Resistance Example
Source: Genesis Financial Technologies, Inc. (www.tradenavigator.com).

market's being supported, and then set up the contingency plan in case your best guess fails.

In Chapter 10 we lightly covered Figure 11.1, but we will look at it again and point out how we could have traded the entry and pluck out the relevant numbers.

As we all know, hindsight is 20/20, but I want you to bear with me a second and learn how our entry and exit setups will lead you to being able to utilize risk management techniques that work.

In Figure 11.1, I want you to ignore everything to the right, beginning in July 2006. Focus on the left-hand side and the bottoming out of the corn market at the end of June 2006. Imagine you are coming to this chart for the first time and you have no idea what to do.

Your indicators are telling you that the market is oversold, but you also know that the trend is your friend. The worst thing you can do is jump into the market on the long side and get steamrolled because you were too early, but you also don't want to jump into the short side and be smacked by the market skyrocketing up off oversold indicators.

You look at the market and you see two potential lines of horizontal resistance. The first line is at the 260 area, and the second is at the 272. The current price is right below 250. What do you do? Do you get in on the long side or short side now and hope for the market to go your way?

If your macro indicators are screaming at you that the market is going to go back up, but the prices have not matched up with the indicators, wait. Use the horizontal resistance point as your litmus test. If the market exceeds it for 48 to 72 hours, you will go long and place a protective short of some sort based on the horizontal resistance now turned horizontal support number of 260.

If the market hits 260 and fails to stay above the horizontal resistance for 48 to 72 hours, then short the market at the 260 and place a protective long.

By waiting for the market to hit its resistance market, what are you giving up?

A 250 to 260 move represents 10 cents, or $500. So in order to employ this type of strategy you would have to wait and potentially give up $500. That's okay, though. The market eventually rallied up a total of 25 cents above the 260 area, reaching 285, and potentially gaining you $1,250. Even if you didn't know that at the time, the peace of mind that comes from being able to trade with a sense of control stops you from attempting to pick market bottoms or tops and focus on the real work of trading—it's worth giving up the $500.

Let's say you didn't see the charts until after the first point of resistance had been broken. You would then look to the second point—in this case, 272—and you could employ the same tactic as before, wait until the market broke it, or you could apply a second tactic.

The second tactic has you enter the market based on the current market movement, long, and you use the new horizontal support as your protective short. Each time the market breaks through resistance, you would employ this technique to initiate a new trade or to add on a contract.

Every single horizontal resistance line then becomes both a profit target—on this chart 260, 272, 285, and 290—and a potential as a protective short. With each target being accomplished, you then must assess your risk-reward ratio of 2 to 1. As you get to the higher profit targets, 285 or 290, it begins to make less sense to risk what you have made in order to make small incremental gains; that is, from 260 to 285 is $1,250 in profits; from 285 to 290 is just $250 in profits. It doesn't make sense to risk $1,250 to gain $250.

This also sheds light on where you are coming in as a trader and if a particular trade has matured too far past your profit target goals to make it well worth your while to get involved.

In Figure 11.2, we see another familiar chart. We looked at this chart back in the macro technical analysis as well. In this instance we see that

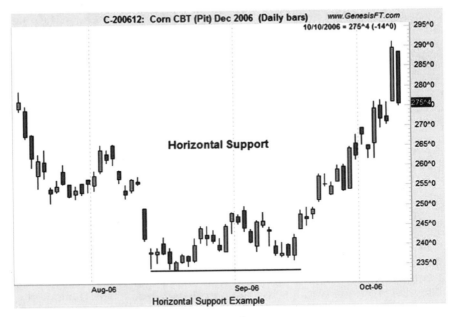

FIGURE 11.2 Horizontal Support Example
Source: Genesis Financial Technologies, Inc. (www.tradenavigator.com).

the corn market was moving sideways from the middle of August to the middle of September.

As a trader, you see that the market is range bound between a low of 235 and a high of 250. Before we see the run–up, the sideways action can be representative of the market's consolidating to collapse or the market's consolidating to do a breakout.

Knowing that the market is having difficulty breaking through the support at 235, it is a fair assessment to go long while at the same time putting on some type of short side protection, just in case the market collapses.

Another way to look at support and resistance is to place limit orders right outside the two numbers: buy limit order of 255 and a sell limit order of 230. This way, you have the ability to catch the market wherever it goes without watching the screen. Once the limit order is filled, you then put on the proper protection at the resistance or support point.

Since the markets operate in a sideways pattern of some sort, 70% to 80% of the time utilizing the limit order based on support and resistance gives trades time to develop and catch momentum before you get in. In this case, if your 255 limit order is triggered, you have the opportunity to make profits from 255 to 290, a 35-cent move with a cash value of $1,750. You give up the potential profit between 235 and 250, 15 cents ($750) by using a limit order, but you are properly risking one to potentially gain two.

This is a more conservative approach, but is just as legitimate as entering the trade immediately. There is nothing wrong with leaving some potential profits on the table to avoid getting whipsawed in the markets.

So horizontal resistance and support does three things:

1. It allows us to become confident in picking a primary trade, long or short.

2. It gives us multiple profit and exit targets.

3. It gives us a gauge of where we are potentially getting into a trade—beginning, middle, or end.

By entering or exiting trades based on the failure of the market to break out or fail at support and resistance levels, you give yourself a sense of control. We know that we cannot control how the market flows, but we can control what we do and how we will react to the market.

Fibonacci Retracements

We utilize Fibonacci retracements in the exact same way that we use horizontal support and resistance. The key difference is that our entries and exits are based on the market penetrating any of the five Fibonacci ratios: 0, 38%, 50%, 62%, and 100%.

In Figure 11.3, the Fibonacci retracement levels for corn give us five target points—the base is at 234, 253, 259, 264 TQF, and 284. Each level is given the pass or fail test. If it breaks through and is sustained, buy; if it fails, sell—purchase a protective short or long based on your entry.

This is identical to how we utilize the support and resistance levels. The only difference is that these numbers may not necessarily be at key points of support or sideways activity. Utilizing the Fibonacci numbers will give you a little more volatility in the triggering.

When you apply the Fibonacci tool on your computer, I suggest that you use a 30-day and a 60-day look at the market, picking from high to low. Since the futures contracts cycle so quickly, you have to be careful using longer time frames because of the smoothing factor. Every futures contract has a large gap in price between each month. On the longer-term charts these gaps are ignored, but in our trading we want to be careful basing our decisions on the smoothing effect.

In Figure 11.3, we look at a wider example of the corn chart that encompasses the time frames before and after the bounce off of the horizontal support. When we draw the Fibonacci line from the former high of 284

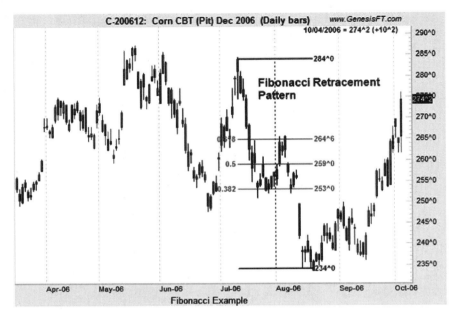

FIGURE 11.3   Fibonacci Example
Source: Genesis Financial Technologies, Inc. (www.tradenavigator.com).

to the then-current base of 234, we find that from top to bottom there is a potential of a 50-cent ($2,500) move if the market turns around.

   If we enter at the base of around 234 and use the first Fibonacci point at 38% as a target, 253, we realize that if the market fails to break through, we will exit immediately. The market makes a first run at the 253 level but collapses at the beginning of September. At the first sign of weakness, particularly this long down day, we exit the market.

   When the market consolidates around the base again, and fails to penetrate it, we have an opportunity to buy back in, still using the same Fibonacci targets. On the second run-up at the end of September, we see huge gap ups until the market exceeds all of the Fibonacci targets: 253, 259, and 264 TQF.

   Every time the market breaks through one of the Fibonacci points, it becomes more and more difficult to enter a new long trade. We begin to look for a failure at one of the Fibonacci points to enter a new short instead.

   The Fibonacci points are good just to give us a number to activate the decision we have already made, not to make a new decision. If the macro technical analysis is not in tandem with the market's prices for the Fibonacci, follow the macro.

Average True Range

While support, resistance, and Fibonacci are used as both entry and exit triggers, average true range (ATR) tends to be a one-trick pony. Once you have entered a trade, you are able to use ATR as a stop-loss indicator or as a way to place your protective short or long.

ATR is a volatility indicator that smoothes out gaps and erratic market behavior to give us the absolute highs and lows of the market. Knowing this range is very important. As we discussed earlier under money management strategies, knowing the ATR gives you a clear example of the worst-case scenario. In the chart in Figure 11.4, the average true range for soybeans is 14, which represents $700. So if you were to enter by buying the high and selling the low based on current volatility, you would lose $700.

You are capable using ATR in one of two ways. The first way is to simply use it as a stop-loss or protective price indicator. In the chart we use a multiplier of $1^1/_2$ times the current volatility to create a loss target of 21 cents; price is 641 TQF.

If you were to enter the trade in the chart based on the current trend, you would be buying in at the absolute high. Using an ATR stop loss lets you get out of the market based on volatility, not on a random decision.

FIGURE 11.4 Average True Range Example

The common use of the ATR multiplier is $1^1/_2$ times, but in fast moving markets or in times of high volatility compared to the past activity, plus your money management thresholds, you can use $^1/_2$ times ATR. In slower-moving markets or during times of lower volatility relative to a market's past operational history, you can use 2 times ATR.

A second way to use ATR is as an indicator of whether a trade you are in has exhausted itself. If the volatility has suddenly decreased after a long rally down or up, it may be time to exit the trade immediately.

Moving Average

The first tool that I learned to use when I got involved with futures trading was the moving average. There were several rules about the 9-day crossing the 20-day, I also learned about the 8- and the 14-day MAs. It was all very exciting stuff. When it came to trading it, I found it difficult.

We are all aware of the fact that technical analysis indicators are lagging, but when it came to waiting for the 9-day to cross the 20-day or the 8-day to cross the 14-day, I found that the price had moved in the new direction already and was actually in the process of rebounding.

I don't believe that the markets can be divined with 100% accuracy, but I would like to know what is going on right now. I don't want to be blindsided by MAs that are incongruous with the price activity I see on the screen.

That's when it occurred to me, MAs are a function of price. The MAs are designed to smooth out the price patterns over a set period of time and give us an idea of what the optimal price could have been had there been complete equilibrium between the buyers and sellers.

This leads us to the next revelation: If the MAs represent the smoothing effect of the market, then the true deviation of MAs comes from the actual price breaking through or bouncing off of the moving average, not the activity of MAs crossing or interacting with other MAs. Price is king. MAs serve the price when it comes to setting a standard and representing deviation, not the other way around.

When I trade I use the 9-day exponential moving average (EMA), the 20-day MA that is built into the Bollinger bands, and the 50-day MA. When the market "price" penetrates any one of these levels for 2 or more days, it can represent an entry signal or an exit signal. Failure to penetrate can represent a renewed buy signal or sell signal, depending on where the price is in relationship to the MA.

Figure 11.5 shows an example of the soybean market's 9-day EMA. If you look at the 9-day EMA price, it is 646 TQF just a few points shy of the ATR stop-loss figure of 641 TQF. If you were entering a new long trade, you would wait until the market pulled back to the 9-day EMA and bounced off.

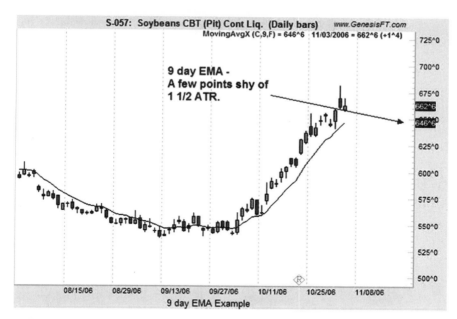

FIGURE 11.5 9-Day EMA
Source: Genesis Financial Technologies, Inc. (www.tradenavigator.com).

If your other indicators are pushing for a short entry, then you have two choices: Wait until the market price penetrates the 9-day EMA and short with a protective long, or short the market immediately with the 9-day EMA as your first profit target.

In Figure 11.6, we see the 20-day MA at $617\frac{1}{2}$. This would be our second profit target or our first profit target, depending on when you enter your short on the 9-day EMA.

In Figure 11.7, we revisit the 50-day MA. As we have discussed before, the market is either bullish or bearish, depending on where the price lies above or below the 50-day MA. What do we do when the price is approaching that boundary where there can potentially be a fundamental shift in the overall tone of the market?

The gold market is quickly approaching the 50-day MA at the $653.70 price point. The momentum is definitely up, but there is no way to tell if the market will make the leap or if this is a temporary retracement. The $653.70 becomes our key entry price when entering the market.

On March 27, 2006, had we waited to enter the market at the crossover, we would have caught a rally from $575 to $750. So by waiting for the price to cross over, we have an opportunity to catch a new rally. However, the

FIGURE 11.6 20-Day MA
Source: Genesis Financial Technologies, Inc. (www.tradenavigator.com).

FIGURE 11.7 50-Day MA
Source: Genesis Financial Technologies, Inc. (www.tradenavigator.com).

market could also collapse and the failure to penetrate $653.70 will be a setup for a short.

The key to successfully trading the MA is to pay attention to how the price interacts with it and how it sets it up. Using the MA numbers as entry/exit and profit target setups puts you in control, as opposed to being a passive observer.

Candlestick Patterns

If you have been trading for more than two weeks, you probably know about candlesticks. They are one of the most innovative tools in enlightening a trader on day-to-day momentum. They are excellent for intraday trading and, more importantly, for this chapter entry and exit signals.

The other four tools—support/resistance, Fibonacci retracements, ATR, and MAs—can give you set numbers to target candlestick charts to seal the deal.

As I suggested in the macro technical analysis, you have to have some redundancy in your trading indicators to answer the core questions, "Where is the market going?," "How fast is it getting there?," and "When will it arrive?" You need the same type of redundancy in the micro analysis of entry and exit. Candlesticks do just that; once you have your favorite entry/exit price selection technique, use the candlesticks to set up the timing.

If you are unfamiliar with candlestick patterns, they employ two-dimensional bodies to depict the open-to-close trading range and upper and lower stems (or shadows) to mark the day's high and low. Steve Nison introduced the United States to candlestick charts, although they had been used in Japan since the sixteenth century.

While there are volumes of books and videos on the various types of candlestick patterns, we have only two goals when we use candlesticks: (1) we want it to confirm our entry or exit into or out of a trade, and (2) we want it to confirm a market's turnaround or continuation.

When we know the price at which we are entering or exiting the market, we want to give it a 2- to 4-day time period to let the proper candlestick pattern to show up to confirm our trade. Once we get the confirmation, we act *immediately!*

I have narrowed down the candlestick chart patterns to 10 key patterns that I watch. You can use my set, or you can use/develop your own set. Even with the 10 that we see here, you will find that you may favor just a few as confirmation indicators.

The trick to understanding how to apply candlesticks is to realize that they can give you information for only a limited time. They are not designed to be a macro indicator, but they are great at gauging the market's sentiment right now. They do not necessarily give you a price to enter or exit; they just tell you the "when," which is important if you already have an opinion of the market, but if you do not have an opinion, you can find yourself chasing every candlestick pattern with little discretion, which can be detrimental in the long run. When you have an overall context on how you are approaching the market, the candlestick patterns are the icing on the cake.

Memorize these candlestick patterns. Photocopy these pages and make flash cards if need be—just remember them so that when you have all of the setups in place, you simply can see the proper candlestick and execute the trade.

There is some overlap between the various entry and exit technical analysis tools and the macro tools, particularly when it comes to answering the question, "When will the market arrive?" That's perfectly fine. We have taken a top-down approach to the technical analysis that will allow us to look at a chart and within a few minutes be able to determine how and when we will interact with the market.

Having exact prices to target is what is all important. Now that we have discovered the prices we are targeting for our entry and exit, we are capable of matching them up with the proper risk management technique that will help us have the optimum opportunity for success.

Top 12 Candlestick Indicators and What They Look Like

1. *Doji:* A doji line that gaps from a long green candlestick. See Figure 11.8.

2. *Bullish engulfing signal:* A bullish engulfing pattern occurs when buying pressure overwhelms selling pressure, reflected by a long green real body engulfing a small red real body in a downtrend. See Figure 11.9.

3. *Bearish engulfing signal:* A bearish engulfing pattern occurs when selling pressure overwhelms buying pressure, reflected by a long red real body engulfing a small green real body in an uptrend. See Figure 11.10.

4. *Hanging man:* A small real body (green or red) with little or no upper shadow. It is a bearish reversal pattern when appearing during an uptrend. See Figure 11.11.

5. *Bearish shooting star:* A candlestick with a long upper shadow with little or no lower shadow and a small real body near the lows of the session. See Figure 11.12.

6. *Bullish hammer:* A bottoming candlestick line with a small real body (red or green) at the top of the trading range with a very long shadow with little or no upper shadow. See Figure 11.13.

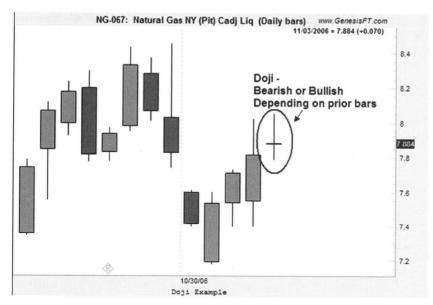

FIGURE 11.8   Doji Example
Source: Genesis Financial Technologies, Inc. (www.tradenavigator.com).

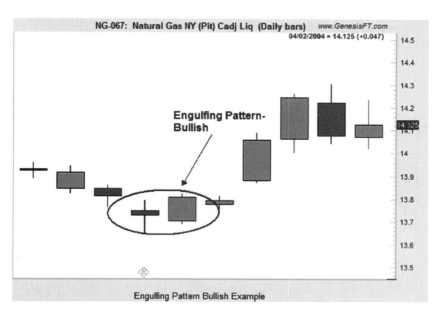

FIGURE 11.9   Bullish Engulfing Pattern Example
Source: Genesis Financial Technologies, Inc. (www.tradenavigator.com).

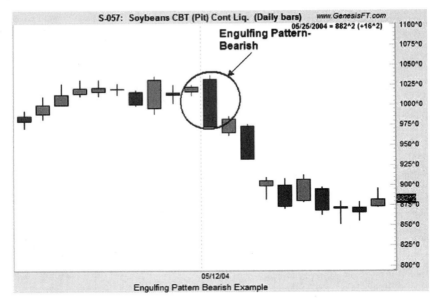

FIGURE 11.10 Bearish Engulfing Pattern Example
Source: Genesis Financial Technologies, Inc. (www.tradenavigator.com).

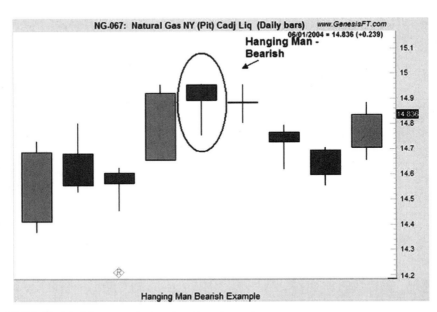

FIGURE 11.11 Bearish Hanging Man Example
Source: Genesis Financial Technologies, Inc. (www.tradenavigator.com).

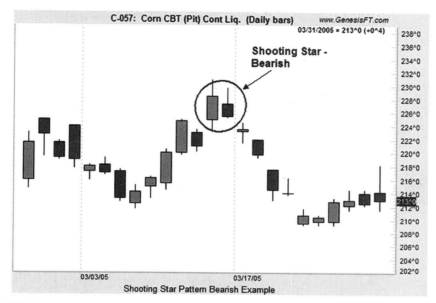

FIGURE 11.12 Shooting Star Example
Source: Genesis Financial Technologies, Inc. (www.tradenavigator.com).

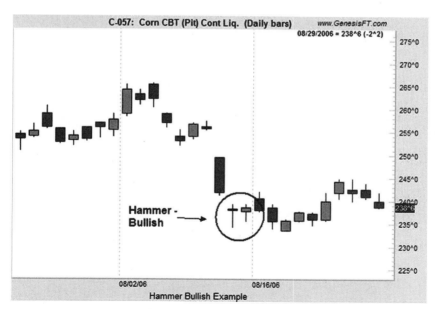

FIGURE 11.13 Bullish Hammer Example
Source: Genesis Financial Technologies, Inc. (www.tradenavigator.com).

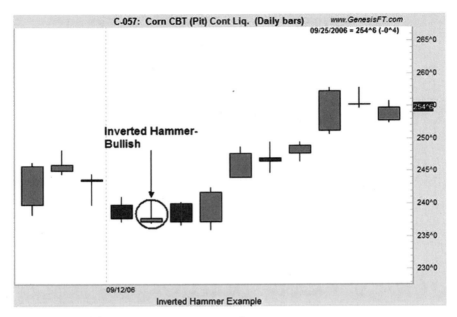

FIGURE 11.14 Inverted Hammer Example
Source: Genesis Financial Technologies, Inc. (www.tradenavigator.com).

7. *Inverted hammer:* A candlestick that has a long upper shadow and a small real body at the lower end of the session. It is a bullish bottom reversal signal. See Figure 11.14.

8. *Bullish harami:* A two-candlestick pattern in which a small real body holds within the prior session's unusually large real body. The harami implies that the preceding trend is getting ready to conclude. See Figure 11.15.

9. *Bearish harami:* A two-candlestick pattern in which a small real body holds within the prior session's unusually large real body. The harami implies that the preceding trend is getting ready to conclude. See Figure 11.16.

10. *Dark cloud:* A bearish reversal signal. In an uptrend, a long green candlestick is followed by a long red candlestick that opens above the prior green candlestick's high. The second candlestick must close well into the first candlestick's real body. See Figure 11.17.

11. *Piercing pattern:* A long red candlestick is followed by a gap lower during the next session. This session finishes as a bullish green real body that closes more than halfway into the previous session's real body. See Figure 11.18.

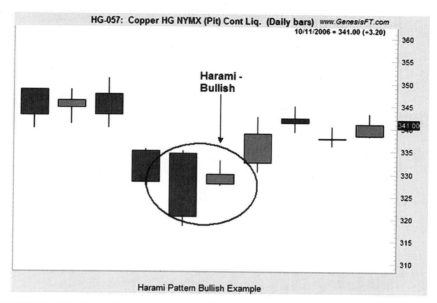

FIGURE 11.15 Bullish Harami Example
Source: Genesis Financial Technologies, Inc. (www.tradenavigator.com).

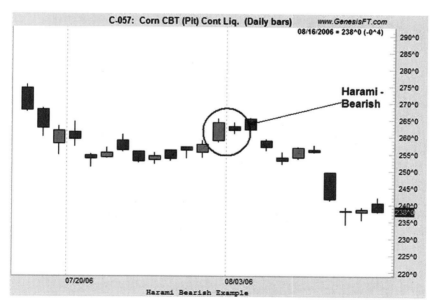

FIGURE 11.16 Bearish Harami Example
Source: Genesis Financial Technologies, Inc. (www.tradenavigator.com).

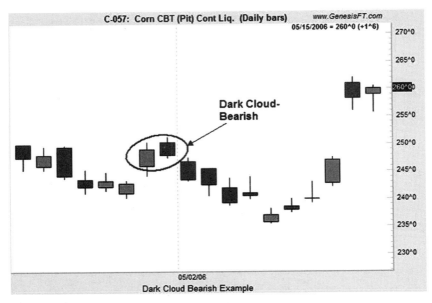

FIGURE 11.17 Dark Cloud Example
Source: Genesis Financial Technologies, Inc. (www.tradenavigator.com).

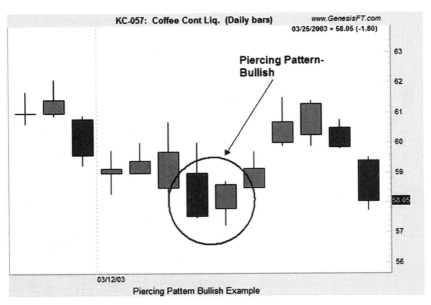

FIGURE 11.18 Piercing Pattern Example
Source: Genesis Financial Technologies, Inc. (www.tradenavigator.com).

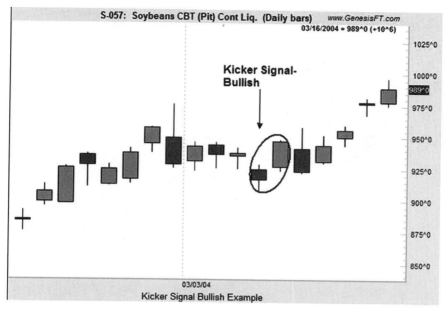

FIGURE 11.19 Bullish Kicker Signal Example
Source: Genesis Financial Technologies, Inc. (www.tradenavigator.com).

12. *Bearish/bullish kicker signal:* The first candle opens and moves in the direction of the trend, either up or down, depending on whether or not it's a bullish or bearish kicker signal. The second day's candle opens at the same price of the previous day and goes in the opposite direction. This means the two candlesticks must be opposite colors (one white and one black). It's important to remember that the candle of the second day should never retrace the previous days trading range. See Figures 11.19 and 11.20.

TRADING IS A TEAM SPORT

So much emphasis and time is spent on technical analysis in books, lectures, and seminars, it is easy to forget that technical analysis is just one component of a whole. There are computer programs and rocket scientists working day and night sifting through data to find and execute solely on patterns. None of this is new; since graphs have been plotted, everyone has looked for the magic trading formula.

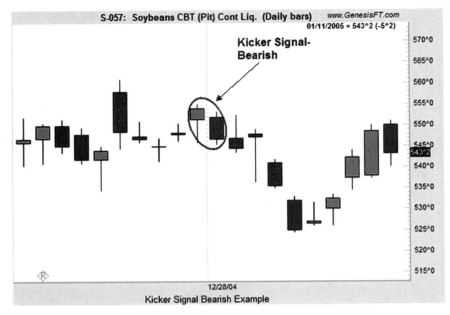

FIGURE 11.20 Bearish Kicker Signal Example
Source: Genesis Financial Technologies, Inc. (www.tradenavigator.com).

For those people with a lot of money and time to spare, the search for the perfect technical analysis tool can be an exciting process. Unfortunately, it often leads to just chasing rabbits down rabbit holes. Everything in life must have context. Rainbows have little significance without rain, aspirin has little use without pain, and technical analysis means little if you are following the wrong indicators for the type of trader you are.

By utilizing the entry and exit strategies here, together with "macro technical" analysis, money management, and risk management, you give yourself a leg up as a trader. You minimize your devotion to technical analysis in exchange for the opportunity to see the big picture. This is not an easy task, especially for the scientifically inclined, but once it's accomplished, you will be able to take a refreshing look at trading that will give you a leg up on your trading competition.

CHAPTER 12

Lesson 5: Analyzing Your Opponents and the Market

Futures predate stocks by several thousand years. One of the earliest recognized futures transactions was the Chinese rice futures of 6,000 years ago. In the seventeenth century, Japan instituted the first organized rice futures exchange. Japanese merchants would store rice in warehouses for future use. Warehouse holders would in turn sell receipts against the stored rice. Gradually, these "rice tickets" became accepted as general currency, and rules were developed to standardize their exchange. The agricultural problem that existed 6,000 years ago in China—maintaining a year-round supply of a seasonal product—reared its ugly head in the U.S. Midwest of the 1800s.

Just like in seventeenth-century Japan, the United States began to deal with its seasonal crops in much the same way. Contracts between buyers and sellers were created to lock in prices. These contracts were well received and became collateral for bank loans. Since these contracts were well respected, both dealers and farmers were able to sell their contracts to third parties.

These third parties were often other dealers and farmers willing to deliver or accept delivery on the contracts. Some third parties also purchased and sold contracts solely to capitalize on weather or market conditions that affected the price of the grains. These parties became known as "speculators" because they never intended to take delivery of the grains. They wanted to simply buy high, sell low or sell high, buy low.

From this system the U.S. commodity exchanges developed. Until this day, we have the same set of market players: buyers, sellers, and speculators. Each group has its own objectives and goals. As a trader, you must find a way to compete on the same level as the actual buyers and sellers while at the same time outsmarting your fellow speculators. The secret to doing that will be your ability to distinguish the difference between money management and risk management.

While the task is not impossible, the majority of traders constantly confuse money management and risk management. The two strategies work in tandem, although they clearly have different end goals in mind. How often you trade, how much you trade, and how much you are willing to lose have nothing to do with the risk associated with what you do in an actual trade. All these questions can be answered before you execute a trade. So what is risk management?

Risk management deals with one thing and one thing only: the trade, and more importantly—losses in a trade. Risk management gives you the guidance on how to minimize and eliminate loss in your day-to-day trading. Risk management does not focus on profits. It cannot help you make money, nor can it determine what trades you should be making. Your money management and technical analysis strategies deal with profits and trade selection. Risk management lets the profits take care of themselves and focuses on what you can control yourself. This is an essential skill that is rarely explained.

If you hope to succeed at understanding risk management, you need to understand who your opponents are—the actual buyers and the sellers of currencies and raw materials—and know how they operate. Unlike the stock market, in which almost everyone has a vested interest in seeing the price of a stock increase, in futures and forex there is an equal amount of pressure in forcing the price down. The buyers want the cheapest price possible for raw materials and products. The sellers want to extract the maximum amount of profit possible.

It is naive for the retail investor to assume that it is easy to figure out the desires of either of these two groups. One prime example is the U.S. economy. In George W. Bush's first term in office, he made it clear that he believed in a strong dollar. At the same time, Treasury Secretary John Snow was asking the G8, "What's wrong with a weak dollar?"

Who's right?

Traders are often caught unaware in the futures and forex markets because of this kind of blatant ambiguity filtered from the top down. Sudden changes in a market's direction will catch them unaware because they have assumed that the motivations of the real buyers and sellers are the same as theirs. So the question to ask yourself is: If there is constant pressure on both the up- and downside, how do the actual buyers and sellers protect themselves from each other?

It is no secret that there is no insurance company that would insure buyers and sellers of actual corn, sugar, or oil against price fluctuations.

The insurer would point out the unpredictability of supply, the volatility of demand, and the uncertainty of people's taste and desires as reasons to avoid insuring companies against price changes. The insurer would go one step further by stating that price changes are inevitable and are simply the cost of doing business.

Because of this reality, the futures and forex market is very difficult to predict. The buyers and sellers don't want to be 100% exposed to uncertainty. Unfortunately, in order to make the futures markets work, they need to entice investors. They need a sucker—someone who isn't going to actually buy or sell the products, someone who isn't a farmer or has no intentions of reselling the goods, someone who has no problem in trying to predict the market. That's you, the speculator.

Speculators really have only one purpose: to provide the capital and liquidity needed to cover the buyers' and sellers' hard cost, thus creating a zero-sum game. The money that leaves a speculator's account gets dumped right into the buyer's and seller's accounts, and sometimes into the account of another lucky speculator.

The average speculator feeds into the system by picking one side to trade, long or short, and bets in hope that one side will win out over the other. While a speculator may win from time to time, eventually he will pick the wrong side and lose. This scenario is played out over and over again. Statistics are dismal for futures and forex traders—95% of them lose their trades. Many speculators will find success early on and eventually become disappointed with their long-term results, all the while blaming the markets and not looking at themselves as the source of the problem.

In the futures and forex markets, the actual buyers and sellers are called the *commercials*. Their knowledge of the underlying mechanics of how the markets operate have them laughing all the way to the bank. The secret to their success is both simple and elegant. Every commercial is always both long and short the market at the same time. It couldn't be any clearer. They call this behavior *hedging*. However, it's an advantage that is not exclusive to them.

By being both long and short, any movement in the markets is a benefit to the commercials. If the buyers want to protect themselves from prices moving up, they are long the futures. What they would like to see happen is the actual cost of the products they intend to buy drop in value; this is known as being *short the cash*. Since they are long the futures and short the cash simultaneously, the likelihood that they will benefit in some way is pretty good.

On the other hand, the sellers want to protect themselves against the price drop, so they are short the futures, and they hope the actual prices of the goods they sell will go up in value, so they are long the cash. Being short the futures and long the cash at the same time is a mirror reflection of how the buyers set themselves up.

Both the buyers and the sellers are well protected from one another. If there is activity in the markets, they have the ability to benefit regardless. This is why a loaf of bread or a carton of orange juice does not always reflect the tremendous price shifts that occur on the charts.

The ability to weather any kind of volatility is a huge advantage for the commercials. Hedging is not the exclusive domain of the commercials, though. Hedging is also a superior way to trade, even for speculators. Once a speculator discovers how to properly hedge, a world of opportunities unfolds before him.

Hedge trading is given preferential treatment throughout the futures industry—lower commissions, lower margins, and lower fees. The clearing firms realize that when the commercials go both long and short the market, at the same time, both the clearing firm and the commercials reduce their level of exposure to risk. This gives the Futures Commission Merchants a level of security that they cannot find with speculators.

So what is risk management?

It is the ability to go both long and short the market, even when you have a market bias, with the goal of minimizing or eliminating loss and the added benefits of enjoying reduced fees, commissions, and margins that the commercials receive.

Money management alone simply cannot reduce your commissions and margins on its own. When you manage your risk in the same way that the commercials do, you put yourself in control of your trading, whether it's futures or forex. You give yourself the opportunity to succeed whether the market moves up or down; you change the way you pick trades and how you approach the market.

In this chapter we will look at what's happening behind the scenes. We will learn how the commercials, actual buyers and sellers, are forced to tell you what they are doing in the markets. We will look at minimum reporting requirements for the commercials and large speculators. We will review the Commodity Futures Trading Commission's (CFTC's) weekly report. We will then take this one step further by analyzing the report and how the activities of the commercials and the large speculators affect the small speculators.

We will then look at the secret language of price action. We will explore contango versus backwardation. We will assess volume, open interest, and option liquidity. By understanding this information, we will get a better understanding of how the commercials operate and how we can mimic them and their hedging behavior.

Once this chapter is complete, we will tackle 10 different strategies that the average speculator can use to put himself on par with the commercials.

MARKET PLAYERS

Monthly futures and forex trading in the world is measured in trillions of dollars. The activity far surpasses the stock and bond markets combined. The key players are the hedgers and the speculators. It's the fight of the century, with the clear winner being the hedgers.

A *hedger* is defined as someone who simultaneously holds a cash and futures position. Hedgers typically use futures as an insurance policy to protect themselves against adverse reactions in price. Their goal is to simply be profitable in the cash market, with as little exposure to price changes as possible.

Many stock investors are familiar with hedge funds, but the reality is that hedge funds don't hedge. When it comes to investing, stocks have won the propaganda war. They have successfully been labeled *securities*, even though the level of risk associated with them is not much better than any other investment. The same can be said about hedge funds. The concept of hedging is meant to imply that you are making an investment that counterbalances, if not completely sidesteps, the level of risk to which your main portfolio is exposed. The majority of hedge funds do not do that. Some will dabble in commodities, but few make a complete commitment to the concept.

Hedgers come in all shapes and sizes. These actual buyers and sellers who use futures as an insurance vehicle include major corporations such as Nintendo, Sony, ABN Amro Inc., Deutsche Bank Securities Inc., Barclays Capital Inc., and Goldman Sachs Inc., along with many of the Fortune 500 companies. In fact, the same banks and dealers that carry cash positions in the interbank markets will also use futures contracts to protect themselves from overexposure to trades and news. There is no true separation between futures and spot forex trading for the hedgers.

There are currently 11 futures and currency exchanges in the United States. They have a total of over 370 active futures contracts. Unlike stocks, futures do not have a minimum number to purchase. Each commodity has its own special "margin" requirements as well as movement frequency and values/movement, with each futures contract operating on its own independent time cycle. There is something for everybody.

Hedging Examples

When it comes to hedging, there are some basic ideas that the commercials follow. First, they consider *futures price* as a change in cash pricing relative to expectations. The actual *cash price* is considered a true reflection of today's supply and demand. Then there is a third concept—*basis*. Basis is the difference between the cash price and the futures price.

If you are a short cash hedger, when you see basis steadily increase, you have the ability to make a nice windfall in profits. If you are a hedger who is long the cash, then when basis decreases, you have the opportunity to make a great profit. Basis plays a significant role in clarifying what is really happening behind the numbers when you trade.

Short Hedge in T-Bond Futures

Cash Market		**Futures Market**
Buy cash bonds at 105–107	Now	Sell T-bond futures at 105–117
Sell cash bonds at 104–118	Later	Buy T-bond futures at 104–120
Loss 0–21		Gain 0–29

Net gain = 0.08
Basis 10 – Basis
2 = 0–08

Narrowing basis is profitable for long cash hedger.

Long Hedge in Corn Futures

Cash Market		**Futures Market**
Cash corn at $2.85/bu	Now	Buy corn futures at $2.96/bu
Buy cash corn $3.10/bu	Later	Sell corn futures at $3.25/bu
Loss $0.25/bu		Gain $0.29/bu

Net gain = +$0.04
Basis 11 – Basis
15 = 4

Widening basis is profitable for a short cash hedger.

The difference between hedgers and speculators and how they look at basis is twofold. While hedgers see basis as par for the business, an acceptable risk that exists, smart speculators look to exploit it for profit. It's called *convergence*. Since only 3% of hedgers actually take or make delivery on futures contracts, there are opportunities when futures and cash converge. This convergence can occur in one of two ways.

If the futures are decreasing in price while the cash is moving up in price, this is reflective of how the markets should be moving. This type of price action is typical of the futures markets. It is known as *contango*. We will delve into it later, but suffice it to say that the short hedge benefits from this type of market.

Normal Market—Contango

Short Hedge	**Long Hedge**
Futures down = gain	Futures down = loss
(Short)	(Long)
Cash up = gain	Cash up = loss
(Long)	(Short)

Short hedgers have convergence gains in normal markets (contango).

The opposite is true when the market prices are inverted. Those hedgers who are long futures will benefit the most.

Inverted Market—Backwardation

Short Hedge	**Long Hedge**
Cash down = loss	Cash down = gain
(Long)	(Short)
Futures up = loss	Futures up = gain
(Short)	(Long)

Long hedgers have convergence gains in inverted markets (backwardation).

Contango and Backwardation

Contango and backwardation are unique concepts for markets that also have a futures component. Common sense dictates that what you want to buy today should be less expensive than something you would want to buy six or seven months from now. There are many variables to take into consideration: supply, demand, storage, financing, and insurance costs. This is what is called *contango*. The front months and cash are less expensive than further-out months, creating what is known as a *negative spread*.

Backwardation is just the opposite. A fundamental shift in supply and demand occurs, forcing the cash and near-term months above and beyond the further-out months. This is a very bullish signal if you can catch it when it first begins and a very bearish signal when it starts to collapse.

Trading Contango and Backwardation   Knowing about contango and backwardation is one thing; trading it is another. Since these concepts directly represent price activity, they can give any trader a clue on how to interact with the markets, buy or sell. They can also give you clues on exactly what kind of risk management tools you can use to make a trade more effective.

They also:

- Are great near-end contract plays.
- Give you the opportunity to watch supply and demand fulfill its course before investing.
- Give you a clear opportunity to take advantage of the contrarian view to investing.
- Show you how to speculate on prices.
- Signal when to buy on switchovers from contango to backwardation.
- Signal when to sell on switchovers from a backwardation to contango.
- Identify when you can combine these price anomalies with notice days.

Notice Days   Notice days play an integral part in the ebb and flow of the market activity. As we learned earlier, futures and options contracts expire in various months. Options typically expire one month before the underlying futures contract. Leading up to that expiration date, contract holders have notice days. This is the main time in which the commercials and the hedgers are on equal footing. Everyone knows that whatever the market sentiment is, long or short, once expiration arrives, you either take delivery or exit the contract. This forced decision is unique to futures and options trading and can lead to interesting trading opportunities.

Understanding notice days can dovetail nicely with understanding how to trade contango and backwardation. Depending on whether the market is in contango or backwardation, various activities will happen. If the market is in contango and the contracts are on the verge of expiring, we will often see a smooth transition of open interest increasing from one contract month to the next. If the market is in backwardation, it can be a coin toss. Since backwardation is a direct reflection of supply and demand, it is difficult to determine if the same shortage or aggressive buying can continue from the front month into later months.

What further adds to the complication of notice days is the "seller's option rule." All commodity contracts, except currencies, are what is known as *sellers' option contracts*. Sellers have the option of making delivery to buyers at any time during the delivery period, but buyers are unable to force delivery from sellers.

Since we know that 3%, or less of futures contracts are ever delivered, you can take advantage of the mass exodus out of and into other contract months that occurs around these notice days. This can often involve putting on spreads, buying one month and selling another, or confidently shorting a market that is in backwardation as it expires.

The expiration of a contract comes in three parts: the first notice day, the last notice day, and the last trading day. Depending on your trading position, long or short, when the notice days occur, there are different activities required and different tactics you can take to attempt to make a profit. Long-term position holders, like the commercials, plan far in advance, scaling in and out of their positions, while the speculators find themselves scrambling around these times.

First notice day. First notice day is one to three days before the first business day of the delivery month. In order to be sure that you avoid taking delivery, you must be out of your long by the close of the day prior to first notice day. In some contracts, first notice day occurs after last trading day.

Last notice Day. In most cases, last notice day is from two to seven business days prior to the last business day of the month. It is the last day of the delivery period on which sellers may tender a delivery notice to buyers.

Last trading day. Last trading days vary from commodity to commodity; however, most occur during the latter part of the delivery month. All futures contracts outstanding after the last trading day must be satisfied by delivery.

Since there are two sides to every market, long and short, there are six different reactions, one for each notice day, that can occur. Depending on what side you are on, long or short, and your level of aggressiveness, you can determine the full extent of the notice-day opportunity you are presented with.

Long Positions

1. First notice day: Speculators have to "sell" their positions. Drives price down.
2. Last notice day: Hedgers begin their selling.
3. Last trading day: Complete market shakeout.

Short Positions

4. First notice day: Speculators have an opportunity to add to a position.

5. Last notice day: Short covering rally.

6. Last trading day: Complete market shakeout and rollover.

When it comes to notice days, most traders react with fear and panic. They get confused by the market activity and enter or exit trades, many times prematurely. They look at the price movements of the market, without the context of the markets relationship to the notice days. By understanding how the market reacts on any given notice day, you gain a better insight into how your opponents, both the commercials and the speculators, are behaving versus how they should behave. That type of knowledge goes a long way to helping you beat the markets.

Speculators

One definition of a *speculator* is someone who wants to profit from the price discrepancy between hedgers. Speculators fall into two categories: large speculators and small speculators.

There are many famous speculators, like George Soros and Jim Rogers, as well as infamous, like the team that collapsed Long-Term Capital Management. Nicolas Leeson, the guy who broke Barings Bank and Amaranth, lost $9 billion trading natural gas futures.

For speculators, it's not all just sad stories. The same Fortune 500 companies, banks, and dealers that make markets for forex also trade in the futures markets for their own accounts or on behalf of their clients. They successfully meet their objectives year in and year out. Goldman Sachs is one of the more famous investment banking firms that trade futures and forex. They have had record profitable years with their Goldman Sachs Commodity Index.

The CFTC decides who is a large speculator. The CFTC is a branch of the U.S. government. They regulate futures and make sure that no market manipulation is going on. In order to successfully do this, they have guidelines that all traders must follow.

In their eyes, the only difference between a large speculator and a small speculator is the reporting requirements. The CFTC has set different reporting thresholds for different markets. Some markets require that you file a report with them when you hold 100 contracts at one time. Other markets require that you file a report if you hold as few as 25 contracts.

Anyone who doesn't have to report is deemed a small speculator. That's where the average retail client fits in. The accuracy of this assessment can be deceiving. There are futures and forex money managers called

Commodity Trading Advisers (CTAs) that work with clients and operate just like the large speculators but may not have the reporting requirements because they trade so few contracts.

Sophisticated Speculators

CTAs are considered the "mutual funds" of the futures and forex industry. CTAs actively work with private investor money and use various strategies to attempt to minimize the speculative risks associated with futures and forex.

Managed futures are the perfect investment for those retail investors who cannot take the time out of their day to follow the markets. It is also appropriate for investors with large portfolios who are seeking diversification. These are true hedge funds. Since futures and forex are not correlated to stocks, any movement in the stock market, up or down, has no true bearing on what happens in these markets. Investors put a small portion of their overall portfolio with a CTA in order to increase their overall rates of return.

Sometimes you can invest indirectly in a managed futures or forex account by participating in a commodity pool. Many commodity pools have small minimums. There is no true uniformity on how commodity pools or managed futures accounts are run. It is best to have a prospectus sent to you and have your futures broker or other professional go over the details with you.

Even though CTAs may not be actively reporting, small speculators have to be aware of their strategies and successes for two reasons. First, by understanding how they operate, you can gain insight into becoming a better trader. Second, since many of their strategies are based in technical analysis, you don't want to get steamrolled by their activity. Whatever the case may be, you have to watch out for them.

GROUND RULES FOR SPECULATORS USING HEDGING TECHNIQUES AS A RISK MANAGEMENT STRATEGY

While hedging techniques are great, there are no guarantees when it comes to trading. These techniques are designed to help minimize your losses. At the same time, you must have realistic expectations of what they can do for you. Many major corporations, banks, and governments have been blindsided because they did not hedge at all or didn't understand how to hedge until it was too late.

We will answer three questions that speculators have to ask themselves if they intend to use the techniques:

1. *Do hedgers lose money?* Of course. That's what hedging is designed to do. When a commercial company puts on a hedge, they have a bias in the marketplace. They may want to buy or sell the actual products, but when they put the hedge on, they determine if the risk they are taking is worthwhile. They know up front that one leg of the position will lose money, and they prepare for it. It's the difference between having a controlled fire and a wildfire.

2. *How important is volatility?* If you are using a hedging technique you have to have volatility otherwise you will lose on both sides of the trade. Markets that don't move at all or move too little to be of significance can and will hurt you.

3. *Is hedging easy?* Once you put on a hedge, you can set it up and forget about it. Let the market work its way out. Prior to putting on the hedge is where all the work is. You must calculate your potential profits, potential losses, and net expenses, depending on the exact hedging technique you use. It's necessary, but it's worth it.

While I have made hedging seem simple, time and time again it is underutilized. Over the past 30 years, we have seen the futures and currency markets attempt to be manipulated, with disastrous results.

In the late 1970s, we saw the Hunt brothers attempt to corner silver and gold. In the early 1990s, we saw George Soros break the Bank of England. The late 1990s brought us the "Asian flu" and almost demolished the Southeast Asian economies.

Then we saw a money management firm, Long-Term Capital Management, run by an Nobel Prize winner in economics, and leveraged by over $1 trillion, almost collapse the world economy because of a refusal to accept that they had made a mistake.

Many of these events had a devastating impact on the speculators who jumped on the bandwagon. For example, gold ran up but they did not have an effective way to protect themselves against the sharp down turn. Understanding and utilizing hedging techniques is the only way the everyday speculator can have a shield against the large commercial enterprises that operate behind the scenes.

Examples of Why Hedging Can Be Important

The rules and regulations governing futures, developed by the CFTC, occurred over time. Several scandals along the way have hurt speculators tremendously. These events happened behind the scenes and were discovered only after much of the damage had already been done. As a trader, it is important to be prepared for any event. The only way to be prepared for many of the events discussed below is to have a countermeasure in place—some type of hedge that would protect you from these trading fiascoes.

Cornering Silver and Gold When the United States decided to take the dollar off of the gold standard, a gold auction was held. The gold auction was held in August 1979 and was more successful than anyone had expected. At the time, the Chicago Board of Trade (CBOT) was the primary place to trade gold futures contracts. In order to slow down the speculation that was occurring at the time, they raised the margin minimums to keep small speculators out. When that didn't work, to stem the tide of activity they limited the number of contracts that large speculators could hold.

At the same time, the Hunt brothers were busy accumulating gold and silver. They were using borrowed money to purchase gold. Every time their gold and silver went up in value, they would borrow more money to buy more. Their activity led to them having the largest gold and silver reserves in history. As too often happens, events outside of their control occurred.

With the CBOT taking an aggressive stand against the exuberant price moves in gold and silver, by 1980 silver had reached $68.00 per ounce. The Hunt brothers were doomed. After the CBOT had forced all of the small speculators out of the market and then limited the number of contracts that large speculators could hold, they dropped one more nail in the coffin. The CBOT used the Olympic boycott to force all speculators into a pigeonhole. They would not allow any new position, and only those with long positions were allowed to close out.

The resulting collapse in the price of gold and silver was phenomenal. By forcing investors and traders to liquidate their positions, they single-handedly changed the face of metal trading. It took gold over 20 years to get back to the $800 level, and silver has yet to reach anywhere near its all-time high of $83.

The Hunt brothers fared no better. Their constant pyramiding of profits and borrowing from banks led them to financial ruin. Their activity forced the Federal Reserve to bail them and the banks out of trouble to the tune of $1.1 billion.

Breaking the Bank of England George Soros is the founder of the Quantum Fund. It is considered to be one of the world's first hedge funds. George Soros, unlike many investment managers, takes a macroeconomic view of investing. One opportunity led him to being considered a pariah in the United Kingdom and brought him the admiration and disdain of many financiers worldwide.

George Soros had discerned that the British pound was top-heavy. He felt that it was long overdue for a correction and that there was nothing the central bank could do to stop the currency from sliding downward once everyone else realized the same thing. So Soros began to build up a highly leveraged short position against the British pound. Over the course of six months, he racked up profits of over US$1 billion. This devastated the British pound and scandalized the government. Ever since, George Soros has been known as the man who broke the Bank of England.

Asian Flu   In late 1996, many Asian countries were being noticed globally for their unprecedented economic growth. Technology and manufacturing were large contributors to the newfound financial strength in Indonesia, Malaysia, Thailand, and Singapore. Victims of their own success, many wondered how long their growth could be sustained. Their main business attraction, undervalued currencies, had gotten significantly stronger.

In early 1997, Soros's groups began heavily shorting Thailand's currency, the baht, and Malaysia's currency, the ringgit, using the exact same highly leveraged tactics as five years earlier against the British pound.

In July 1997, in order to stimulate their weakening economy, Thai officials devalued the baht. This action set off a wave of devaluations throughout Asia, particularly Malaysia. South Asia still has not successfully rebounded from such an aggressive currency attack.

Prime Minister Mahathir Mohamad of Malaysia has vocalized to the world his disdain for George Soros and his currency crippling strategies.

Collapse of Long-Term Capital Management   Long-Term Capital Management (LTCM) was a hedge fund company founded with Nobel Prize winners Myron Scholes and Robert Merton on the board.

LTCM had developed a trading style that focused on arbitrage. They focused their efforts on trading U.S., Japanese, and European sovereign bonds. The arbitrage focused on a simple concept. Over time, the value of long-dated bonds issued a short time apart would tend to become identical. Since the bonds that were trading at a premium would have to decrease in value and the bonds trading at a discount would have to increase in value, the profits between the two were guaranteed. This risk-free profit would become more and more apparent every time a new bond was issued.

Since the profit opportunity was very thin, LTCM needed more leverage than normal in order to make the program worthwhile for their investors. In 1998, the firm started out with equity of US$4.72 billion. They used that to borrow over US$124.5 billion, with leveraged assets of around

$129 billion. They then used these positions to convince banks to give them off-balance-sheet derivative positions amounting to US$1.25 trillion.

Initially, this heavily leveraged strategy produced returns in the double digits. The "risk-free" profits stopped in August 1998. Russia defaulted on their sovereign debt. Investors lost faith in Japanese and European bonds. U.S. Treasury bonds became the bonds of the hour. The expected bond narrowing not only stopped but quickly began to diverge. LTCM lost US$1.85 billion in capital.

Since LTCM had daisy-chained so much leverage, if they failed, the effect would not only be a loss of capital but a banking crisis to the tune of US$1.25 trillion.

To save the global economy, the Federal Reserve Bank of New York, without putting up any taxpayer money, organized a banker bailout of US$3.625 billion. By the end of the fiasco, the total losses were found to be US$4.6 billion.

Collapsing Barings Bank   It can be said that Barings Bank made a mistake when they hired Nick Leeson, but the true mistake was not watching his activity as closely as they should have. Before the earthquake, Nick Leeson was long futures positions of 3,000 contracts.

A month after the earthquake, he had increased his position size to 19,094 contracts.

By February 27, 1995, he was holding on to Japanese equities and interest rate products to the tune of US$27 billion.

In order to cover losses, Nick Leeson sold 70,892 Nikkei options with a value of $6.68 billion. All of this activity was going on, and the bank's reported capital was only $615 million.

WHAT CAN WE LEARN?

What we can learn from all of these stories is that the whims of the market can be fickle. You have Soros taking a big bet against the Bank of England and succeeding. You have Nick Leeson taking a big bet on the Japanese economy and losing. There are market forces that are aggressively vying for attention. You have Nobel Prize winners at LTCM almost collapsing the world financial markets. No amount of money, knowledge, and pedigree can protect you. You have to raise your level of awareness in order to succeed against these types of competitors. The only way to do that is by acting and operating more like the hedgers and less like the speculators.

Analyzing the Markets: Volume, Open Interest, and Liquidity

When it comes to trading stocks, volume is king. The number of shares exchanging hands can be tremendous—billions of shares on a daily basis. There is no such luck when it comes to trading futures or over-the-counter (OTC) currencies. When you trade futures, you have the opportunity to successfully trade markets with a volume of 5,000 contracts as easily as you have the opportunity to trade markets with a few hundred thousand contracts.

Unlike stocks, futures are a leveraged investment. The actual volume of contracts does not reflect the true value of those contracts being traded. For instance, if you traded corn and saw the volume at 50,000 contracts, you wouldn't be impressed. A stock trader would assume that there was no liquidity.

However, if we looked at the true value of a corn contract, we would quickly realize that it was worth $20,000. Multiply $20,000 dollars by the 50,000 contracts, and we have $100 million in activity. So volume is not a good indicator of whether there is liquidity in the futures markets.

To take it one step further, we know that there are two players in the markets—hedgers and speculators. The hedgers have a long-term objective—that's why they buy or sell futures in the first place. They are not interested in entering and exiting the markets on a daily basis. So a better reflection of the true activity of a futures market is the open interest. Open interest accurately counts the number of long, short, and spread positions that are out there. Often, you can easily see a market with a volume of 2,000 to 3,000 contracts but open interest of 125,000 long and short positions.

The ebb and flow of the open interest is what gives us our best insight into what is really happening in a market. This is particularly helpful for spot currency traders. The spot market doesn't have any data on the true volume of activity that goes on at any time. So an easy way for spot traders to see if they are taking the right stance on a market's direction is to look at the futures open interest of those particular currencies that they trade to get a bead on the overall market condition.

If you are familiar with options, you may already know about open interest. *Open interest* is defined as the total number of derivatives contracts traded that have not yet been liquidated. There are two ways that open interest can change, it is offset either by another derivative transaction or by delivery. Since we know that the largest number of contracts of any market are held by the commercials by monitoring open interest, we can see the strengthening or weakening of bullish and bearish momentum.

Let's look at how a typical oil contract would operate:

A believes oil prices are going lower, so he sells one futures contract.

B believes oil prices are going higher, so he buys one futures contract.

These two positions combined together, one long and one short, equal one unit of open interest.

When the oil market attracts attention, C buys a contract from D. Open interest increases to two units.

E buys a futures contract from B, who was long. E takes over B's position, leaving open interest the same.

C and D decide to close out their long and short contracts simultaneously. This decreases open interest by one unit.

Open Interest Rules of Thumb
- Open interest increases when a new long buys from a new short.
- Open interest decreases when an old long sells to an old short.
- Open interest does not change when an old long or short is simply replaced by a new long or a new short.

When it comes to trading based on open interest, you also have to match up the increase and decrease of open interest with the actual price activity occurring at that time. The open interest will give you an idea of the momentum of the markets. It will let you know if you are getting in on the beginning or tail-end of a market's new high or low.

Price = up	Open interest = up	Technically strong
Price = up	Open interest = down	Technically weak
Price = down	Open interest = down	Longs are exiting, temporary pullback
Price = down	Open interest = up	Potentially more selling ahead—bearish

There are two ways to see open interest, either plotted on a graph or by downloading the Commitments of Traders report published the CFTC.

Commitments of Traders (COT) Report   The COT report is a weekly publication. The report includes information data on the numbers of traders in each category. Until 1995, the report was a fee-based publication, but has since become freely available on the CFTC's website. The weekly reports for *Futures-Only Commitments of Traders* and for *Futures-and-Options-Combined Commitments of Traders* are released every Friday at 3:30 PM Eastern Time.

There is no way that I know of to trade the COT report by itself. It simply allows you to get a clear picture of market activity and sentiment. This is the insider information that you can't find in the stock market.

MASTERING FUNDAMENTAL REPORTS

There is a constant ongoing debate on which type of trading is better, technical analysis or fundamental analysis. When it comes to trading commodities and forex, if you don't stay on top of fundamental reports, you are bound to be blindsided in your trading. While you cannot trade directly based on fundamental information, by knowing when these announcements occur, you give yourself the upper hand in discovering what your chief trading opponents, the commercials, are worried about or planning for.

Depending on the type of trader you are—active, swing, or position—you approach fundamental reports based on your own needs and goals. You will utilize fundamental information either to protect the position you are in, to start a new trade, or to add on to your positions. Having a thorough knowledge of the when and what the reports are will make your trading more robust. The ability to know what the commercials are looking for and what they are expecting from key data makes you an insider as well.

As we discussed before, however, there is a lot of information to filter through. It's impossible to know how or if the market will react at all to the news. Often, the news will be bullish and the market will tank because the information has already been incorporated into the price activity of the markets. Use fundamental reports only as guideposts of the state of the markets, not as gospel.

Some of the most prolific fundamental information sources are the various economic reports that come out every month. They deal with interest rates, labor statistics, import/export numbers, and so on. The trick to incorporating this fundamental information into your trading is by picking and choosing the reports that will have the greatest impact on volatility, whether you are adding to your position or establishing a new position. The following economic reports do just that.

Labor Department—Consumer Price Index (CPI): 10th business day of the month

Commerce Department—Durable Goods Orders: 10th business day of the month

Labor Department—Employment Figures: 1st Friday of the month

Commerce Department—Gross Domestic Product (GDP): 20th business day of the month

Commerce Department—Housing Starts: 15th business day of the month

Federal Reserve—Industrial Production: 15th business day of the month

Commerce Department—U.S. International Trade: 3rd week of the month

National Association of Purchasing Management—Composite Index of New Orders: 10th business day of the month (inventories, employment, production, supplier deliveries)

Commerce Department—Retail Sales: Mid-month

Labor Department—Unemployment Insurance Claims: Every Thursday

Major USDA Agricultural Reports:

World Agricultural Supply and Demand: Monthly

Grain Stocks: Quarterly

Prospective Plantings: End of March

Crop Production: Monthly

Crop Progress: Weekly

Cattle on Feed: Monthly

Grain Transportation: Weekly

USDA National Agricultural Service: Monthly

Tip for Active Traders

If you like to be in and out of the market in the same day, the best way to take advantage of fundamental reports is one to two hours before and one to two hours after. While much of the pricing may already be built into the trade, you have the opportunity to trade a lot of the momentum that small and large speculators bring to bear on the markets. Combine this activity with key candlesticks, and you will come out ahead. These are prime times for e-mini traders and forex traders.

Tip for Swing Traders

The typical swing trader is looking to buy and sell tops and bottoms. By paying attention to key reports and open interest, you will be alerted to whether or not a pullback is on the horizon or the market is continuing with its momentum. Ride out the momentum until it reaches your risk management points.

Position Traders

Fundamental reports will either validate or invalidate your long-term position if the market breaks that all-important 50-day moving average. If the

50-day moving average isn't violated, you may want to add to your position; if it is violated, take stock of the market and don't hesitate to peel off the trade if it looks unfavorable.

CONCLUSION

In this chapter we took a look at hedgers and how they approach the markets. We took a look at the role of speculators and the havoc that they have wreaked on the markets over the years. Then we looked at volume, open interest, and liquidity and what we need to look for in determining how strong the markets are or aren't, even if the price seems to have a lot of momentum. Finally, we took a glance at some of the fundamental reports that are out there and discussed how you can potentially trade them.

The goal of this chapter was to help you change your mind-set and begin to look at the markets from the point of view of the actual buyers and sellers. By thinking like them, the goal is to behave like them. Don't get caught trading one side of a market and to read their behavior in such a way that you are able to ride along with their wave of activity and not be crushed by it.

The bottom line is that no one knows your trade better than you. Do the trade and let the trade prove itself. Just know that most of the time your trades will fail and there's nothing you can do to change that. The market will do what it wants; you simply want to lose less on the losing trades, so you have enough capital left over to find those potential winning trades. By properly applying some, if not all, of the hedging techniques in the next chapter you should be able to do just that.

CHAPTER 13

Lesson 6: Managing Risk

You cannot know if you will be successful or not. You can only prepare for battle, and it must be done with all of your heart and with all of your consciousness.

—Sun Tzu, *The Art of War*

In Chapter 12, we went in depth on how hedgers and speculators operate. We also took a look at their motivation for why they trade. The secret to becoming a better trader hinges on your ability to look at the market through the same eyes as the hedgers and to act accordingly. As with many important things in life, on the surface it is simple to conceptualize, but difficult to execute.

This chapter puts the tools in your hand to execute the necessary combination of longs and shorts to help represent yourself as a hedger in the larger trading community. You must be committed to the idea that you are capable of succeeding in your trading and that you can keep a constant vigilance on the trading demons of fear and greed. Once that type of consciousness is developed, then the resistance to this type of trading diminishes quickly.

As with any rules of engagement, we must lay the groundwork for some beliefs you will have to incorporate in your trading experience in order to make it successful.

STOCK INVESTMENT TRUISMS

When it comes to investing, the first market that anyone is introduced to is the stock market. Throughout your entire stock market learning experience, there are multiple truisms that you learn. These truisms are designed to make you trade smarter and show you how to manage your risk and exposure to market downturns.

The problem occurs when a stock investor attempts to apply these same truisms to futures, forex, and options trading. The following six truism can easily have a way of backfiring on you and destroying your account. Putting these truisms in perspective and knowing when and how to apply them will make your trading experience less confusing.

Stock Truism 1: Buy low, sell high.

In futures and forex you can go short as easily as you go long. Don't have a buy-side bias.

Stock Truism 2: Let your profits run and cut your losses.

When using any of the risk management tools we've discussed, one side will be losing while the other side profits. This is necessary so that you can weather fluctuations, particularly on position and swing trades, and catch the largest momentum move possible.

Stock Truism 3: Quantity of accuracy is not as important as quality of accuracy.

When it comes to leveraged investing, you want to be able to be in as many optimum trades as possible. Constantly scalping 1 point here and 1 point there only to get caught on the wrong side and give away 20 points in one go is not our goal. Focus on getting into the trades with the best opportunity for larger profits, and you won't have to worry about being constantly in and out of the market.

Stock Truism 4: You need to know where the market is going to profit from it.

In the end, none of us can know the future. We make our best guesses and estimates, and still we are wrong. The right money management tools act as our safety net and help make up for our mistakes. As long as you set aside your ego and let your tools operate to protect you, you will find them all valuable.

Stock Truism 5: Picking tops and bottoms is the only way to succeed.

This is a variation of buy low–sell high, but it needs to be addressed. Too many traders believe there is a perfect entry and exit price, and in focusing this way they lose sight of the big picture. Often, it's enough just to get started in the trade. Leave the timing to the timing experts and the money making to the money-making experts. Don't get bogged down.

Stock Truism 6: It's not a loss until you take it.

This is the worst concept to bring to the futures market. Every dime you make in these markets belongs to you; every loss you take belongs to you. Do not get lulled into a false sense of security in believing that you are immune to or somehow separated from your profits and losses. Be proactive and constantly be vigilant of what you are making and losing, so you can correct it if need be.

Attempting to apply these six stock market investment truisms to futures and forex can quickly backfire on you if you are not careful. They can cloud your risk management judgment when it comes to futures and forex investing. Eliminate the dogmatic stock market approach to trading and you will find a world of doors opening to you.

WHAT YOU SHOULD BELIEVE

Now that we beat up the stock market truisms, the question becomes what should you believe when it comes to managing your trading risk. In this chapter we will take a look at nine different risk management techniques. Some you will be familiar with; others you may recognize vaguely. Each one of them will seem to be counterintuitive to how you would trade the markets.

In order to understand the logic behind these risk management tools, you have to establish a basic foundation of belief. Once you accept these beliefs, it becomes easier to properly execute the risk management techniques without second-guessing yourself.

Belief 1: Being Both Long and Short the Market Is Not the Same as Being Neutral the Trade

In a seminar I conducted in San Diego regarding a few of the concepts laid out in this book, a man raised his hand and asked me, "If I am long a contract and short the same contract, aren't the trades canceling out each other?"

The answer is a resounding *"no!"* When we use risk management strategies, one side is the insurance, and the other side is the trade. There are different levels of commitment, in both capital and price, so don't get bogged down with this belief.

In much the same way that a corn farmer is not neutral in expecting the value of corn to go up, but still protects himself with options just in case the price falls, so does the sophisticated speculator manage his trading positions.

Belief 2: These Markets Were First Designed as Insurance Vehicles, Not to Be Speculated On

While it's exciting to look smart at a cocktail party in knowing the direction a market is going—higher oil, weaker dollar, and ethanol expansion—knowing or presuming to know these things has little bearing on your ability to trade.

Look at the futures market as first being an insurance vehicle, and recognize that there is "daisy-chain effect" when it comes to trading based on the insurance aspect. The futures market protects the spot market; the options market protects the futures and/or spot market. Each alternative increases your leverage and diminishes your exposure to the underlying risk that the cash market may be experiencing.

So while the futures market leverage may be only 5% to 10% of the total value of the spot market, option contracts may be worth only 5% to 10% of the futures contract. Use this disparity to your advantage.

Belief 3: It Is Too Difficult to Understand/Learn

Earning money is not easy. Trading the markets, forex, futures, or options, can be the most difficult activity to succeed at. While thousands of people get involved in the market year in and year out, 95% of them fail in their trading.

Knowing those odds, as a trader you are better off learning how to trade correctly from the outset. Utilizing the risk management techniques puts you head and shoulders above the 95% of traders who are simply picking a market side, the same way they would pick horses or roulette numbers.

Learn how to use these risk management techniques, and you will find yourself head and shoulders above the competition.

Belief 4: There Are Only Three Ways the Market Can Move: Up, Down, and Sideways

This is trading 101. Yet the concept is either forgotten or overlooked or assumed to mean that you must only trade one of the three possible scenarios to the best of your ability.

This is not the case. By picking "long or short," you handicap your ability to trade by cutting yourself off from two thirds of your opportunities. As we learned in our technical analysis, by utilizing the 50-day moving average (MA), we can gain a tone for the overall market, but that doesn't guarantee us the market will head in that direction.

With the proper risk management techniques, you can be both long and short, as well as trade sideways markets. You don't have to pick—you just have to be prepared.

Now that we've tackled your belief system, later on we will discuss the ideas and concepts behind various risk management strategies and take a hard look at what makes it different from money management. There will be various before-and-after examples to see how each one of the nine risk management techniques can help you increase your chances when you trade. Finally, we will pull it all together to help you have a more enjoyable trading experience.

SUCCESS AND FAILURE IN TRADING

Once you have committed to a trade, you must prepare for success. Part of that preparation is understanding that 95% of traders fail in futures and forex trading and 80% of options expire worthless. Therefore, in order to succeed in a trade, you need not be overly optimistic. You must have a high level of realism in believing that the trade you have picked will most likely be wrong.

Instead of focusing on how much money you could make on this trade, one thought that should consume your mind when you execute a new trade: "What if I am wrong?" Without this thought coming to the forefront, you are doomed to lose not only the various trading battles, but also the trading war.

You may not like what I am about to say, but it's true: Profits are easy to make. That's right, profits are easy to make. There is little that you have to do except be in the trade. There is little to no active participation on your part. They happen all of their own volition.

Just like magic, economic factors align, CNBC talks your trade up in their latest news report, the moon is retrograde to Jupiter, and all is good with the world. In fact your actions have little to do with the success of the trade. You were just there, the right person at the right time. This confluence of events is a trader's dream, yet too often novice and experienced traders alike attempt to take undue credit. They assume that they are smarter than the market. Some traders say, "I'd rather be lucky than smart," because the moment you think you have the markets figured out, they surprise you.

So what do you do when you are wrong about the trade?

Statistics tell us that we will be wrong more times than we are right, so how do you react when the charts don't align, the Federal Reserve Board is talking on CNBC against your position, Jupiter crosses Mars, and all is wrong with the world?

Too many potentially good traders become bad traders because they are not concerned about risk in the right way. Pareto's principle states that 80% of our efforts produce 20% of our results, while at the same time 20% of our efforts produce 80% of our results. By fixating on how much money you are going to make, you are falling right into the 80/20 trap.

It is important to be positive-minded and self-encouraging; it is also important to be forewarned and forearmed—be proactive. There is a constant barrage from system and black box sellers promoting 80% and 90% accuracy in picking markets. This constant marketing has distorted the reality of trading.

There has been a shift of the retail client in believing that if he can just pick the right markets, he will be a great trader. This dynamic has placed an unfair burden on the average trader to be almost perfect, if not perfect, in order to succeed at trading. This simply is not true. Eighty percent of a trader's time is eaten up in finding the holy grail of market entry, when in reality it accounts for only 20% of a trade's success.

Futures magazine did a survey of commodity trading adviser (CTA) money managers, and there was one theme that was consistent: loss. Out of every 10 trades, 6 were losers. Of the remaining 4 trades, 2 were break-even or small losses and the final 2 made up for all of the losses and then some. So even with just 40% accuracy, there are CTAs who are managing tens of millions of dollars. If accuracy mattered, then these CTAs should not even have one client. So let's avoid the distortion of the 80/20 rule by placing our attention on the 20% that gets often ignored.

Before we go any further, I want you to ponder this: In a trade, when and where do you make your money?

Make sure you think about this before you go further. Are you ready?

You make money when you exit your trade.

The exit is the most important time in a trade's life cycle. Yet the typical amount of effort that traders put into what they will do when they exit a trade is small. This is a shame. In order to be successful at exiting trades, whether you expect to make money or diminish losses, you have to plan out your activities far in advance; this is before you ever put a dime in the market.

The secret is in knowing, before you commit to a trade, your profit targets and your loss targets. Calculate your potential returns or losses based on both the margin you will be putting up and overall account balance.

By focusing on the end results first, you put yourself in control of the demons of fear and greed. By knowing what the end result is, good or bad, you can be in control of your emotions and your knee-jerk reactions. This is how you turn your trading into something you can control, not something that controls you. This is the true mettle of a speculator: the willingness to replace chance with design. By understanding how you will exit the market every time you trade, you no longer are a gambler.

Keep in mind that knowing how you will exit is different than knowing when you will exit. This is not about market timing. None of the traders I know have a crystal ball; even if they did, I don't think they would be sharing with me. Since that's the case, the goal for the average trader is to manage the lines of probability that they are presented with.

Whether you use the technical analysis strategies we used when we answered the question, "When will the market arrive?," or you have some other methods to determine tops, bottoms, highs, and lows, the goal is simply to give yourself a framework within which to trade. This framework is the foundation of each trade you make and will set the tone for how you approach the markets for the rest of your life.

By having some type of profit-and-loss target at your disposal, you give yourself the opportunity to effectively set up risk management scenarios that will optimize profit potential and, at the same time, diminish potential losses. As traders, that's all we can ask for.

WHAT MAKES IT DIFFERENT FROM MONEY MANAGEMENT

In the beginning of the book, we separated money management from technical analysis and risk management. There is a clear distinction between money management and risk management, but the subtleties tend to get lost in the shuffle. When I ask new traders what their risk management strategies are, they tell me "stops"; when I ask them what their money management strategies are, they tell me "stops."

The best way to clearly delineate money management from risk management is to think of it this way: Money management is how you deal with the capital you have in your account. If you were to never execute a trade, how would you treat the money in your account? That's why we discussed things such as earning interest on your account, how much you would risk if you took on a trade, what your risk-reward ratios were, and what type of markets fit your personal volatility as well as the capital in your account.

Risk management has to do with one thing and one thing only—how to protect yourself from the risk of loss. So while stops may be a type of risk management tool, they are definitely not a money management tool. In the case of this book, we definitely did save the best for last. Risk, risk, risk! That is the name of the game. We know we will lose money trading—in fact, it is guaranteed that we will have losing trades. The goal is to use risk management techniques that will help us minimize our losses so we can stick around long enough to let the winning trades handle themselves.

Don't Expect a Miracle

If there is a holy grail of trading, I haven't found it yet. The strategies presented in this chapter are designed to do three things: make you appear like a hedger to the exchanges, make you think like a hedger, and make you act like a hedger. All the while you are still speculating and have the most to gain when you do succeed.

By looking like a hedger to the exchanges, you will enjoy reduced margin requirements, better commissions, and hopefully a more stable account balance.

By thinking like a hedger, you will not be afraid to have an opinion of the market, because you will be able to minimize your losses and have the opportunity to profit regardless of the direction that the market ultimately takes.

Finally, by acting like a hedger, you will reduce the amount of pain and frustration that the markets can bring. It is easy to punish ourselves and beat ourselves up for failures that we may experience in the markets, without realizing that part of the process of success is loss.

The nine strategies that are included in this chapter are by no means the only risk management tools available to you, nor do they incorporate some of the more exotic and sophisticated option strategies that exist today. They all represent tools from which you can pick and choose in order to get a better grasp on preparing for loss.

Along the way you may discover that the risk management position that you put on is making money. Great! But keep in mind that's not what it was designed for. It was meant to protect your initial market bias. So once you know where the market is going and have the answer to the next question, "When will it arrive?," you can build up any risk management strategy around it.

You then take a look back at how far the market has come. Use average true range or horizontal support, the Fibonacci, or cold hard money management percentages and "set your trap."

Can you lose money using these or any other risk management strategies?

Of course, you can. Ask any farmer who has hedged his crop and lost on his futures position, then lost on his sell of the crop at the market; or any banker who was using dollar futures contracts to protect his euro spot position, only to see the dollar rally and the euro position collapse. There are no guarantees when it comes to trading, and you can get wishboned in your trades if you do it wrong.

These are tools that you use, but they are not 100% autopilot. Make sure you are putting the hedges on properly and calculate all of your worst-case scenarios in advance. There will be some risk management tools that will be less aggressive than others and there will be some risk management tools that will be more appropriate because of the circumstances of the market, even though they may be more aggressive. Take the time to pick and choose the right ones for your trading style and objectives.

Keep in mind that the risk management strategies are there to help those traders who may be right about the market but wrong about how to trade it. These strategies help eliminate that problem.

Stops—A Bad Habit

I don't condone murder, but let's kill the stop—as a risk management tool.

In the past, you would have been told to set your stop and forget about it. It was and is the number one risk management tool promoted by brokers, educators, and sometimes even fellow traders. Yet those with experience in trading know how dangerous using stops can be. By attempting to use stops as your sole risk management tactic, you not only put the current trade in danger, you also put your entire account at risk.

It's like driving with only the emergency brake. Although it may get the job done, in the end the wear and tear on your car, not to mention the pedestrians, would be horrific. This is not to say that you can't use a stop; you just don't rely on it as your sole risk management tactic.

There are smoother ways of exiting trades. There are better ways of reacting to the markets without panic and with a steady hand. It is no secret that markets rarely go straight up or straight down. What too often happens to traders is that the dips and the pullbacks shake them out of the market before they can get a chance to actually profit.

When it comes to investing, how do you protect yourself from the inevitable fact that you will be wrong?

The majority of investors, because of their stock background, fall back on a "stop loss" to protect them. In the stock market, a stop loss is the right tool for the job. The stock market has an inherent long-side bias, so anytime the prices are dropping, it's because investors are selling. There is nothing wrong with having a circuit breaker in that kind of system.

Before we go any further, let's define a stop. The Commodity Futures Trading Commission (CFTC) defines a *stop* as

> *... [A]n order that becomes a market order when a particular price level is reached. A sell stop is placed below the market; a buy stop is placed above the market. Sometimes referred to as a stop loss order.*

In futures and forex, it's not so simple. The nature of the market is based on the duality of buyers and sellers. So when the price is dropping, it doesn't mean that people are just jumping ship; it means that people are actually obtaining contracts on the sell side. This is why understanding open interest is so important to knowing the rhythm of the market.

If new sell-side contracts are being created and you are using a stop to get out, you may find yourself chasing the markets. This level of sophistication in a world where new buy- or sell-side contracts can be created at any time, based on the market needs of the moment, makes the stop as a risk management tool ineffective.

A second problem that a stop order has is the fact that it is converted into a market order when it is activated. A market order that occurs as the result of a stop order can be filled at practically any price; this is known as *slippage*. Slippage is the difference between where you placed your stop order and where the order is filled. This alone can mean the untimely demise of a small trading account.

For instance, let's say you bought (long) gold at $570 and you have a stop-loss order at $565. Each $1 move in gold is equal to $100. Your goal as a trader is not to lose more than $500 on this trade. If the market moves against you, and your stop loss is triggered at $565, it immediately turns into a market order. You are not "filled" at the $565, in fact, because of the volatility; the price that your market order gets filled at is $560. So even though you wanted to lose only $500 on the trade, due to slippage, you are $1,000 in the red.

For a small $10,000 or $15,000 account a $1,000 loss in trading capital is significant.

A stop-loss order that gets executed when new sell (if you're long) or new buy (if you're short) contracts are being initiated is a recipe for disaster. The commercials, the actual buyers and sellers, rule the markets and set the tone for the activity. If you are on the wrong side of their flexing their market muscle, you could even find yourself "lock limit" on the wrong side of a trade.

Stops can't:

Protect you from gaps.

Protect you from whipsawing.

Protect you from slippage.

Protect you from your emotions.

Be used with a good-till-canceled order in electronic markets.

They are the last resort of a desperate trader!

Traders who use only stop orders lose on three fronts: (1) they can lose more on a trade than expected; (2) they diminish an account's leverage capabilities; and (3) there is the opportunity cost of not being able to switch their position around fast enough to take advantage of the market's new direction.

There are nine tactics that can give you much greater control of your losing trades that far exceed the abilities of a stop-loss order alone. They are used by institutional traders, money managers, and successful speculators. They are accessible for anyone to learn.

Power of the Limit Order

Limit orders are a step above stop orders because they give you some control. Unfortunately, they still force you to be very accurate in your predictions. If you don't get the numbers just right, you could find yourself missing opportunities or, worse, in losing trades because of a few points getting you into a trade.

The definition of a *limit order* is "an order placed with a brokerage to buy or sell a commodity at a specified price or better." Limit orders also allow an investor to limit the length of time an order can be outstanding before being cancelled.

Problems with limit orders include the following:

- They can't guarantee entry in a market.
- They can't guarantee exit in a market.
- They can't protect you from market whipsawing.
- They can't be used with a good-till-cancelled order in electronic markets.
- They are better than stop orders, but still incomplete!

DETERMINE WHAT TYPE OF TRADER YOU ARE

To be a successful risk management user, you also have to know the type of trader you are or aspire to be. Too many traders attempt to pigeonhole themselves into titles and trading styles that often do not match their personality or goals.

As I have said time and time again throughout this book, be true to yourself and your ambitions. The farther you stray from them, the more difficult it is for you to succeed. You end up pushing boundaries and envelopes that may exceed your skill and learning curve.

I developed the list of the types of traders. There is no Oxford Dictionary or Investopedia listing behind these. The words are just my interpretation of what I have seen over the years.

Once you define yourself as a trader, the field of risk management may narrow down from nine techniques to two techniques. Regardless of the type of trader you may want to become, keep in mind that your lifestyle may not accommodate that type, and it's okay. Recognize that you will constantly be evolving and developing your skills as a trader. You may change which definition will apply to you as time goes on. Until then, enjoy.

Day Trader

This is your standard e-mini, forex, and bond trader. They are in and out the same day with the maximum gain, attempting to achieve the minimum loss. They typically don't see the big picture; they are attempting get a specific point or pip spread, or they are attempting to make a specific amount of money every day.

The disappointment that these types of traders see every day is that they rarely understand the level of time commitment involved. They also find it difficult to justify their winnings because when they calculate man-hours spent to total income earned, it quickly becomes apparent that they could have made more working in the retail setting.

The common pitfall of every day trader is overcoming the mantra of "do not chase the markets." Unfortunately, technical indicators are lagging, so by the time you get into a trade, the potential momentum simply may not be there.

Swing Trader

Swing traders are typically betting on time. They are looking for 3- to 10-day streaks of the market's momentum. The goal is to do your best, within a short time span, to picking the most recent tops and bottoms and to profit by catching the retracement.

The swing trader's job is the most difficult. Picking the highs and the lows of a market can be the most impossible task to accomplish. Unless you have tools that can approximate where they can be, it is easy to get stuck in a trade assuming that you have picked the top or bottom and then get steamrolled by the market going in the opposite direction.

If you can catch the beginning of one of these moves, that's great; you simply need the tools that will protect you just in case you didn't pick well.

Position Trader

The position trader is going for the gusto. He is looking to catch the big waves, for example, oil from $12 to $76, gold from $300 up to almost $800, and the euro run from $0.89 to over $1.30. Although not very common in futures and forex trading, there is room for it.

By weathering all market fluctuations in pursuit of the maximum profit on the long-term trend, you have an opportunity to be rewarded. The trick is to successfully roll over money and purchase the right protective hedges to get your trade to behave properly as months and years roll by. When done properly, since the futures market is a "mark to market" account, you can actually take profits along the way and still maintain your position.

The hardest part is to just be at the right place at the right time.

WHAT RISK MANAGEMENT TOOLS CAN DO FOR YOU

Being able to effectively use risk management techniques puts you in an elite status of trading. When done right, risk management techniques can:

- Reduce margin requirements.
- Improve control of trades.
- Eliminate exposure to unnecessary risk.
- Put you in control of fear and greed in your trading.
- Increase your percentage of successes.
- Bolster your account returns.
- Change the way you think about trading!

In this chapter we will explore nine distinct risk management techniques. I would suggest that you study them, paper trade them, and gain a firm grasp of the type of trader you are and the trader you want to be, so that you can find the right risk management tools for you. Once that's accomplished, you open up a whole new world of possibilities for yourself.

NINE RISK MANAGEMENT TACTICS

I neither invented nor created the nine risk management tactics that follow. Each concept can be found in multiple books as definitions or concepts. What makes this book unique is the fact that we have addressed and aggregated various risk management tactics as a way to help elevate your trading and round out your overall trading plan.

These techniques are designed to give you as much leeway as possible in being wrong, while at the same time opening your mind up to the style of trading practiced by the hedgers and CTAs we discussed in Chapter 12. Combining these tactics with the proper money management technique and macro/micro technical analysis presents you with a rare opportunity to take a holistic approach to your trading.

The following nine risk management techniques will be defined and presented in a before-and-after format by the charts. Again, I did not invent any of these risk management techniques, nor do I claim to have perfected them. They have all been around in some form or fashion. Various authors and educators have usually taken one of these risk management techniques and elaborated them to the point of being a panacea of trading.

Of the nine, I like none better than the others, nor do I feel that any are inherently better than the other ones. They are all tools meant to be used in your arsenal to protect you from the risk of loss. Be fluid in your use and experimentation of each of the various tools until you find one that resonates for you.

Later in the chapter I break down which risk management techniques I feel are best applied to day/spot traders, swing traders, and position traders. While I don't believe my suggestions are set in stone, the breakdown will give you a sense of my logic and give you the ability to choose to use them or not as I suggested.

The nine risk management strategies that we focus on in this book are as follows:

1. Synthetics
2. Spread trading
3. Hard stops
4. Covered options
5. Hedges
6. Collars
7. Straddles
8. Strangles
9. Ratio spreads

In no way are these the only risk management tools that money managers use. These are techniques that I feel are easily accessible for the retail client and may open your mind to doing a little more research to learn more about these tactics as well as others.

The nine risk management strategies are simply introduced to stretch your comfort zone away from the old fashioned "stop" or "stop limit" techniques and to get you to utilize any one of these techniques on a regular basis in conjunction with stops and stop limits if necessary.

All of these techniques are best traded in the front months of a market; otherwise, make sure that the option you are hedging with and the futures contract always share the same month as well.

1. Synthetics

Action: Long futures—buy put

Short futures—buy call

I call them the synthetics, but technically what we have created is a "synthetic option." The reason why traders enjoy options so much is that, unlike futures, which have unlimited risk, they have a limited risk, but unlimited gain potential. The problem with trading options by themselves is threefold.

First, in order to succeed when purchasing an option outright, you have to be skilled at picking the right strike price. The strike price has to be far enough away to be of a reasonable price and a reasonable likelihood of the market's reaching it. Otherwise, you may find that the volatility of the option has driven the price up so much that the likelihood of your making a decent return on the option becomes difficult. This leads to the second problem.

Just because the underlying futures or spot market has hit your targeted price doesn't mean you are suddenly making money. In order for an option to become profitable, the market must hit your strike plus the premium you paid in order to obtain the option. Many a new option trader has been baffled by the fact that the market is at or slightly exceeding their strike price, and yet the value of their option is below where they purchased it.

Which brings us to a third problem—delta. The delta represents the rate of speed at which the option market moves in relation to the underlying futures or spot contract. Even if the option is in the money, there is no guarantee that the value of the option will move in tandem with the underlying market. It could move faster, but often it moves slower. A one-point move in the underlying contracts can mean that the option moves at half the speed, 0.5 or, at 80% of the speed, 0.8, of the underlying market. This can be frustrating and can sometimes mean that trading the options may be more trouble than they are worth. After all, 70% to 80% of options do expire worthless.

There are "synthetic futures," but I believe they are a little advanced for this book and don't serve the purpose of being truly risk management techniques by themselves.

Now let's talk about the "synthetic option" and why it is superior to the regular option.

As we have talked about the daisy-chain relationship among the spot market, futures, and options, so should the hierarchy of trading be. If you can trade full-size futures and spot contracts by putting up 80% or better of the face value, that is your best trading bet. Money management–wise, you will be able to weather more of the up-and-down fluctuations and really be able to see how trades come to fruition, much like the stock market.

Your second best bet is to use leveraged futures or leveraged spot. While you are not as capable of weathering huge fluctuations, you are putting up a little money to be able to earn money just as if you were an actual banker, farmer, or major wholesale buyer. The futures markets move in tandem with the spot and have the most volume next to the spot market. While the futures market is meant to be insurance for the spot market, it still functions pretty close to the way the stock market does.

Your last resort should be the options market. Options may be the least expensive, but they also lack significant volume, based on the strike price, and they are the least like the spot or futures market. They really are designed as insurance tools.

For the most part, I recommend that you use the futures or spot contract every chance you get, and let options operate as your primary insurance tools.

In a synthetic option position, that is exactly what happens. When you put on a futures position, you have unlimited risk and unlimited gain potential. Stops are used to mitigate your risk, but they can be incomplete. By using an "at-the-money" option, tied directly to your futures contract, you have effectively limited your risk, while still retaining your opportunity for unlimited gain.

By creating this synthetic option, you get the benefit of the regular option with none of its drawbacks. You don't have to worry about whether delta is one for one, you don't have to worry about selecting the right strike price because you are in "at the money," and you are in control of your "premium." If the market is going your way, you do not have to retain the option you purchased. You can exit it any time, minimizing the amount that you paid for it, while still having gains in your primary futures position.

So you can have all of the benefits of a futures position and the key benefit of an option position—limited risk—at your fingertips. This is one of the simplest, yet most overlooked, risk management techniques I know.

A little later we will look at something similar—hard stops. There are some subtle differences, so watch out for them.

Let's tackle a few charts. Figure 13.1 is a typical example of a chart I would use on my screen. It has all of the technical analysis tools that I use and the setup points that I would use to determine exactly where I would place my futures and options contracts to create a synthetic.

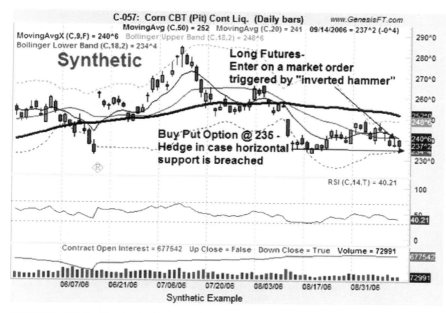

FIGURE 13.1 Synthetic Chart (Before)
Source: Genesis Financial Technologies, Inc. (www.tradenavigator.com).

Some of you may recognize this chart; it's an example of the corn chart but a little more hectic than previous examples. There are a lot of things going on, but that doesn't stop me from asking the main technical analysis questions: Where is the market going?, How fast is it getting there?, and When will it arrive?

While the market is underneath the 50-day MA, 252, it has also based out on the horizontal support line around 235. Since the goal is to catch the market on any potential upswing from this support level, we go long at the first entry signal we see; in this instance, we put an "entry signal" at the inverted hammer. We search out a protective put option close to the 237 entry price, and we put on a 235 put option to protect ourselves.

The price distance between 237 and 235 is $100—fairly close protection. Our first profit target is 252, 50-day MA, potential $850, and the option we purchased for $400. Using our 50% money management rule on holding on to options puts us with a potential loss of $300 to gain $850—well within the "risk one to gain two" money management rules.

In Figure 13.2, we see the follow-up to our activity. The corn market holds steady to its horizontal support at 235. After a few days, it breaks through the 50-day MA and gets up to 264—a horizontal resistance point. From 235 to 264 is 29 cents or $1,450. If you had exited the put option at

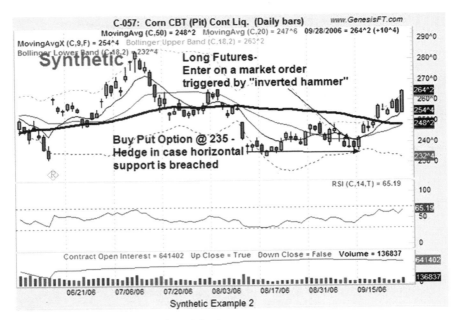

FIGURE 13.2   Synthetic Chart (After)
Source: Genesis Financial Technologies, Inc. (www.tradenavigator.com).

the 50% rule, you would have had a net profit of $1,250. If you had held on to your put option instead of selling it, in anticipation of a later turnaround, you would have netted $1,000 on the synthetic call.

There are several reasons you may want to execute a synthetic option instead of purchasing a call position outright. The first reason is the cost of the call option. The closer an option's strike price is to the current futures month, the more expensive it is, particularly if it is in the same direction that the general market sentiment is going in.

Second, options don't always move one for one in price with the futures contract. So by having your futures position, you are accruing gains faster. Finally, synthetics allow you to ride out larger fluctuations in the marketplace, while giving you the opportunity to hold on to larger positions for a longer period of time.

What's the Worst That Can Happen?   *Scenario 1:* If the market stays sideways, the time value of your option erodes and you lose all of your option premium of $400.

Scenario 2: The market tanks, so on your futures position you lose the $100 distance between your 237 entry and the option kick-in at 235.

Depending on the delta of the put option, you would need to reach 231 or better before you could begin to make profits off of your option position.

You have the opportunity to lose $100, or you could make money from your put position without chasing the market or being whipsawed—not a bad opportunity.

The great part about it is that you can calculate all of your opportunities for profit and loss in advance.

2. Spread Trading

Spread trading has long been the domain of seasonal commodity traders, whether it was to take advantage of old crop–new crop opportunities in agricultural commodities or to take advantage of interest rate discrepancies. Spread trading is simply the buying and selling of the same futures contract but in different months.

When an average investor decides to spread trade futures contracts he receives favorable treatment. This is similar to the favorable treatment that hedgers (those who actually buy and sell the actual commodity) receive. Since a spread trade is considered to have diminished risk (one side is long, the other side is short), the margin requirements are one half to one fourth the price of a stand-alone contract.

Let's take the gold futures, for example. The futures margin is $2,025. If you decide to spread trade, the margin is only $608. This is a $1,417 difference.

There are many different criteria for why you would choose spread trading over an outright contract. You may believe that there is a discrepancy in price (contango versus backwardation activity), believe in the market's long-term bullishness or bearishness, or weak or heavy supply and demand.

Regardless of what you use to determine your spread trade, it is definitely one of the most flexible of the risk management tactics. At the same time, it can be one of the more dangerous risk management techniques as well.

Figure 13.3 shows an example of the November 2006 and January 2007 orange juice contracts.

In this example we are looking at an opportunity to take advantage of the November orange juice contract. The contract has a small bullish hammer developing, and we decide to go long the November contract.

In Figure 13.4, just two short days after we entered the November orange juice contract, we see a huge up day. The November contract flies from 150 to 200 in just three days. What makes this scenario interesting is that the November has now exceeded the January 2007 orange juice price.

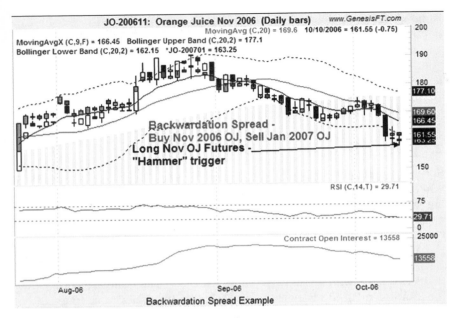

FIGURE 13.3 Spread Trading Chart (Before)
Source: Genesis Financial Technologies, Inc. (www.tradenavigator.com).

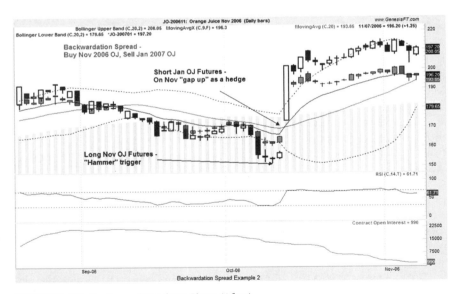

FIGURE 13.4 Spread Trading Chart (After)
Source: Genesis Financial Technologies, Inc. (www.tradenavigator.com).

This is known as an example of backwardation, when the front contract months exceed the value of the further-out months.

As a precautionary act to lock in profits and potentially catch any future giant leaps we go ahead and short the January 2007 contract while simultaneously maintaining the November 2006 position.

What's the Worst That Can Happen?   Pick your spreading opportunities carefully. The worst thing that can happen is that you can lose on both legs of the spread. So even though you are gaining a reduced margin, if the November position starts to go down in value and the January position starts to go up, opposite of your current situation, you will mount twice as many losses.

The trick to working with spreads is twofold. First, you have to have a strategy. I prefer working with spreads when there are backwardation opportunities. We know that backwardation is unnatural, with the front months being more valuable than further-out months. When this occurs, there are opportunities to buy or sell the market. Depending on the expiration date and notice days, you will pick and choose which contracts to buy and sell.

Particularly around contract expiration dates, there are opportunities to benefit from price convergence. At this time the spot market and futures contracts prices have to match in order to eliminate excessive arbitrage opportunities. The only reason why backwardation exists is that there has been a fundamental shift in either supply or demand that has driven up the value. This change in value self-corrects when the futures contract reaches expiration.

When using spreads, use a two-pronged trading strategy. The spread is the first line of defense; the second is money management parameters backed up with stop limits.

3. Hard Stops

As we have learned, stop orders or "soft stops" are inherently flawed because they turn into market orders and allow slippage to creep in.

Hard stops are just the opposite. A hard stop has the ability to actually stop your losses at the exact price you want. The secret? Use an option. By purchasing an option that is opposite to your futures position, at specific price points you are capable of limiting if not eliminating your slippage loss.

What makes using an option as a hard stop different than making a "synthetic option" is the fact that it is not necessarily close to the futures contract price. The goal is to set the option price 5%, maybe even 10%, in losses outside your futures entry price. You may even use a stop to exit

FIGURE 13.5 Hard Stop (Before)
Source: Genesis Financial Technologies, Inc. (www.tradenavigator.com).

the futures position and hold on to the "hard stop option," waiting until the futures price rebounds back in the direction you expected.

In Figure 13.5, we look at the corn market. We find that there is horizontal resistance around the 270 area. So we purchase a 270 call to protect ourselves. The actual futures market has failed to break through the 20-day MA and has penetrated horizontal support. We look to enter at the current price of 260'6, with a first profit target of 250 and a second profit target of 245.

Between your entry of 260 and the protection of 270 is 10 cents or $500. $500 is 10% of a $5,000 account and 5% of a $10,000 account. This is a significant amount of leeway between your protection and your trade. The benefit is that you don't have to worry about slippage because you know your losses can't exceed that specific price; otherwise, the option begins to gain in value.

In Figure 13.6, you are able to see how the market evolves. The price drops down to our first profit target of 250 before it rebounds, giving us a profit of $500. The difficult part of using the option as a hard stop is maintaining the discipline to exit the option at no more than a 50% stop loss. If you hold on to it, it will diminish the overall profit that you make and defeat the purpose of why you used it in the first place.

FIGURE 13.6 Hard Stop (After)
Source: Genesis Financial Technologies, Inc. (www.tradenavigator.com).

What's the Worst That Can Happen? Timing is everything! By using the option as a hard stop, you have to be conscious that you do not want your futures trade to go against you. If you hold on to your futures trade as it is going against you and you have an option "hard stop" out $500 or $1,000 away from your entry price, you end up simply locking in your losses.

It's no fun seeing a trade rack up losses and knowing that you can do nothing about it. If you exit the futures contract and book your losses, there is no assurance that the option will continue to be successful.

Never let your futures contract meet or match your option strike price.

4. Covered Option

A popular way for people to generate income from trading is by selling options. While it is no secret that 70% to 80% of options expire worthless, the problem with selling options is the tremendous risk associated with it. While the income derived from selling options is fixed, the amount of risk that a trader takes on is unlimited.

So for those that want to actively sell options as a way to generate income, the goal is to diminish the risk while at the same time generating the most assured income available. This is where the "covered option" comes in.

If you sell a call, go long a futures contract; if you sell a put, go short a futures contract. The futures position protects you from exposure to the potential of unlimited risk while you generate the income from selling the option.

There are two ways to take advantage of the covered option: You can sell one option and obtain one appropriate futures contract to protect yourself, or you can play around with delta.

Since we know that options move at varying rates to the futures contract, you may be able to sell multiple options and protect them with one or two futures contracts. This is typical of options that may be out of the money. Often, these options can move at one fifth, one fourth, or one third the actual futures value.

In Figure 13.7, we have a corn contract. We look at the simplest type of covered option, a one-for-one. You sell one put option and you cover it with a short position. You can sell an option at around the 250 level to gain the most premium, around $750 in this instance.

We picked this area because it is sitting right on top of horizontal support. If the market breaks, there is a stop limit to help you enter your short contract, so that your losses can be minimized; if it doesn't break through and rebounds, we never have to establish the short position.

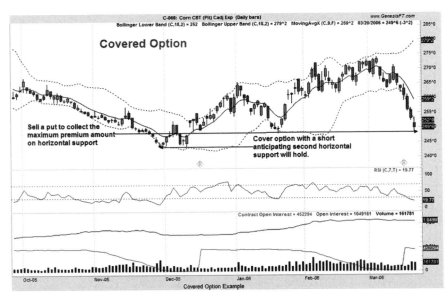

FIGURE 13.7 Covered Option (Before)
Source: Genesis Financial Technologies, Inc. (www.tradenavigator.com).

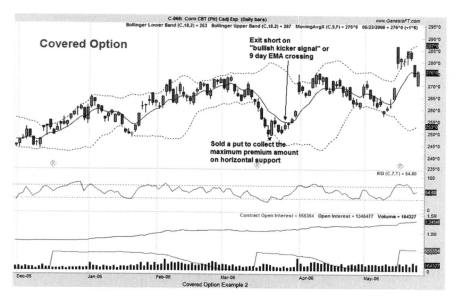

FIGURE 13.8 Covered Option (After)
Source: Genesis Financial Technologies, Inc. (www.tradenavigator.com).

If you choose to be more conservative in your trading and establish the short position simultaneously as you sell your put option, you must have a trigger that will get you out of your losing future position. In Figure 13.8, we use the "bullish candlestick kicker" signal to get us out of the trade.

Unfortunately, the amount of losses that we accrue in our short position is subtracted from the premium we collect in order to give us our net profit. In this instance we lost 3 cents or $150 on our $750 in collected premium. Netting us a total of $600.

What's the Worst That Can Happen? If you have sold an options contract, you have to understand that the risk of selling based on delta percentages can be severe. If the market moves against you, the delta of the options can change to match the futures, and the three, four, or five options that you have sold may begin to move rapidly against the one futures contract with which you were protecting them. You can quickly find that you bit off more than you can chew.

5. Hedges

There is a misunderstanding by everyday investors as to the true nature of the futures and options markets. Since the creation of the "forward"

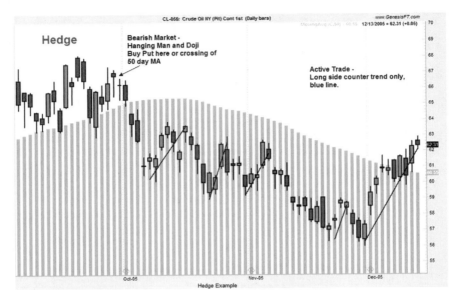

FIGURE 13.9 Hedges Short
Source: Genesis Financial Technologies, Inc. (www.tradenavigator.com).

contract, the precursor to the futures contract, some believe as far back as Egyptian times, the goal has been to "limit" risk or to create "insurance" against unforeseen price fluctuations due to supply and demand.

The everyday investor rarely takes advantage of the inherent daisy-chain insurance effect. The spot market is protected by the futures market. The futures market is protected by the option market. The option market can protect the spot market.

The best way to exploit this relationship is by using technical analysis to determine the long-term trend of the futures or spot market; use the macro technical analysis tools to identify this. Once that's determined, purchase an option that follows that long-term trend.

When you trade the futures or spot market, you then use micro technical analysis tools to determine entry for the countertrend and to exit the market when it begins to follow the trend.

In Figure 13.9, we take a look at the crude oil contract. The gray bars represent the 50-day MA. Once the crude oil market's price crosses the 50-day MA, purchase an at-the-money or slightly out-of-the-money put option, in this case.

Now, as an active trader, you can focus on only one side of the market—the long side. The option is taking care of the short side, so every time the proper entry tools show the market moving countertrend to the overall trend—in this case, long—you buy the market.

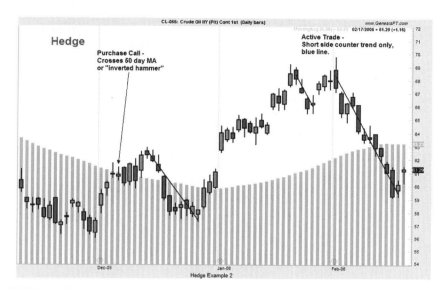

FIGURE 13.10 Hedges Long
Source: Genesis Financial Technologies, Inc. (www.tradenavigator.com).

My indicators showed five opportunities on a swing-trading basis. If you are an active day trader, there will be more buy-side signals.

In Figure 13.10, we see the crude oil prices crossing the 50-day MA on the long side and only three countertrend sell opportunities.

What's the Worst That Can Happen? I believe that there is little downside risk, but there are three tools that you must have:

1. The ability to identify the trend.
2. The ability to identify the countertrend.
3. The discipline to exit the counter trend *immediately* when it is no longer going your way.

For effective day traders, this system can be a boon for you. You will find your trading flowing more smoothly and your skills will become honed as a buy-side or sell-side specialist. No more whipsawing, no more chasing the market.

6. Collars

A collar trade occurs when you combine a hard stop tactic or a synthetic call or put tactic with the selling of an option.

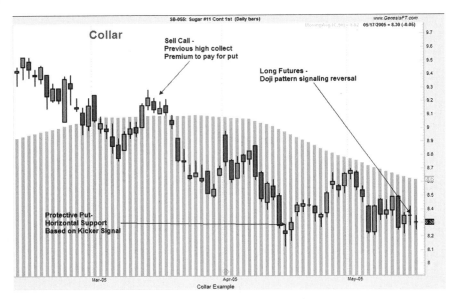

FIGURE 13.11   Collars (Before)
Source: Genesis Financial Technologies, Inc. (www.tradenavigator.com).

This is a way for you to get the market to pay for your option that you are using as an insurance tool. For smaller accounts, this is a way to offset the cost yet still relish in the protection.

In Figure 13.11, we put on a sugar synthetic call position, buy a futures contract at $8.40, buy a $8.30 put option, and then sell a $9.30 call option.

By selling the $9.30 call option, you would be paid a "premium." This premium has the ability to discount or offset the total you spent on purchasing your gold $8.30 put option, effectively making your futures trade very structured and limiting its risk.

In Figure 13.12, we see that the futures contract made a total of $1,232. Once the futures market reaches the same price as the sold call, any profits above and beyond are forfeited to the option purchaser at $9.30.

What's the Worst That Can Happen?   Once you put on a collar, you have to set it and forget it. You can't use moving options to protect your profits, you can't buy back the sold option, and you simply cannot touch the trade whatsoever.

Once you set it up, the numbers work in equilibrium, but you have to take the trade until its logical conclusion. This is only when the futures trade is going in the direction you expect it to go.

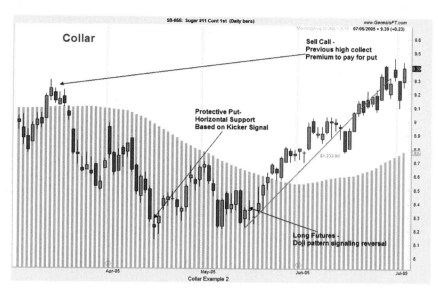

FIGURE 13.12 Collars (After)
Source: Genesis Financial Technologies, Inc. (www.tradenavigator.com).

If the futures market is not moving in the direction you expect, make sure you use your money management stop-loss technique. Exit the futures trade and let yourself collect the premium from the call you sold and revert your option that you were using as loss protection into your new trade.

7. Straddles

The purchase or sale of an equal number of puts and calls, with the same strike price and expiration dates.

As a trader, the question you have to ask yourself is: Is it more important to be right about the markets or to be profitable? Your answer should be profitable!

No one has a crystal ball on where the markets will go. This is particularly true before critical announcements and when a market is range bound.

In our example we take the Treasury bond market when it is moving in a sideways pattern and purchase a put and call at the 110 area, total cost $2,500. The market breaks out to the upside in Figure 13.14, and we leave the put on the wayside.

What's the Worst That Can Happen? This is a very expensive trade. You have to purchase two in the money options oblivious to what the

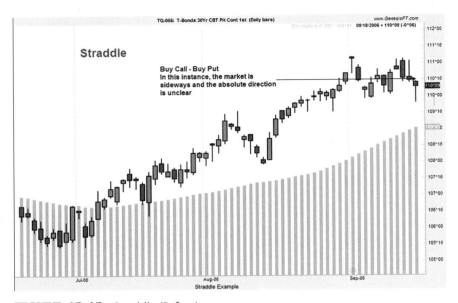

FIGURE 13.13 Straddle (Before)
Source: Genesis Financial Technologies, Inc. (www.tradenavigator.com).

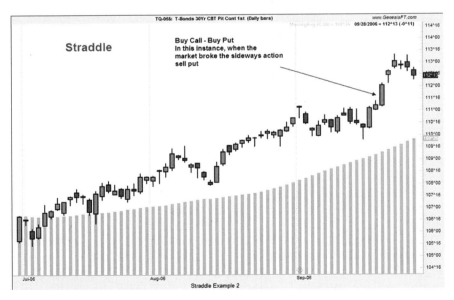

FIGURE 13.14 Straddle (After)
Source: Genesis Financial Technologies, Inc. (www.tradenavigator.com).

outcome is. You must then be able to pull the trigger on the nonworking option as quickly as possible. For a smaller account, it can be difficult to execute this kind of trade. This is not for people who hesitate.

8. Strangles

Strangles are slightly different from straddles. We discussed before about finding horizontal resistance and support. By purchasing a call just outside of resistance and a put just outside of support, you are able to wait out sideways trading activity.

By purchasing this call and put option away from the current price (out of the money), you will pay significantly less than if you put on straddle, but you will have the same opportunity to profit on any news that is volatile to either side.

In Figure 13.15, we are looking at the same Treasury bond chart as the straddle example. This time, we look at two significant candlesticks in the horizontal resistance and support lines. On the resistance line, we see a former hanging man at the 111'04; we look to purchase a call at the 111 strike price.

On the support line we see the hammer tail around 109'24. We purchase our put at 110' because 109 is too far away from the action.

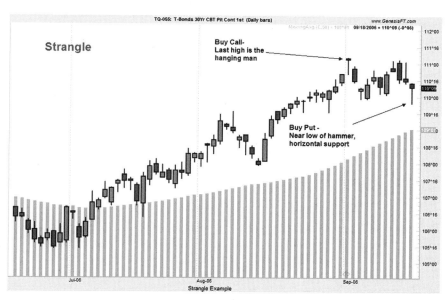

FIGURE 13.15 Strangle (Before)
Source: Genesis Financial Technologies, Inc. (www.tradenavigator.com).

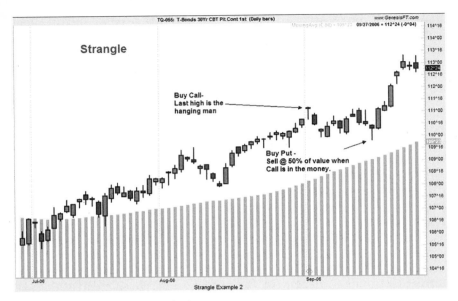

FIGURE 13.16 Strangle (After)
Source: Genesis Financial Technologies, Inc. (www.tradenavigator.com).

The cash difference between the 111 call and the 110 put is $1,000. The costs for both options were $1,843, $625, and $1,218, respectively.

In Figure 13.16, we see the call gain in value and make it to 113, approximately a $2,000 profit. Subtract the one half the cost of the put that failed—$609—and we end up with a net profit $1,391.

What's the Worst That Can Happen?   We know that there are three directions a market can move in: up, down, or sideways. You can get caught in a situation where the market simply doesn't break out of the range or briefly breaks out only to slump back in. In that situation, just like a straddle, you can lose all of the premium for both your put and your call.

9. Ratio Spreads

Ratio spreads are similar to collars in the sense that you get the market to pay for part of your trading. The concept is simple, you sell an in-the-money put or call to collect enough premium to purchase to slightly out-of-the-money put or calls, the same direction as you sold the option.

One option that you buy is designed to cover your risk associated with selling the option to collect premium. The other option is partially or fully paid for from the selling of the "in-the-money option" and is designed to

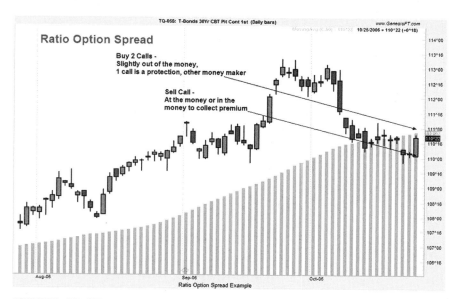

FIGURE 13.17 Ratio Spread (Before)
Source: Genesis Financial Technologies, Inc. (www.tradenavigator.com).

cover the gap between option you bought and sold and to become your money maker.

In Figure 13.17, we take the Treasury bond chart and decide to sell an in-the-money option call at the 110 price level. We collect a premium of almost $1,800. We then purchase two slightly out-of-the-money call options for only $2,000. So we purchase one option for protection, and for the second option, our money maker, we only paid $200.

This second option is designed to cover the distance between 110 and 111, or $1,000, and pay for the $200 we paid to obtain it. So we know that in order to make this trade successful, we need for the price of Treasury bonds to exceed 112.

In Figure 13.18, the market does just that. The options we bought at 111 get to a high of 113.16. This generates a profit of $2,406 per contract. Subtract the $1,000 you have to cover for the distance between the option you sold and the options you bought and you have a subtotal of $1,406.

In the end, you risked $200 to make $1,406. In any universe this risking 1 to potentially gain 7 risk-reward ratio works out.

What's the Worst That Can Happen? You have to have a market bias when you take advantage of a ratio spread. You will have three call

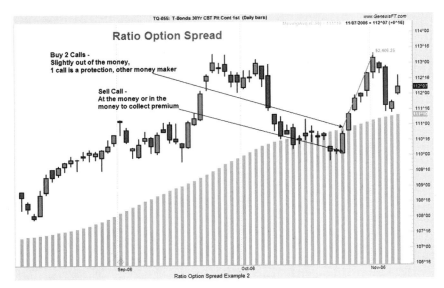

FIGURE 13.18   Ratio Spread (After)
Source: Genesis Financial Technologies, Inc. (www.tradenavigator.com).

contracts or three put contracts and you will be heavily committed to the position. So there are two worst-case scenarios.

In the previous example, if the market collapses, you will have collected premium in the amount of $1,800 and spent $2,000. You are upside down in the trade for $200.

Another bad scenario is if the market moves slightly up but for the most part stays sideways. If it moves up to 111'51 or around there and hovers around 112. We know that in order for a seller to be willing to collect or exercise his option he is looking for the strike price to be reached along with the premium. The option we sold was at 110 so his exercise number is 111'51. At that point we give back the $1,800 in premium we collected.

Our options are barely in the money; we need our options to exceed 112 in order to exercise them. If it doesn't, then we are on the hook for the $1,800, plus the $2,000 it cost to purchase the option minus anything we can salvage to offset our expenses. This can easily be a $3,800 loss if you do not manage it right.

RISK MANAGEMENT TOOLS BEST SUITED FOR YOUR TRADING STYLE

All of the risk management strategies/tactics I have presented in this chapter can be mixed and matched together. They can be used in part or in whole. You have full discretion on how you can manipulate and use these tools to your benefit.

As long as you keep in mind your primary objective, minimizing your risk, you can work out the numbers in advance and discover for yourself the endless possibilities for profiting.

Below is my recommended list of best tools for various styles. These are just suggestions, apply any of the tools as necessary to your trading to help you succeed. Keep in mind you can still use limits and stops, but place them on trades where you have risk management tools in place—do not rely on them to be your sole means of risk management.

Suggested Day Trader Risk Management Tools

Straddle: The purchase or sale of an equal number of puts and calls, with the same strike price and expiration dates.

Strangle: An options strategy involving a put option and a call option with the same expiration dates and strike price that are out of the money.

Hedge: Long or short your position protecting yourself with currency futures contract or option.

Suggested Swing Trader Risk Management Tools

Collar: Sell an option with a synthetic.

Option as a hard stop. Use your money management rules against absolute loss.

Suggested Position Trader Risk Management Tools

Synthetic: Long futures—buy put, short futures—buy call.

Futures spread. Buying and selling the same futures contract but in different months.

PROPER RISK MANAGEMENT

Risk management deals with loss. Too many traders come to trading not understanding that the loss can be managed and sometimes even eliminated, if you use the right tools. The nine strategies in this chapter are just the beginning. You can mix and match them together, you can select one or two as your favorite, or you can discover ways to manage risk that were never mentioned in this book. Regardless of what you do, constantly be prepared for loss—it is inevitable—and more importantly, be able to turn that loss to your favor.

CHAPTER 14

Lesson 7: Building Confidence

You cannot know if you will be successful or not. You can only prepare for battle, and it must be done with all of your heart and with all of your consciousness.

—Sun Tzu, *The Art of War*

There are programs out there that claim you can be a multimillion-dollar trader in just 30 minutes a day, or that if you follow the green and red arrows, untold riches will be yours. To be truthful, I hope these programs work. More often than not, beginning traders use these programs as a gateway into learning that trading is difficult.

That's what this book has been all about. There is a systematic way to approach trading, and you are capable of learning it and executing it. As the saying goes, it's simple but not easy. This book is not intended to replace anything that you may currently be doing that is successful. It has been designed for you to pare away the things that may not have been working in your trading while helping you round out your trading plan by utilizing a three-step approach.

My intent has been to make you a complete trader—a trader who incorporates money management, technical analysis, and risk management strategies, together, in order to be successful. If you believe that one strategy is superior to the other, then I have failed in my job in helping you succeed in your trading. The reality is that every trading plan has to go beyond technical analysis, beyond stops, and beyond simply the percentages of loss. I hope that you can come to that same realization.

By having a systematic approach to the markets, you will know why you make money and, more importantly, why you lose money. Understanding both of these occurrences will catapult your trading from just an art into a customized science that you can control. I want you to use my ideas that make sense for you and discard the ones that don't. I want you to mix and match my concepts and add your own spin on each one of the trading plan areas.

As students of the markets, we are all evolving the "what we do" of the way we do things; that's natural. "How we do it" need not change. As long as you are constantly conscious of the three components—money management, technical analysis, and risk management—then you have placed yourself in the elite company of the 5 percenters.

In this chapter we will explore three key areas so that you can better improve your trading over time. First, we will explore the 10 mistakes that all traders make; second, we will tackle how to properly demo and paper trade; and, finally, we will look at three tools that can help reinforce the concepts of the book.

10 MISTAKES ALL TRADERS MAKE

Trading is not easy. In fact, it can be one of the most difficult endeavors anyone can take on. Whether you have been trading for 6 months or 30 years, bad habits have a tendency to creep up. While there are many ways to lose money in the markets, there are 10 common mistakes that every trader, new or experienced, makes over and over again. When you can identify the mistakes, you give yourself a leg up in making sure they don't affect you.

1. Misuse Leverage

Leverage is the only thing that separates futures and forex from all other investments. It is both misunderstood by the novices and misused by the semiexperienced. Leverage is the cornerstone of why every trader both succeeds and fails in futures and forex investing.

This is both a blessing and a curse. While it is so exciting to imagine the possibility of making thousands if not tens of thousands of dollars from a few thousand, little attention is paid to the "what if" of loss.

This can express itself in one of three ways. Either they don't understand the true value of the futures or forex contracts they are trading, they are looking to put too much money in one trade, or they trade too many different types of markets. Or it can be all of the above.

The key way to avoid misusing leverage is by taking the time to really understand what it can and cannot do. While leverage can help a good trader be successful, it cannot make a bad trader do better than he already is doing. In fact, it will actually magnify his poor decision-making skills and inability to trade.

If you have and use discipline when applying leverage and money management techniques consistently, then you will be able to have your use of leverage under control.

2. Confuse Speculation with Gambling

Speculation and gambling are not the same. As we have discussed before, gambling involves chance, while speculation doesn't. More importantly, how traders express their attitudes toward their money is the best example of the view they have of what they are doing.

The most disturbing of these views is the belief that the money they make in the market is actually "house money." Somehow the money you make in the market is inferior to the money you brought to the market. This can be extremely dangerous in trade choice, stop-loss execution, and how profits are plowed back into your account or within various other trades.

Remember the words from *The Richest Man in Babylon:* Part of what you earn is yours to keep. This is too often overlooked when it comes to trading. You are trading to make money, don't make the mistake of trading your profits back into the market solely because of some misconceived notion that you are trading with the market's money. It's all your money—don't gamble it away.

3. Improperly Funding Account

Trading is a business, plain and simple. Like many businesses, it fails due to either too much capital or, more importantly, too little capital. When there is strong volatility that meets high ego, with a healthy dose of too little money in the account, disaster will ensue.

While there are commercials advocating trading spot forex with as little as a few hundred dollars, the question you must ask yourself is: Am I a "subsistence" trader or am I looking to thrive?

It's been said that the average investor 20 years ago would invest $5,000 in the futures market. Fast forward to the present; that same investor still invests $5,000. With no adjustment for inflation and little thought to what the real-world equivalent should be, traders are still throwing $5,000 at the markets to get started.

Once you understand the markets you want to trade, you will then properly place the right amount of capital into the markets. Or you will change your approach to how you trade the markets. Whatever the case may be, attempt to find equilibrium, capital versus market, that will work for you, and don't trade above that.

For markets where you may want to day trade, utilizing boosted or geared leverage is fine. Simply don't trade the full number of contracts that you are capable of. If you have a $2,000 account that is allowed to be traded like a $20,000 account, don't be afraid to use only one half or one fourth of the total amount available to you.

This goes for the spot forex market as well; just because you have 500-to-1 leverage doesn't mean you have to use 500-to-1 leverage. Manipulate your leverage to your liking in order to make the capital you have last as long as possible.

4. Choosing Costs over Quality

Execution is only one aspect of commissions. There are many companies that offer barebones commissions in return for zero service. In fact, they do not even keep any licensed professionals on hand to deal with your problems and require that you keep a second account somewhere else to offset your trades in case there are any glitches.

Unlike many other investments, futures and forex in no way have reached critical mass, yet for those that are current traders price has been falsely been perceived as a "unique selling point" to the total abandon of all of the ancillary, but important features necessary to have an enjoyable trading experience.

Look for a mixture of full-service hand holding and fast execution in order to have a happy trading experience. If you don't, you will find yourself in the same boat as 90% of most traders that switch brokers at least three times in their trading life.

5. Misunderstanding the Differences of Trading

Just because the most recent guru promotes "day, swing, or position" trading doesn't mean that you are capable of emulating that same kind of trading. In fact by focusing on a style of trading instead of the markets to be traded will prove the downfall of the majority of novice traders time and time again.

It's more important to become familiar with the margins, volatility, and rhythms of the market you are trading as opposed to artificially opposing time constraints on the market you are trading.

To recap the different types of traders:

Day trader: A trader who holds positions for a very short time (from minutes to hours) and makes numerous trades each day. Most trades are entered and closed out within the same day.

Swing trader: A style of trading that attempts to capture gains within one to four days

Long-term/position trader: A commodities trader who holds a long position for the long term, usually five to seven months.

6. Trading without a Plan

Not operating with a trading plan is like going on a trip without a map. A proper trading plan assesses your risk tolerance and your profit goals. It is also the best tool to help you navigate between the demons of fear and greed. Unfortunately, too many traders confuse technical analysis systems with a trading plan.

You have to incorporate money management, technical analysis, and risk management together in order to make a proper trading plan.

7. Not Keeping Records of Your Trading

Statements are insufficient to keep accurate records. If you have ever read a futures or forex statement sheet it is one of the least friendly financial documents ever invented. Deciphering your activity can be like reading runes. So while the statement may show pluses and minuses in your account, they do not represent the logic behind the trade.

The best kind of record keeping for your trading activity is by keeping the charts, before and after a trade, and writing your notes directly on the chart. It helps you develop perspective on your logic and it is the most accurate real representation of your activity.

8. Looking for Trading Confirmations

There is a trading tool called the "Bullish Consensus" put out by Market Vane. Since 1964 they have tracked over 30 different markets. With this market sentiment index, they track various commodity trading advisers (CTAs) through their newsletters and advisory services.

The funny thing is when the Bullish Consensus reaches an 80% level of agreement, 80% of CTAs are bullish, and the market typically goes the opposite way. While newsletters and services have their place for "informational" purposes only, it is a sincere mistake to rely on someone else to give you your opinion.

Ownership of your decision-making process is infinitely more rewarding and reliable in the long run.

9. Options Are Not the Only Leveraged Investment

There is a misconception that options are easier to trade than futures. While 70% to 80% of options expire worthless, new traders get caught in the trap of feeling that if they know how much they are risking up front, as opposed to the freewheeling activity of futures and spot trading, they are safe. The problem with this logic is that there is a presumption that once you know the risk up front, then the risk is worth taking.

With so many components to option contracts, the Greeks, the strike price, the underlying spot and futures, if you trade options only, you will be disappointed. The key to investing success is by diversifying among the daisy chain of interdependence of futures, spot, and options. Let the trade dictate the actions, not the product.

10. Lack of Understanding Regarding Money Management

If you think that money management is about stop losses, then your battle has been lost even before you began. Money management is multifaceted and requires a set of money rules for losing trades as well as a set of money rules for winning trades.

You have to have well-developed money rules for trades that don't develop and the proper number of contracts for your account size and risk level. You also have to be capable of having rules for trading frequency.

DEMO ACCOUNTS AND PAPER TRADING

Demo-trading accounts and paper-trading accounts can be an invaluable learning tool for all types of traders. If you are a novice it can give you the confidence to try out and learn new ideas and theories. If you are an experienced trader, it can give you a way to take a break in your actual trading and become more confident when things aren't going well.

When it comes to demo trading and paper trading, I find them fairly synonymous. One you can use on the computer, the other you do by hand. They both reach the same conclusion, becoming a better trader by practicing first.

The key problem with most demo trading and paper trading is that it is useless. The average trader does not take it seriously enough to make it of any use in their real trading. The typical trader will demo/paper trade with an unrealistic amount; they will typically trade end-of-day information only; and, finally, they will constantly retro grade their results to make their paper trading seem more successful than it really was. Combine that with lack of planning and breaking any of the 10 rules we just mentioned, and demo trading can be a letdown.

The secret to successfully demo trading is threefold:

1. Trade with the amount that you would normally use if you opened an account. If you only have $3,000 to trade in reality, then trade the same amount in your demo account.

2. Treat your demo account as if it were your real account. If you want to be a day trader, day trade the demo. If you want to be a position trader, trade the demo as a position account.

3. Create a trading plan for the demo account, just like you would your real account. This is the easiest way to make sure that there is consistency in your efforts when you make the transition.

They say that practice makes perfect. I have heard that perfect practice makes perfect. If you operate the demo account just like your real account, you can overcome the primary lament that since you are not using real money your emotions are not involved. As long as you plan your trades and trade your plan, your demo trading will far exceed your expectations.

Whether you trade with an online demo account or with a paper-trading account, there are some pros and cons to each. Only you can determine which of the two types of trading will work for you.

When you are using an online demo account, you are able to test out various ideas and strategies. Some of the more sophisticated demos will even allow you to program or back-test your ideas. This can be particularly beneficial when you are curious about a new program or system, but don't feel confident in putting up any money yet.

Online demo accounts are also able to give you exposure to various trading platforms. Since the majority of traders execute trades on their own, understanding how to place an order in a noncritical situation leads to fewer mistakes when real cash is on the line.

Most importantly, demo account trading can be a real confidence booster. By simulating real-time trading, you are able to learn how to control your emotions. You can sense when you are feeling greed and fear, and you are better able to recognize it when you are actually trading.

The key drawback to demo account trading is you, the trader. If you don't take it seriously, it won't be of any use to you. In fact, it will be like a fancy video game, with little rhyme or reason.

When it comes to paper trading, it has all of the benefits of demo account trading, but it has two key drawbacks: time and lack of emotions. Since you have access to only end-of-day data, it is primarily useful for position or swing trading. With such limited data, you simply cannot learn any day-trading tactics.

Out of this time problem comes the lack-of-emotions problem. Looking at the market at the end of the day cannot effectively convey the emotions and stress associated with trading. Even for position traders, there is a high level of emotional commitment that comes from being in the markets with real cash. Many paper traders find that they have great success on paper, but when it comes to the actual markets, they crumple. It's the lack of emotional commitment that does them in.

If you find that the limitations of demo account trading and paper trading are too much, there is a third option—a test account.

TEST ACCOUNT

While demo trading and paper trading have a place, the best thing you can do for yourself is to set up a test account. Don't bet the whole farm, simply a portion of it to get a feel if trading is for you. The reality is that trading futures and forex is not for everyone. The majority of them would be better off having someone managing their investment portfolio.

Unfortunately, my book, or any other book, cannot change your fundamental personality. If you are prone to cutting your profits short or riding your losses or worry, there is no amount of reading that will fix that. The typical response is for the average trader to assume that if they can't master it, no one can. This is the wrong assumption.

On the other hand, you have the demo whiz kids who do super great and then assume that because they were successful, anyone with a computer and a chart can trade. They suffer from the flipside of the assumption emotions of being too confident.

Both groups need to set up a test account to really understand themselves. Up until that point, it is just a theory—an unproven theory. Each trader needs to be humbled, but in a slightly different way. The worrywart trader needs to have a few successes in a real account or see a few successes slip through his fingers because of his emotional impediments to realize that the potential for success exists, but they may be better off working with a money manager of some sort.

The demo whiz kid needs to trade in a test account to introduce the emotions that are necessary to be disciplined in his trading. While the demo account was easy to operate through a level of discipline devoid of feelings, by putting a little money on the line, you are able to test your mettle. Do your palms get sweaty, do you second-guess your technical analysis, and are you hesitating to pull the trigger?

The whiz kid will end up doing one of three things: He may decide that a money manager would be the best solution, he may battle through and get to the next level, or he may get caught up in trying to recreate his demo-trading experience so much that he may lose sight of the problem himself, and continue to attack the market.

Of paper trading, demo trading, and a small test account, the small test account, when done properly, wins hands down. The point to take away from a small test account is that it is a stepping stone to your larger account. Even if you already have an account, open a test account every time you want to try a new idea or market. It will be in your best interest to keep your new trading segregated from your old trading style. It will show you what is and isn't working and how to replicate it in the future.

While setting up a test account may seem daunting, it can be a very simple task, with only a small commitment of time and money, but the emotional long-term benefits will last a lifetime.

First, your test account does not have to be the same amount as what you would actually trade with. The goal is to get you comfortable with the emotions of fear and greed, while at the same time having as little money as possible at risk to accomplish this. For different people this means different amounts, but a test account with $2,500 or less can get the job done.

By working with a small amount, you can try out new strategies, learn how the platform you are trading works, and have the opportunity to see what would have been potential profits in a demo- or paper-trading account, actually on the bottom line. The biggest drawback for the test account is that you may lose money. If this is a true problem for you as a trader, then you have to either reconsider the amount you are putting in your test account or reconsider if trading is appropriate for you at all.

TRADING PLAN, TRADE WORKSHEET, AND TRADING JOURNAL

In Chapter 7 we discussed the three Ts to becoming a speculator: trading plan, trade worksheet, and trading journal. Without a doubt, if you want to develop trading into an avocation or you want to improve your demo trading, or you wish to trade for a living, you cannot ignore either of these three tools. This particularly goes for your demo-, paper-, or test-trading account. Utilizing these three tools effectively makes your day-to-day trading go a lot smoother.

Trading Plan

In my book *Futures for Small Speculators: Companion Guide*, I lay out the 30 questions of the trading plan and how you can answer them. Earlier, in Chapter 7, we looked at the first five "prequestions." Now we will look at the first five questions from the trading plan questionnaire and see how they can anchor you and build your confidence in what and why you are trading.

The first question you have to ask yourself is: What markets do I want to trade?

How you answer this question will ultimately determine your longevity in trading. There are many factors that determine which markets are best suited for you. Do you want to trade very volatile markets or low-volatility markets? Do you live on the West Coast where it's difficult to see the 5 AM opening bell for some markets? Do you travel a lot and you can't stare at your screen all day long? The market or markets you pick to trade should best suit your lifestyle.

It is also important to pick only two to three markets that you sincerely want to trade. It is difficult to understand and trade the subtleties of every single market available. While technical analysis can be applied across the board, as a specialist, you begin to understand what actually makes a particular market tick. You can then manage your money and your trades according to the rhythms in that market. By focusing on a handful of markets, you can become a specialist. Without a doubt specialists in any field tend to fare better.

The second question you have to ask yourself is: What am I trading for?

Knowing why you are trading futures, forex, and options is imperative. Is it for fun, like a gambler, or is it a true desire to speculate? Or are you trying to "hedge" your overall investment portfolio? What many investors forget about trading markets like futures and forex is that there are two aspects to it. It can be both the riskiest investment and the least risky investment at the same time, if you use it properly.

For example, during the dot-com bubble, many investors had mutual funds and stocks that closely matched the Nasdaq 100. When the market began to slow down and investors found themselves in the precarious position of not knowing if they should liquidate their tech stock and investment portfolios, they could have simply used Nasdaq futures to protect themselves from any quick drops in value.

By looking at futures from both sides, speculating and hedging, you can come up with more versatile strategies of managing your money over the long haul.

This leads us to questions three through five: What am I hedging against/for?, How many contracts would it take to accurately hedge part of my portfolio?, and How many contracts would it take to accurately hedge my entire portfolio?

These questions are designed to get you to think outside the box as a futures and forex trader. Look at how your current investments are linked to interest rate fluctuations, the S&P 500, or the Dow Jones Industrial Average. Calculate how much you stand to lose when these markets move against you, and from there you can figure out how best to hedge yourself.

None of these markets operate in a vacuum; there are ways for you to protect yourself from stock market adversity if you open your eyes to the hedging side of futures and forex investing.

Trade Worksheet

The trade worksheet is designed to break down the numbers of any trade you are planning to execute before you enter it. It is designed to ask some fundamental questions. Once these questions are answered, you can see in black and white what the potential profit is, what the potential loss is, and if the trade is worth taking at all.

The vital information that it gathers is:

1. Entry price
2. Profit exit price
3. Loss exit price
4. Margin level
5. +/−% return on margin
6. +/−% return on account
7. Cost of option

We have premade forms that you can fill out, but they are not necessary. A notebook that you can write in on a consistent basis will suffice. The goal is to get you used to doing the numbers.

For day traders, the trade worksheet will be of most help to you with your option, if you decide to use one as a hedge, but little else on an intraday level. Since day traders are in and out of the market, it is difficult to sit around doing the calculations before each trade you execute. I do suggest that you do the calculations afterward, though.

Keep track of the trades you entered and exited throughout the day. Tally up your profits and losses and how much you risked attaining your results. The information just may be the food for thought you need to help you make better choices during your trading experience.

Trading Journal

It's been said that you don't know where you are going unless you know where you have been. The trading journal does just that. Throughout your trading career, you will have multiple journals. In fact, you should do your best to never stop journaling when you are a trader.

If you cannot, a great alternative is to journal in 20-day trading cycles at a time. By journaling your trades, you will be able to understand why you do the things you do and when you do them. If they are good habits, keep them; if they are bad habits, do your best to modify them to help you succeed.

The typical trading journal should have the following:

- A copy of your trading plan, so you can constantly refer back to it.
- At least 20 trade worksheet forms, complete one for *every* trade you execute.
- A copy of the entry chart of every trade you execute, along with a small three- to five-sentence synopsis on why and how you entered the trade, including your feelings and emotions at the time.
- A copy of the exit chart of every trade you execute, along with a small three- to five-sentence synopsis of the profits or losses and why and how you exited the trade, along with your feelings and emotions at the time.

By consistently documenting your experiences, you will become an expert at knowing how fear and greed wreak havoc on your decision-making process.

A question I always hear is: "Should I do this with my demo trading?" My response is: "Perfect practice makes perfect." If you can't create a trading plan, work out the numbers on a trade worksheet and journal for an account where no money is on the line, imagine how you will operate when you have capital in the account—not much better. Develop some good habits in your demo trading and you won't find it a waste of time.

That's what this entire chapter has been about: Demo trade properly and with the right frame of mind so that you can move forward into your actual trading with little to no remorse.

In the next chapter I will break down how you can get started over a three-month time frame in taking yourself from a novice or an advanced trader who just keeps making the same old mistakes, to thinking and operating like a professional trader.

You will be amazed at how differently you will approach the markets.

BUILDING CONFIDENCE ISN'T EASY

They say that in order for a new activity to become a habit, you have to do it 30 times consistently. Trading is no different. Avoiding the top 10 mistakes of trading, putting together a trading plan, working with a trade worksheet, and utilizing a journal are all activities that have to be done consistently in order to build confidence. While your confidence boost won't happen overnight, one day you will wake up and find yourself a skilled and confident trader.

CHAPTER 15

Getting Started (The Three-Month Plan)

Y ou have come a long way! You have gone from having maybe a basic understanding of futures and forex to, I hope, a greater appreciation of what it takes to be a professional in these trillion-dollar marketplaces. While the transition hasn't been easy, especially for me over these several years, it is necessary.

There is no holy grail, there is no magic, and there is only a little hard work and a little dedication. In a lot of ways I wish my approach to the markets could be a little sexier or a little more glamorous. Unfortunately, that is not my personality, and a lot of investors and potential traders may be turned off by my basic approach. I would tell you to keep in mind that all that glitters isn't gold. Fool's gold is just as shiny as real gold, if not shinier and more attractive, yet it has little intrinsic value.

As a trader, don't get caught in the various traps and trading myths that abound that have been rehashed and retooled for the next set of suckers. Look for actual "values of wins" over percentages of wins, don't let "hypothetical" results make your buying decisions for you, and don't get pulled into believing that there is a "magic bullet" that will solve all of the trading ills.

Most importantly, don't be tricked into believing that "trading is easy." Corporations spend millions of dollars hiring some of the best minds on the planet to eke out small double-digit returns, if that. They pay the money because they want traders who can balance risk and reward while keeping in mind the need to preserve capital. Should your thinking be any less?

You have the means and the tools to become exactly like your professional counterparts; now let's put it to the test.

I felt it was important to round out your education by giving you some practical step-by-step advice and pattern to follow to help you form new habits. It is said it takes 30 times of consistently doing something in order for it to become a habit. So while I could have made the program a 30-day intensive reeducation process, I was also content to break it up like a workout routine. Do something in regard to your trading three times a week for 12 weeks, which gives you a total of 36 days. So you have a few days to spare, just in case life gets in the way.

My approach to the market will not stop you from losing money, what it will do is give you control. Part of that control is about actually trying these ideas on paper before you ever actually commit any money to them or, if you do commit money, you use a small test account, like the one we spoke about in Chapter 14.

By taking your time, you will find your own rhythm and what works for you. You will become a professional on your own terms and at your own pace. But in the end, you will be a professional. It has been said that "ignorance is bliss" because once you know something, you cannot go back to a state of not knowing.

What you now know is that futures is an insurance game. It works with spot markets and option markets, and they are all meant to protect each other in a daisy-chain effect. You know that those who take advantage of the insurance aspects are given preferential treatment in margin and commissions. Finally, you know that you are not excluded from the club. In this book there are at least nine different ways for you to appear like a hedger and share in the same benefits that major money managers and corporations have been using for years.

As with anything, it is a lot easier said than done. I will share with you the same regimen that I have been giving private clients and mentor students for the past several years and the characteristics I have seen in them that have helped them succeed.

FOUR STEPS TO SEVEN LESSONS

There has been so much information so quickly that I recommend that you read and reread this book as many times as you can. Highlight it, check my facts, cross-reference with other books—make this book a living guide to help you improve.

I am a student of the markets. I have learned a great deal from Larry Williams, Mark Douglas, Alexander Elder, Tom Busby, Dr. J, and a slew of others. So in no way do I feel that this book is the definitive book that ends all research and study. My book has been meant to be a complement to what you are already doing or whatever you are reading or studying at this time.

Take what you can from each lesson that you have gone through and apply it as necessary or ignore it altogether. I do not intend for you to throw away what has been working for you. I simply want you to replace what hasn't been working. If you don't have a set approach to trading, use this book and my ideas as a framework, but by no means stop learning and adding to the frame you acquired.

Every day I learn something new from the markets, and what I believe or ascribe to today may be completely modified or changed in the coming years. I am not the trader I was 10 years ago, nor will I be the same trader 10 years from now. I hope that your experiences will lead you to the same conclusions. At the same time, I won't sell you out to the hype. Money can be made in the futures and forex markets. It simply takes focus and effort on your part, plus a healthy dose of patience.

At the end of the day, there were three steps outlined in this book that will go a long way to your trading success. The first step was money management, the second step was technical analysis, and the third step was risk management. By combining all three of these together you will become a complete trader. As long as you attempt to trade with only one or two of these areas developed, you will never get the best possible results that you can achieve.

Each step was broken up into two lessons, to make a total of six lessons, with a seventh lesson to pull the pieces together. There were specific ideas and concepts that I wanted you to learn along the way, each a building block on the next. In case you have skipped to this section right away, I strongly suggest that you go through the chapters that cover these areas as well. As I have said along the way, there are no shortcuts to successful trading.

This is also a small refresher of the topics, so that as you go through the process of applying what you have learned over the next three months, you will be able to quickly reference what you learned throughout the book and go back to that chapter to review it, if you have forgotten.

Money Management

Money management is simply how you treat the capital that you use when you are trading. It is meant to be a guideline for what you will do regardless of whether your money sits idle, you are in a winning trade, or you are in a losing trade.

Lesson 1: Developing Your Trading Plan A trading plan is not simply knowing what technical tools you will use. A proper trading plan incorporates your risk, reward, and volatility levels. It then couples this vital information with your goals, market expectations, and capability.

This is the essential tool of every trader and allows him to grow from being a novice to becoming a professional in the highest sense. While it seems easy to get started trading, by spending a little prep time on developing the trading plan, it quickly becomes evident who will succeed and who is doomed to repeat the same mistakes over and over again.

Can you trade without a trading plan? Possibly. Can you succeed without a trading plan? Possibly. While there are the superstars in any industry, those with incredible talent, I suggest that when talent meets preparation, there is a tendency to succeed to the highest level of our potential.

Lesson 2: Preparing To Speculate   Using a "stop loss" is not a money management technique. It is a risk management technique—one that may not be that successful, but a risk management technique nonetheless.

There are so many benefits available to the average trading account as well as capabilities that are either ignored or misunderstood that traders are doing a disservice to themselves when it comes to really managing their capital.

There needs to be an understanding of how to buy T-bills, sweep accounts, how margin operates, and what volatility really means in cash values for your account. Couple this with the four pillars of money management, and you will treat your money like you should—as a tool.

Technical Analysis

Technical analysis is not a holy grail to trading—it is a tool. If the tools you are using are not answering one of the cardinal questions (Where is the market going?, How fast is it getting there?, and When will it arrive?), then what use are they? There is no one-size-fits-all technical tool, and you have to be able to distinguish between technical tools that give you an image of the big picture and technical tools that give you an image of the small picture.

Lesson 3: Choosing Your Technical Indicators   I am constantly asked what my favorite technical analysis tool is. I really don't have one. For the spot forex market, I may use slightly different tools and different time frames from my futures position trading. As long as the tools answer one of the three questions, then I am satisfied. I don't need 10 or 15 technical analysis tools to get my answers, nor do I need to monitor 3 or 4 computer screens to accomplish my goals.

Of the three questions, the most important question you will need to ask yourself is: When will it arrive? This is the cornerstone of our basis for the risk management strategies. If you cannot answer this question, it becomes difficult to know if you are pre-anticipating a move or if you are involved in the current move.

You must also use your broad or "macro" technical analysis tools in order to understand if you are trading the trend or countertrend. This gives you an idea of what to expect of the current trade movement that is occurring.

Lesson 4: Developing Tactics for Entering and Exiting the Market   Knowing how to enter and exit trades is a different skill from understanding the direction of the markets or trend and countertrends. This is an important skill to know, but for the most part is misunderstood. Every trader I have met focuses so much energy on the perfect trade entry that they lose sight of the fact that entering a trade is not the same as "trading" the trade.

Entering a trade and exiting a trade are functions of fine-tuning your current opinion of the market, not cultivating an opinion. Too many traders find themselves being whipsawed back and forth by entry and exit signals because they jump at every potential opportunity with little regard to what the overall market is doing.

Commodities and currency markets trend; utilize entry and exit signals as a function of those trends. If done properly, this "micro" technical analysis will reinforce your opinions.

Risk Management

Trading futures, options, and forex should never be done singularly. These are interconnected, interdependent markets that set the tone for each other. The most sophisticated traders follow the lead of their corporate counterparts and actual buyers and sellers, hedgers, in incorporating all aspects of these seemingly disparate markets together to protect themselves from too much loss and to maximize gains. The belief, and rightly so, is that profits take care of themselves; risk (i.e., losses) is the side of the equation that all of your attention should be focused on.

Lesson 5: Analyzing Your Opponents and the Market   Unlike stocks, futures and forex trading has less to do with other speculators and more to do with real-world supply and demand and the people who need these products. Your competition is banks, farmers, corporations, importers, and exporters—the hedgers. Their motivations may be different from yours, and their decisions will have a direct impact on how you interact and react to the markets.

Your strength of conviction will come from your understanding that the movements of these markets may be counterintuitive from a speculator's perspective but make absolute sense from a hedger's perspective.

Lesson 6: Managing Risk   The hedgers understand and know how to use options combined with futures and the spot market. Why shouldn't you?

If you believe that a stop is sufficient, ask your hedging counterparts if they use only stops. Their resounding answer will be "No."

For them, a balancing act is initiated whenever one of these hedgers puts on a futures or options contract against their spot position. They are constantly gaining on one side and losing on the other side, knowing full well the consequences.

If more speculators traded like hedgers, their interpretation of loss and gain would change. The willingness to lose a little to gain a lot would make a world of difference, as opposed to just being afraid to lose.

There is an old philosophy that says where the head goes, the body will follow. If you are fixated on the fear of loss, you will lose. If you can feel comfortable with loss, because you feel in control of it, you will be able to let the profits take care of themselves. Knowing risk management strategies will teach you how to do that.

Pulling It All Together

There is no point in trading new ideas or a new way unless you have spent the time to experiment first. Through experimenting, you give yourself the opportunity to narrow down what works and what doesn't work for who you are as a trader. The point of experimenting, though, is to make it relevant to your everyday trading life. The further it's removed in actual capital, style, or market selection, the less use it is to your learning process.

Lesson 7: Building Your Confidence   You have read, you have studied, and now's the time to just get started. While it may be easy to say but difficult to do, it's a necessary evil. Applying the concepts in this book will take a commitment on your part. This is best accomplished by starting off slowly and testing out ideas on paper, or in demo accounts, or putting a little bit of money into a test account.

The success comes not from simply "trying" it out, but in making your simulated account, no matter what it is, as close as possible to what your actual account would be like. Only then can the real benefits and the real learning begin. If you "play around" in your simulated account, how can you trade your real account with the level of seriousness and dedication that it needs?

They say that practice makes perfect, but the better saying is "perfect practice makes perfect." Operate your demo account as you would your real account, and your success flourishes.

THREE MONTHS OF WORK

How long does it take to learn how to trade properly?

It could be one day, one year, or a lifetime. For me it was a seven-year trial-and-error process to understand my feelings about the market. In the meantime, the market changed and evolved into something else entirely from when I started.

At the same time, key fundamentals stayed the same. So as long as I did not get excited about the price fluctuations or the shift in supply and demand or the growth of spot forex for the average trader and stuck with fundamentals, I knew that I would be okay.

This book is about the fundamentals. Everything that we recapped in the seven lessons hasn't changed since the inception of the markets themselves. There are still hedgers and speculators. The markets are primarily an insurance vehicle. Risk management deals with one thing and one thing only—loss.

How we apply these skills in order to learn good habits is immensely vital.

So how long does it take to learn how to trade properly?

It's been said that it takes 30 times of performing a new action before it becomes a habit. This is key. So while it may take you longer or not as long, depending on your schedule, I have broken down a set of actions you can take over the course of 12 weeks, three times a week, to help you apply what you have learned. That totals to 36 reminders that you can trade the markets in a different, more lucrative way.

For the first month you will tackle the "structure" of your trading. You will define the markets and your trading on your own terms.

For the second month it is all about "trial and error"—watching and studying, with an idea to finding out what works and doesn't work for you.

Finally, in the third month, you will "perfect your trading" to fit your lifestyle. You will know how to trade the markets on your own terms, not on an artificial set of parameters that come from a market guru or from perceived belief that money can only be made a particular way.

Each item should not take you more than 30 to 60 minutes to complete, but will make a world of difference in your overall success.

Month 1: Structure

The latticework that we use to frame the structure of our success becomes all important in how we interact with the markets. While we would love to believe in our own self-importance, no matter how much capital we have, it is dwarfed by the trillions of dollars floating around the futures and forex markets.

The first month is dedicated to helping you carve your niche in the marketplace and to really understand how your goals fit in with the overall scheme of things.

Week 1: Develop your trading plan.
Day 1: Complete the 30-question trading questionnaire.
Day 2: Assess what markets you want to trade.
Day 3: Run your seven-point checklist to determine which markets match your volatility levels.

Week 2: Research the markets you wish to trade.
Day 1: Discover what makes your markets tick, importers, and exporters.
Day 2: Read the financial statistics that influence buying and selling decisions.
Day 3: Learn to read the raw data and distinguish news from hype.

Week 3: Research the brokerages you could work with.
Day 1: Look at various brokerage firms and discover if they have the tools you need.
Day 2: Compare and contrast the features and benefits.
Day 3: Plug those numbers that you discover into your trading plan to help you with calculating profits and losses.

Week 4: Set up your demo account.
Day 1: Set up your demo account (paper traders subscribe to a financial publication).
Day 2: Modify your demo account to match your expected commissions and account size.
Day 3: Execute test trades to make sure they will allow you to put on options, futures, and spot simultaneously.

Month 2: Trial and Error

Mistakes must be made in order to learn. In the second month, you have gone beyond your prep work and now you are playing with a little fire. You have to test and play around with your charting service. We use Genesis

Navigator in our trading and back-testing. While I can't go into a Genesis Navigator tutorial here, it is important that you know your software inside and out before you trade with real money.

That way, you will be able to manipulate the recommended indicators in this book and back-test your own theories and ideas about what the market is doing.

Week 5: Subscribe to your charting service.
 Day 1: Get familiar with the technical analysis tools.
 Day 2: Understand the ticker symbol parameters.
 Day 3: Program your preferred markets.

Week 6: Narrow down your macro technical indicators.
 Day 1: Pick the technical tools that answer the three main questions.
 Day 2: Back-test the tools in the demo or charting software account.
 Day 3: Create your set of primary and redundant tools that you feel comfortable with.

Week 7: Fine-tune your entry and exit.
 Day 1: Study and learn the top 10 candlestick markets by heart.
 Day 2: Overlay your macro technical indicators with your micro technical indicators and match up profits and losses.
 Day 3. Pick at least 10 entry and exit points based on your overlay in order to calculate your potential profits and losses.

Week 8: Begin your trading journal.
 Day 1: Create or acquire a set of trade worksheets.
 Day 2: Figure out how to type directly onto your charts and print out.
 Day 3: Purchase a trading journal book.

Month 3: Perfecting Your Trading

In the final month, you are refining the tools that you played around with in month 2. By refining your tools, you have now begun to tailor your trading for your lifestyle and goals. Although you are far from being an expert trader, you have now elevated your trading to the professional level. You can now execute your first real trade with all of the tools at your disposal: money management, technical analysis, and risk management.

The power of your trading no longer comes from having an opinion about the markets, but in being able to prepare for potential failure if your opinion doesn't pan out. This is a huge step up for the 95% of traders who thought that picking the right market, long or short, somehow guaranteed success.

Week 9: Choose your core risk management techniques.
> Day 1: Go back to your 10 entry and exit, macro and micro technical analysis charts, and play around with various risk management techniques scenarios.
> Day 2: Narrow down your selection to two to three risk management techniques that match your risk-reward profile.
> Day 3: Run several real-time scenarios of what your potential risk management techniques would look like. Use the trade worksheet.

Week 10: Use the Commitments of Traders report.
> Day 1: Download or review the Commitment of Traders (COT) report from the Commodity Futures Trading Commission (CFTC) for the past month
> Day 2: Learn how to read the long form and short forms of the COT report.
> Day 3: Match the COT activity with price fluctuations based on hedgers and speculators.

Week 11: Execute your first trade.
> Day 1: Set up your trading account.
> Day 2: Design your trade using your trade worksheet and trading plan.
> Day 3: Execute your first real trade with risk management and based on your trading plan. Document your activity in the journal.

Week 12: Evaluate your progress.
> Day 1: Depending on whether you are a day, swing, or position trader, evaluate the trade or your knowledge and document in your trading journal.
> Day 2: Monitor your trading accordingly.
> Day 3: Begin again at week 11, day 2, and find your next trade.

WHAT I WANT FOR YOU AS A TRADER

At the end of the day, all I want to do is see you succeed—move from a Type A trader to an in-control Type B trader. The markets work better when there is efficiency. The goal of the markets is to have the true buyers and sellers "discover prices" that reflect true supply and demand. Your goal is to profit from the price discrepancies as often and as long as possible.

The more educated you are, the more you understand the mechanics of the financial instruments you use, and the more disciplined you are, you will benefit and thrive in this environment. I lose nothing when you succeed; in fact, I gain and you gain as the markets become more predictable and smooth in their movements.

Will there be fundamental shifts in supply and demand that will cause huge swings from time to time?

Of course!

And you will be prepared for them with your risk management tools. In the end, as a trader with a complete trading plan that incorporates money management, technical analysis, and risk management techniques, you will be handsomely rewarded. I wish you good fortune and good luck in all of your trading endeavors. More importantly, I look forward to seeing you on the trading screen.

About the Author

N oble DraKoln is the author of the books *Futures for Small Speculators, Futures for Small Speculators: Companion Guide, Single Stock Futures for Small Speculators*, and *Forex for Small Speculators*. He has also completed a three-part video seminar series entitled *Speculating with Futures, Forex, and Traditional Commodities*

Mr. DraKoln operated as interim editor for *Futures* magazine's newsletter, "Trends In Futures," in 2004–2005. He has written educational articles for *Traders Magazine, Futures* magazine, *Currency Trader, Technical Analysis of Stocks and Commodities, Pristine View*, and *Cornerstone*, as well as eSignal.

He is an international speaker and has spoken on commodity futures and forex investing in Romania, Paris, Germany, New York, Las Vegas, Los Angeles, and Chicago.

In Romania he spoke at the first ever Risk Management Conference on behalf of Romania in front of the European Union ascension representatives. He currently holds a Series 3 license, the only designation that is approved by the government to service the commodity futures industry. His mission is to help retail investors learn how to use the commodity futures markets as an integral part of their overall investment portfolio.

He started off his career working for a commodities broker at the age of 17. He received his first Series 3 license at the age of 19. For several years he succeeded as a commodities broker and an import/export trader.

In 2000, he founded the commodities investment firm Liverpool Derivatives Group in order to service a diverse and growing investment community. Under the group umbrella are three separate entities:

1. *Liverpool Capital Management,* a money management group that helps investors with IRAs and 401(k)s find futures and forex investments with proven track records of success.

2. *Liverpool Trading Company*, which provides professional traders with direct access to the markets and deep discounts to retail traders.

3. *Speculator Academy*, which provides trading courses, mentorship, books, videos, and seminars to help traders improve their trading in the futures and forex markets.

Index